'1998'

Jubb,

Merry Christmas Jubb! I hope you enjoy this book as much as I did!

Lots of Love,

Jan

GOD Bless you Jubb.

"Profound insights! Culturally relevant! Life-changing! *The Great Commandment Principle* is the work of a lifetime with a transforming message. Read it, apply its message, and your ministry and relationships will never again be the same." **Josh McDowell,** Josh McDowell Ministry

"In an original and convincing fashion, David Ferguson clearly explains how the Great Commission can be carried out only through personal commitment to the Great Commandment." **D. James Kennedy, Ph.D.,** Senior Minister, Coral Ridge Presbyterian Church

"Too long have we as evangelistically minded believers focused on 'being right' instead of loving greatly. Here is a foretaste of a new genre I believe the Holy Spirit is seeking to beget as we step into a new millennium." **Jack W. Hayford, D.Litt.,** Pastor, The Church On the Way, Van Nuys, CA

"Dr. Ferguson's inspired insights will help us allow God's Spirit to be manifested and glorified in all our relationships, for the blessing of all. This is truly life-changing." **Dr. Bill Bright,** Founder and President, Campus Crusade for Christ International

"*The Great Commandment Principle* is an incredible book of fresh, God-anointed teachings that, when understood and applied, will place the church at the center stage of relevance in an increasingly secular world. No one has demonstrated more genuine concern for the families of our church leaders than Dr. David Ferguson." **James T. Draper Jr.,** President, The Sunday School Board of the Southern Baptist Convention

"In *The Great Commandment Principle,* my friend David Ferguson powerfully, practically, and compellingly presents the essence of New Testament Christianity. Thank you, David, for giving us a road map to wholeness." **Dr. Crawford W. Loritts Jr.,** Speaker, Author, Campus Crusade for Christ

"Finally, a book that clearly explains how relationships are established, maintained, and grown. This book will enlarge your heart for God and others. Read it!" **Dennis Rainey,** Executive Director, FamilyLife

"I have watched the teaching offered within this book transform many leaders' lives, ministries, and marriages. I highly commend this resource to you. It is a resource you will want all of your leaders to be exposed to!" **Dr. Dann Spader,** Executive Director, Sonlife Ministries

"Living out the Great Commandment is of the greatest importance. [I]t has been said that if you don't live out the Great Commandment, you are not going to be able to effectively live out the Great Commission." **Tony Campolo,** Author, Professor, Eastern College

"David Ferguson's calling to explore the application of *The Great Commandment Principle* in the context of personal, marriage, family, and church life biblically redresses the imbalances of a culturally premised sociology, education, and psychology." **Ramesh Richard, Ph.D., Th.D.,** Professor, Dallas Theological Seminary

"I heartily recommend *The Great Commandment Principle* as a book which will confront the reader with the power and practicality of the Word of God." **Dr. Robert E. Fisher,** Director of Ministerial Care, Church of God (Cleveland, TN)

"*The Great Commandment Principle* is outlined here by one of the great communicating people of our time. Read it and reap!" **O. S. Hawkins,** President/CEO, Annuity Board of the Southern Baptist Convention

"David Ferguson has done it again! He's given us a book of practical scriptural teaching on 'The Great Commandment Principle' of love. He challenges us, as individuals and the church, to reach out in love and be relevant in making an impact for eternity. Every believer should read this book." **Dr. Dal Shealy,** President/CEO, Fellowship of Christian Athletes

"This is a clear call to need-meeting, relational ministry within the family, church and community . . . a practical, instructional, and inspirational guide to loving, intimate relationships." **Dr. Anthony L. Jordan,** Executive Director-Treasurer, Baptist General Convention of Oklahoma

"This is not just a book but a toolshed of resources for building health in both family and church." **Owen Connolly,** Chairman, Institute of Christian Councellors, Ireland

"[A] great, practical handbook on how to be men and women used by God as loving examples of His grace in our families, businesses, neighborhoods, and ministries." **Phil Downer,** President, CBMC of USA

"This excellent book issues a challenge in the dying years of the present millennium to the Church of Christ to make it more relevant. Human needs are impacted and hidden issues exposed. Crucial to growth and unity!" **Marquess of Reading,** House of Lords, Great Britain

"Dr. Ferguson presents a compelling argument for the persuasiveness of Great Commandment love when communicating the gospel." **Dr. R. Peter Mason,** Northeast Regional Executive Director, CBAmerica

"David Ferguson's book is profoundly important. . . . Christians can only fulfill the Great Commission by committing to truly honest relationships humbly, courageously, and vulnerably." **Mr. Charlie Colchester,** Executive Director, Christian Action Research and Education (UK)

"The message David Ferguson shares with us in this book has significantly benefited my own marriage and family and ministry as a church leader, and helped deepen my own relationship with God. This book will bring positive change in marriages, families, and friendships, and transformation in church ministry. It needs to be read." **Reverend Alister Mort,** Vicar of St. Mark's Church, Leamington Spa, England

"David Ferguson's anointed book, *The Great Commandment Principle,* provides another opportunity to see the significance of Christ's words for reaching one's family and the world." **Dennis G. Lindsay,** President/CEO, Christ for the Nations

"Th*e Great Commandment Principle* proposes a rebirth of this great biblical truth for today's congregations. This book will assist churches in connecting with a culture which desperately needs to know we care." **Dr. Jack Graham,** Senior Pastor, Prestonwood Baptist Church, Dallas, TX

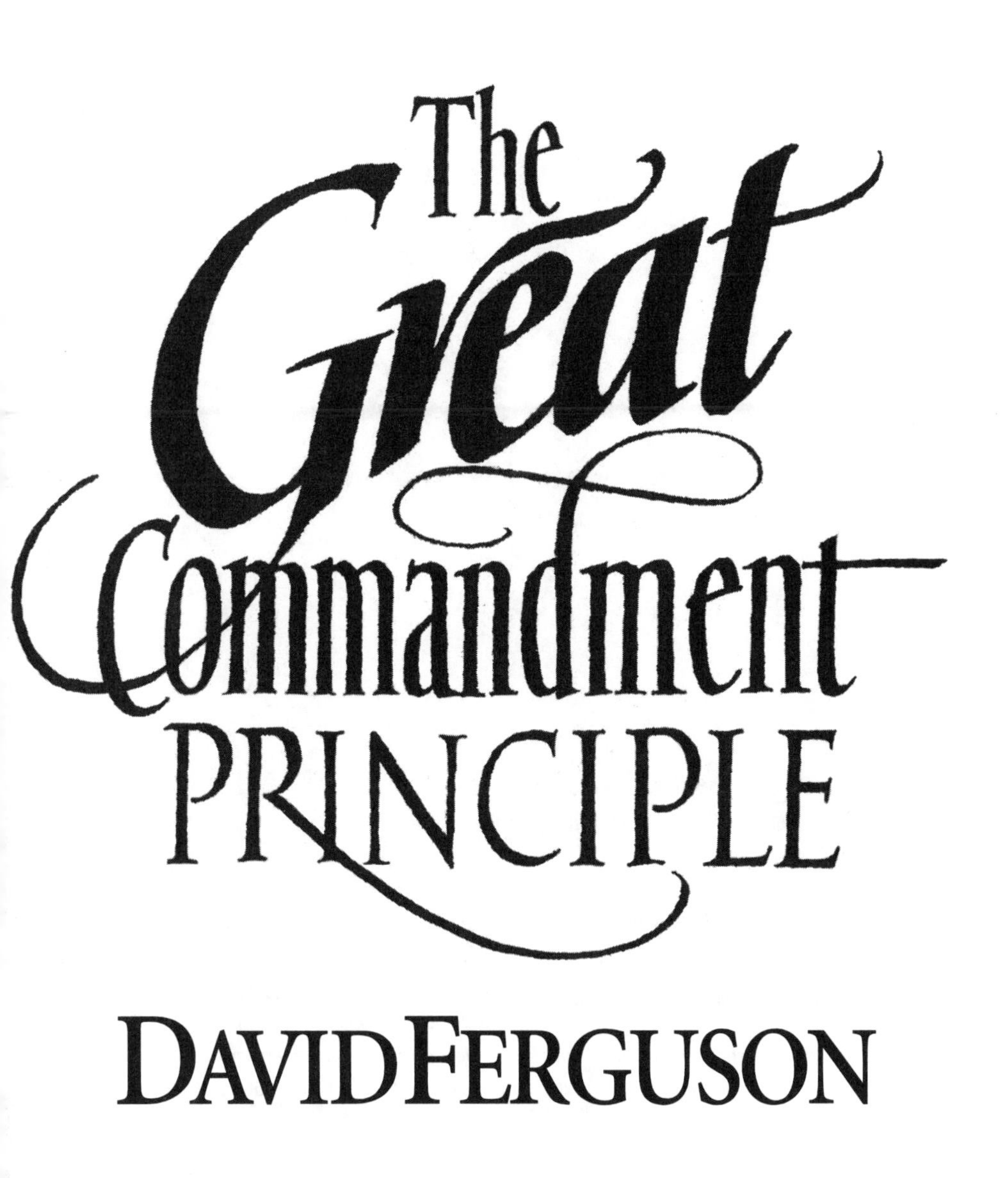

DAVID FERGUSON

Tyndale House Publishers, Inc.
Wheaton, Illinois

Visit Tyndale's exciting Web site at www.tyndale.com

Edited by David Horton

Designed by Timothy R. Botts

Library of Congress Cataloging-in-Publication Data

Ferguson, David (David L.), date
The great commandment principle / David Ferguson.
p. cm.
ISBN 0-8423-5576-6 (pbk. : alk. paper)
1. God—Worship and love. 2. Love—Religious aspects—Christianity. 3. Christian life. I. Title.
BV4817.F39 1998
241.5—dc21 98-17530

Printed in the United States of America

04 03 02 01 00 99 98
7 6 5 4 3 2 1

CONTENTS

Part Three: Modeling Love

ACKNOWLEDGMENTS

Countless people have helped shape the message of this book. I wish to thank the following for their extraordinary contribution and collaboration:

My wife, Teresa, along with my family, who have "journeyed" with me in our efforts to experience the message of this book before writing it;

The Intimate Life Ministries team and the growing network of pastors and ministry leaders, for their constant encouragement, nurture, accountability, and grateful hearts, which humble me often;

Dr. Jimmy Draper, for his passionate heart of love, and for giving consistent support and sacrificial care to me and the ministry in our effort to compile this work;

Dr. Dann Spader, for his vision of healthy churches with Great Commission priorities and how his partnership with us has brought an essential complimentary message to this book;

My friends and colleagues Josh and Dottie McDowell, for evaluating the manuscript extensively and for their support of our Galatians 6:6 retreats, where much of this book's message is experienced firsthand by Christian leaders;

Donnie and Carolyn Dixon, Jim and Vicki McGee, Mark Pecina, Allan Regg, Bennie Carlisle, Lance Herst, Bill and Shelley Schreyer, Rich Tompkins, Maria Munoz, John and Fran Leiss, Michael and Suzanne Schulte, Ashton Cumberbatch, Win and Caroline Baggett, Glenn Wood, and Mike and Myrna Schoenfeld, for participating in the focus group and providing such insight and guidance in the shaping and remolding of the book's theme and emphasis;

Dave Bellis, who provided creative vision to me and to the message, spent countless hours structuring and restructuring the book, and collaborated with me overall as a product developer to maintain the central focus for this book;

Becky Bellis, for her patience and tireless effort in typing the many revisions of this work;

Ed Stewart, whose finely honed writing skills made each scene and character, illustration and concept come alive to touch both mind and heart, who partnered with me and Dave Bellis over many months to bring this book to completion;

Tyndale House Publishers, who—more than just a publisher—is also a partner in passionately propagating the Great Commandment message: Ron Beers, who captured and conveyed a personal vision for the book from the outset; Ken Petersen, who gave such wise counsel and advice in the reshaping of the book, for all of his sacrificial time and attention and his commitment to me and this message; Mark Taylor, whose testimony of the manuscript's personal impact gave me such encouragement to press on; and Dave Horton, who brought his editorial skill, insight, and direction to the manuscript, greatly enhancing the work;

And finally, I am grateful to the God of all mercy for allowing me to experience his love as I seek to better love him and those around me.

CHAPTER ONE
A Cultural Crisis: The Need for Relevance

IT WAS a balmy November evening in Titusville, Florida, and the Friday night service was nearing conclusion. I was speaking to about a thousand pastors and lay leaders gathered for one of our regional ministry training conferences. My text was Romans 12:15: "Rejoice with those who rejoice; mourn with those who mourn." During our time of worship we experienced the first part of that verse, rejoicing together in God's goodness and grace. Then I emphasized the testimony of love that results when we share our hurts and discouragements *with* one another and receive God's comfort *from* one another as the Bible instructs.

At the close of my message I encouraged everyone to turn to someone nearby—spouse, family member, or friend—and share a memory of personal pain. It could be as small or great a pain as they cared to disclose, something recent or from the past. As each individual spoke, his or her partner was to listen and express godly comfort.

As people shared their hurts and comforted one another, many exchanged spontaneous, tender embraces, and a few tears began to flow. I slipped away from the platform and circled behind the crowd near the main doors, rejoicing as I contemplated the Father's joy. His children were moving beyond hearing his Word to actually experiencing it.

While I stood there watching, the door opened behind me, and a man walked in. He was about thirty years old, nice looking, and casually dressed. I found out later that Ray, who was not a believer, lived in the neighborhood and was out for an evening walk. Curious about why the church parking lot was full on a Friday night, he had stepped inside to take a look.

He walked over near me and surveyed the sea of people. Obviously perplexed at the sight, he asked, "What are they doing?"

"They're comforting one another," I explained.

Ray continued to watch the people share their hurts and tenderly embrace—married couples, single adults, and entire families. Tears formed in his eyes, and there was a longing in his voice. "That's what *I* need."

Sensing a divine appointment, I said, "Are there stressful or painful things going on in your life right now?"

Ray nodded. He explained that his job at the nearby Kennedy Space Center was in jeopardy due to cutbacks. Furthermore, he had just gone through the pain of placing his mother in a nursing home. At about the same time, his fiancée had broken up with him. This young man was in a world of hurt!

Others gathered around Ray and shared God's love with him by comforting him. The unexpected outpouring of love from total strangers lifted a great burden from Ray, and before the evening was over, he committed his life to Jesus Christ. Today he is involved in church and a singles ministry. Through new friends in the church, Ray found a better job. And the church's ministry to shut-ins is sharing the love of Christ with Ray's mother in the nursing home. The love and comfort Ray found that warm November evening continue to bless him.

Are We Relevant?

Isn't this what every one of us prays for? Don't we fervently desire to see people like Ray drawn to Christ by what they see in our lives? Don't we long for increasing numbers of hurting people to look to us and our churches for refuge, hope, and healing?

But are we providing this kind of place in the world today? In moments of honest reflection, many of us would probably respond, "Sadly, not as often as we want to be or should be." Unchurched friends and neighbors may attend services when we invite them for Christmas or Easter or "Friendship Sunday." But how many of them come back seeking answers for their troubled lives? And how many total strangers like Ray enter our Christian gatherings saying, "This is what I need"? Again, answering honestly, many of us would say, "First-time unchurched visitors are few and far between, and return visitors are even more rare." Or we may lament, "Whenever I try to share the gospel with unbelieving neighbors or coworkers, they're not interested."

Why is this so? Why do the people who need our message the most seem the least interested in it? Why aren't there more people like Ray coming through our doors? Why do so many of the unchurched walk away from us saying in effect, "I see what you have, and I don't need it"?

I believe I can answer these hard questions with one word: relevance. After more than fifteen years of ministry to Christian leaders who struggle with these questions, I am convinced that the body of Christ frequently fails at being relevant to the needy world around us. What does it mean to be relevant? According to Webster, something is relevant when it has "significant and demonstrable bearing on the matter at hand." A relevant solution is clearly applicable and pertinent, significantly impacting the needs of the current situation. A solution that does not meet the obvious need is deemed irrelevant or extraneous.

People are not streaming to us or to our gatherings for answers because they do not perceive our message as relevant to the deep needs of their lives. To a vast number of the unchurched, we are answering questions they are not asking, we are providing solutions to problems they don't face, we are scratching where they don't itch. We are irrelevant to the people we most need to reach.

"But wait," you may object. "The gospel is the solution to humankind's deepest needs. God and his Word are thoroughly relevant to our problem-plagued culture." And you are right. God and his eternal Word are relevant to the needs of every relationship, every culture, and every period of history—including the present. So to whatever extent we are irrelevant to the world around us, it is not God's fault. Something is getting lost in the translation. Somewhere between God's ultimate solution and the world's crying need, the message of hope is becoming garbled. The problem is not in the message; it's in the medium. The problem is not in the vision; it's in the vehicle.

If we are going to reach a hurting world with biblical, Christ-centered solutions, we must be a showcase of God's relevance.

Most people around us do not listen to our message because they do not see how God and his Word can solve their life struggles. What they need is a relevant solution to their problems modeled right in front of their eyes. Our neighbors are desperate to see the living Word of God applied to the real needs of real people in the real world. Once they see that what we have is real, they will want to know where it comes from. If we are going to reach a hurting world with biblical, Christ-centered solutions, we must be a showcase of God's relevance. We must be people who prompt the watching world to say with Ray, the wide-eyed young man in Florida, "That's what I need."

BRIGHT HOPE, PAINFUL IRONY

The world is full of hurting, needy people like Ray. If I had to characterize the general population in only a few words, I would say we are people who are alienated, disconnected, and alone. I believe the outward manifestations of crime, drugs, rebellion, abuse, addiction, and family breakup plaguing our culture spring from alienation at two levels. First, people are alienated from God and his Word. Second, people are alienated from one another, feeling empty, unloved, and alone. They rush through life at a helter-skelter pace, hardly noticing each other.

Many husbands and wives relate at a surface level but fall short of developing true intimacy. Many single adults feel ignored and unimportant in a world that seems to cater to couples and families. Parents talk *to* their children but not *with* them. No wonder one teenager wrote, "I am so lonely I can hardly stand it. I want to be special to someone, but there's no one who cares about me. I can't remember anyone touching me, smiling at me, or wanting to be with me. I feel so empty inside."[1]

This young person speaks for vast multitudes of lonely, alienated people in our world. The hurt is real. The pain is deep. Anxiety, emptiness, and disconnectedness reign in the human heart as our culture tumbles from crisis to crisis.

The World Isn't Listening

Do we have an answer for pain-filled people in a crisis-filled culture? Absolutely! The bright hope gleaming in the darkness of a hurting generation is the person of Jesus Christ and his message of love and forgiveness. Christ is the answer. We believe it wholeheartedly. We preach it and teach it with conviction and passion.

But does the hurting world find our message relevant? By and large, no. Studies confirm that our words and actions fail to clearly communicate Christ's message of hope. The spiritually and relationally needy around us often dismiss the gospel as the solution to their troubled lives because they fail to see its relevance in us.

On the one hand, many unbelievers seem to be very God conscious. A recent national survey reveals that 57 percent of the unchurched consider religion very important to their lives.[2] We find that many unbelievers look to God and the church for help in times of discouragement or trouble. From this data we might expect the world to beat a path to our door for the answers and solace they seek.

Ironically, another study shows that an astounding 91 percent of non-Christians feel that the church is not sensitive to their real needs.[3] In other words, what they hear and see in us is largely not applicable or pertinent to their situation. They find us irrelevant. What a tragedy! Hurting people may come to the right place but far too often go away empty because the way we relate the answer does not apply to their glaring need.

Rick Warren, pastor of Saddleback Community Church in Orange County, California, and author of *The Purpose-Driven Church,* made a similar discovery. Before he opened the doors at Saddleback Church, which now welcomes ten thousand in weekly worship attendance, Warren conducted a house-to-house survey in the community. He discovered four common complaints about churches:

- Church is boring, especially the sermons. The messages don't relate to my life.
- Church members are unfriendly to visitors. If I go to church, I want to feel welcomed without being embarrassed.
- The church is more interested in my money than in me.
- We worry about the quality of the church's child care.[4]

Is the world coming to us for bread, only to be served a stone? That's what the unchurched seem to be saying. I am concerned that we may be losing the battle for truth in this generation because we are not relevant, vital models of God's solution to a hurting world.

Missing the Mark among Our Own

You may be surprised to learn that recent evidence suggests we are failing the test of relevance inside the church as well as outside. A 1994 Josh McDowell Ministry study of 3,795 church-attending youth reveals:

- Fifty-three percent of our church-attending youth feel alone in trouble or crisis.
- Fifty-two percent say they don't want a marriage like their parents'.
- Fifty percent say they are stressed out.
- Fifty-five percent say they are confused.
- Forty-four percent do not believe their church is relevant to their lives.[5]

If our church-attending youth find themselves lonely, stressed out, and confused, can it also be true that a comparable segment of adults are also lonely, stressed out, and confused? Research confirms it. A staggering 74 percent of today's Christian adults claim that the church is not sensitive to their needs.[6]

There are obviously thousands of churches effectively sharing the message of God's love. But among a broader group of the approximately 350,000 churches in this country, something is significantly missing. When a majority of Christian adults claim that the church's message doesn't meet *their* needs, is it any wonder non-Christians find the church irrelevant?

Week after week, men and women come into services and go out unchanged—knowing that they have not been changed.

LARRY RICHARDS,
A New Face for the Church

Loneliness at the Top

Ministry leaders and their families are not immune to the painful alienation plaguing our culture, nor is the message of hope we proclaim always perceived as relevant to those who seem most deeply committed to it. According to a recent survey, 23 percent of Protestant pastors have been officially terminated or forced to resign at least once during their ministries.[7] H. B. London and Neil Wiseman begin their book, *Pastors at Risk,* with the sobering words, "Contemporary pastors are caught in frightening spiritual and social tornadoes which are now raging through home, church, community and culture."[8]

A study by Fuller Institute of Church Growth found that a staggering number of ministers are hurting and finding little relief among those they serve:

- Eighty percent of ministers believe that pastoral ministry negatively affects their families.
- Ninety percent feel they were inadequately trained to cope with ministry demands.
- Seventy percent do not have someone they consider to be a close friend.
- Thirty-seven percent confess to having been inappropriately involved sexually with someone in the church.[9]

Another survey reveals that 41 percent of ministers struggle with anger toward their spouses. Forty-five percent of ministers' wives claim to have no close friends.[10]

Something isn't working. When the message of Christ's love and forgiveness is not being applied to resolve the personal and relational pain of so many of those who proclaim it, we have a crisis of irrelevance in the ministry.

THE HEART OF THE ISSUE

Where have we missed it? We are the body of Christ, ordained by God to proclaim the Good News. So why do we seem to have so little impact on a hurting world, not to mention our own members and leaders?

I propose that our culture no longer sees us as a relevant solution to its needs because we have lost touch with the very heart of who we are. As the people of God, we may hold the "right" views on sin, embrace the "right" concepts of truth, and proclaim the "right" steps to salvation. But if we are out of touch with why we do what we do, our ministries will be irrelevant to the needy world. In my judgment, this is precisely why hurting people are not flocking to our churches today, where the solution to their deepest needs awaits them. And it is also the reason why so many church members are hurting and unfulfilled.

We have lost touch with the very heart of who we are.

What is our essential motive for the ministry of reaching and teaching people in Christ's name? I like to use the term *Great Commandment love.* In one of the most defining moments of his ministry, Jesus was asked which commandment was the greatest. He answered, "'You shall love the Lord your God with all your heart, and with all your soul, and with all your mind.' This is the great and foremost commandment. The second is like it, 'You shall love your neighbor as yourself.' On these two commandments depend the whole Law and the Prophets" (Matthew 22:37-40, NASB). This Great Commandment to love God and love people defines the true identity of those who are called his church. Great Commandment love is at the heart of who we are and what we do.

The Great Commission capsulizes what we *do* while the Great Commandment embodies who we *are*.

Compare Christ's Great Commandment with the equally important Great Commission: "Go therefore and make disciples of all the nations, baptizing them in the name of the Father and the Son and the Holy Spirit, teaching them to observe all that I commanded you" (Matthew 28:19-20, NASB). The Great Commission to declare God's truth on the vital issues of sin, Scripture, and salvation, and to call people to bow in obedience to God, relates more to the *mission* of the church. The Great Commandment to love God and others defines our *identity* or *heart* as a church. The Great Commission capsulizes what we *do* while the Great Commandment embodies who we *are*. What I refer to as the Great Commandment Principle is the accomplishing of the Great Commission within the context of the Great Commandment.

Both are vital to our ministry to the churched and unchurched. We cannot effectively do what we have been called to do unless we embrace and live out our identity as people who love God and others. In fact, when we adhere to the Great Commandment Principle of loving God and one another, we can "do" church effectively because we are "being" his church.

As the Great Commandment Principle comes to more clearly define who we are, it will be God's love that prompts our activity, empowers our work, and becomes the explanation for any "success" we might have. This principle will bring the evidence of his love into every relationship we enjoy and every message we share. "Therefore be imitators of God, as beloved children; and walk in love, just as Christ also loved you" (Ephesians 5:1-2, NASB).

Embracing the Great Commandment Principle does not mean we are soft on the vital issues of sin, Scripture, and salvation. For example, Jesus compassionately said to the woman caught in the act of adultery, "I don't condemn you," but he also said, "Go and sin no more." Great Commandment love connects us to the very heart of God, where we are empowered to minister truth to people whose lives are scarred by sin, disobedient to Scripture, and spiritually lost. Indeed, only when the truth is spoken in love will people be moved to conform to the truth.

Right on the Issues, Wrong in the Heart

During the first century, a group of religious people clung doggedly to their positions on sin, Scripture, and salvation. They upheld ethical absolutes and did not shrink from denouncing sin. They condemned immorality and rejected Roman paganism. If anyone could claim religious "rightness," it was the Pharisees.

But these champions of "proper" doctrinal correctness were the least responsive to Jesus' mission and message. In addition to missing the mark on real truth, something just as vital was missing from their "ministry," making them irrelevant to the needs of their culture. When Jesus compassionately healed a man racked with disease, the Pharisees objected because it happened on the Sabbath when no "work" was to be done. Jesus offered forgiveness and a new start to the woman caught in adultery, but the Pharisees wanted to stone her. Jesus displayed his love for sinners and drunkards by dining with them, while the Pharisees fraternized only with the "righteous."

The Pharisees were obsessed with correct doctrine and performing religious duty, but they lacked a heart of love. No wonder Jesus had such harsh words for them: "Woe to you, scribes and Pharisees, hypocrites! For you are like whitewashed tombs which on the outside appear beautiful, but inside they are full of dead men's bones and all uncleanness. Even so you too outwardly appear righteous to men, but inwardly you are full of hypocrisy and lawlessness" (Matthew 23:27-28, NASB); "Go and learn what this means, 'I desire compassion, and not sacrifice'" (Matthew 9:13, NASB).

Being relevant is not only about believing and behaving; it's also about loving.

Jesus, who is truth incarnate, did not compromise on sin in his expression of love and compassion. He called people to obedience and promised dire consequences if they failed to obey. Jesus *believed* correctly and *behaved* correctly, but most significantly, he, unlike the Pharisees, *loved* correctly. It was his compassion and love that drew people to him. It was his compassion and love that reached out to resistant hearts. It was his compassion and love that made his message of submission and obedience to God attractive, compelling, and relevant.

Being relevant is not only about believing and behaving; it's also about loving. It not only means fulfilling the Great Commission to reach and teach others; it also means fulfilling the Great Commandment to love God and people. It is essential to take a biblical stand and teach the truth on all the right issues. But without a passionate heart of love for God and others, such efforts are as appealing to people as noisy gongs and clanging cymbals.[11]

All across church history we find those who, like the Pharisees, inflicted much pain and hindered the ministry of the gospel in the name of believing and behaving correctly. The Crusades, the Inquisition, the defense of slavery in our own country, the bombing of abortion clinics—all were done in the name of "truth." Where did these people fail? They missed the heart of love behind the truth, and in doing so they actually perverted the truth. They were obsessed with the mission while oblivious to the heart of love that is to motivate the mission.

Relevant, biblical ministry means fulfilling the Great Commission with Christ's constraining love permeating every aspect of our lives.

Relevant, biblical ministry means fulfilling the Great Commission with Christ's constraining love permeating every aspect of our lives. Minimize Great Commandment love in the church, and you have irrelevant ministry. It's that simple. Seeking to advance Christ's cause without demonstrating God's compassionate heart still tends to turn away more people than it attracts. Sadly, this is the state of many churches at the dawn of the twenty-first century.

THE CRITICAL CHALLENGE

As we begin to restore Great Commandment love to our personal lives and ministries, we will be increasingly attractive to the hurting, needy people around us. Two critical questions must be answered in order to effect this vital restoration. First, what does Great Commandment love look like in our lives and ministry? Second, how does restoring Great Commandment love to our lives and ministry make our message relevant? In the pages ahead, I will attempt to paint a word picture of Great Commandment love in action. I will show how this kind of love results in relevant ministry without compromising God's truth about sin, the absolute authority of Scripture, and man's fundamental need for God. And I will share with you the dramatic difference Great Commandment love has made in my own life, marriage, and ministry.

In order for our lives to demonstrate Great Commandment love and impact our world in a relevant way, three things must happen.

1. We must identify and meet the real needs of people. Take Ray, for example. The message of the gospel reached him that night in Florida because he was first touched by the love of God expressed through someone who identified his need for comfort and met that need. In the environment of love, Ray was drawn by the Holy Spirit into a personal relationship with the one who is love! Relevance springs from a body of believers who are deeply in love with God and are able to identify a "neighbor's" needs for comfort or acceptance or security or approval and lovingly meet those needs.

Such a message does not ignore a person's fundamental need to be in right relationship with God and love him with heart, soul, and mind. We must love God first; it's the "first and greatest commandment." But we must go further. Jesus always linked love for God with the second-greatest commandment: love for people. An intimate relationship with the God of love, comfort, encouragement, and hope always challenges us to pass along his love, comfort, encouragement, and hope to others. When we tell people to love and obey God but fail to love them ourselves, our message is irrelevant. But when the love of God, expressed through a few loving Christians in Titusville, met Ray at the point of his needs, he readily welcomed their ministry to his deeper spiritual need. That's relevant ministry!

Jesus always linked love for God with the second-greatest commandment: love for people.

In the chapters that follow, you will learn how to express Great Commandment love in your ministry to others by identifying and meeting real, scriptural needs.

2. We must help people experience God's Word at the point of their need. We must call people to adhere to the absolute truth of God's Word—that's essential. But we must go further than challenging people to believe the right things. We must challenge them to experience the Word of God until it affects every aspect of their lives. Paul wrote, "Knowledge makes arrogant, but love edifies" (1 Corinthians 8:1, NASB). Our relevance in the world is sacrificed when we misapply God's Word, applying it only to the rational mind.

Great Commandment love is expressed when God's Word is experienced in the human heart and lived out through a loving, obedient life.

Think about Ray again. Simply quoting a few Scripture passages to him or giving him a spiritual pep talk would not have met his need for comfort. Great Commandment love in that Florida church included believers' compassionately and lovingly experiencing, with Ray, Romans 12:15, "Mourn with those who mourn," and 2 Corinthians 1:4, "Comfort others," (NLT). A few people mourned Ray's hurts with him and comforted him as the Scriptures direct. They ministered God's love to him. He responded to this outpouring of love and was greatly blessed.

Great Commandment love is expressed when God's Word is experienced in the human heart and lived out through a loving, obedient life. It's the difference between those who only hear the Word and those who do what it says.[12] In this book you will discover how people can experience God's Word personally at the point of their need.

3. We must communicate the true character of God. Ray was a sinner in need of forgiveness when he entered the doors of the church that night. Had we minimized or ignored his sin and need for a Savior in our ministry to him, we would have done him no favor. In ministering to the needs of others, we cannot be soft on sin. But we must go further than challenging people to confess their sin. As we boldly declare Christ as God's provision for sin, we must also reveal the Father's true character, the heart of love behind the gift of his Son.

We misrepresent God's character when we claim that he is concerned only about removing our sin. We must also convey that he loves the sinner! When we demonstrate God's love for people by meeting their needs, we gain their attention, just as Ray's heart was moved by the loving believers in Titusville. And when we tell people that our love comes from God, who yearns to forgive their sin and enjoy a loving relationship with them, many will be reached, just as Ray was. This book will help you to capture and communicate the compassionate heart of God in your life, your relationships, and your ministry.

A Daring Promise

What will happen when we begin to restore Great Commandment love to our lives and ministries? The answers to this question may amaze you. But seeing the biblical principles of Great Commandment love implemented in individuals and churches across this country and abroad over the past fifteen years has confirmed to me that great rewards await those who live and lead according to the Master's model.

You will experience a level of spiritual health you may have thought unreachable this side of heaven. Great Commandment love fosters spiritual health. Personal, family, and ministry crises are averted or quickly resolved when needs are lovingly met according to God's design. When a group of believers expresses God's love, they experience community, and petty divisions and territorial squabbles diminish. When people experience compassionate care in their relationships, they spend less time untangling interpersonal problems, and they invest more time in spiritual development and concern for others.

You will experience growth you may have thought impossible this side of the book of Acts. A Great Commandment church is a growing church. When love is expressed to people at the point of their need, curious sightseers and hungry seekers alike will return and bring their friends. Rick Warren, Saddleback Community Church pastor, writes:

> Look beyond the hype of every growing church and you will find a common denominator: They have figured out a way to meet the real needs of people. A church will never grow beyond its capacity to meet needs. If your church is genuinely meeting needs, then attendance will be the least of your problems—you'll have to lock the doors to keep people out.[13]

The principles in this book are not church growth principles per se. But when you discover how the truth of God's Word is relevant to the real needs of people and communicate that truth within the context of Great Commandment love, the world around will take note that you have "been with Jesus,"[14] and growth will occur.

You will experience fulfillment in your relationships that you may have thought unattainable this side of Eden. Great Commandment love produces healthy marriages, healthy families, and healthy friendships. As you explore how God's Word meets the real needs of people, you will discover that Great Commandment love enables you to meet needs in the lives of your family members and friends. This discovery literally revolutionized my marriage and family life, then overflowed into my church ministry, producing incredible health and growth. For my wife, Teresa, and me, the message of Great Commandment love continues to be the focal point of the ministry God has given us that has expanded to thousands of Christian leaders.

You will experience intimacy with God that you may have thought unspeakable this side of the throne of grace. A Great Commandment follower of Christ enjoys the presence of God in his or her life and ministry. Why? Because in order to love God with heart, soul, and mind and love our neighbor as ourselves, we must be in touch with the loving heart of God. We cannot love at all apart from God's love. The apostle John stated, "We love because he first loved us" (1 John 4:19). Great Commandment love cannot be manufactured; it is God's love and compassion flowing in and through his people to draw a hurting world to himself. And as you deepen your love relationship with God, the most immediate benefit is the intimacy you enjoy with him.

OUR WORLD needs a relevant, vibrant body of believers who will serve as a shelter in the storm, a refuge from the pressures of life, a sanctuary of hope where hurts can be healed and spiritual needs can be met. Christ is the answer—we sincerely believe it. But the needy world has every reason to question the relevance of the answer if our lives and our ministries fail to exude Great Commandment love.

Are you aware of people in your community, in your circle of ministry, and perhaps even in your own home who are in need of a shelter, a refuge, a sanctuary? Do you long to provide solutions that are real, relevant, and revolutionary? Do you believe that God is the answer and that he desires to use his people as his ambassadors for communicating the answer to a hurting world?[15]

If so, you have much in common with a growing movement of pastors and lay leaders across this land whose ministries are relevant and growing. Your colleagues in this movement are committed to fulfill the Great Commission out of a Great Commandment heart of love that meets people at the point of their need. You are among a growing throng who will lead relevant churches into the twenty-first century and experience unprecedented fruitfulness in ministry. This book is about perpetuating the Great Commandment movement—one person, one family, one friend, and one church at a time.

PART ONE

CHAPTER TWO

People Need God and One Another

A PASTOR and his wife approached me during a break in one of our conferences. They wanted to talk about Rachel, a woman in their church they had been counseling for months. As a little girl, Rachel had been sexually abused by her father. Anger and resentment were eating her life away.

"David, we have tried everything we can think of to help her forgive her father, but she won't let go of her bitterness," the pastor lamented. "We remind her that God has forgiven her for things she has done, so she must forgive also. We tell her that forgiving is for her own freedom and that it doesn't mean what happened to her was right in any way. We have gone through all that and more, but nothing works. She is as bitter as ever."

"As you have come to understand Rachel's pain from her past," I said, "what kinds of feelings for her has it prompted in you?"

The couple's response was classic. "Feelings? Just as we said, we feel she needs to forgive her father."

"Yes, Rachel needs to forgive," I agreed. "But what do you feel for Rachel as you consider the painful trauma she experienced?"

I received blank stares, so I rephrased the question. "Can you imagine how God feels toward Rachel for all she went through? This innocent little girl was betrayed and violated by someone she trusted. She probably lay awake in terror countless nights, dreading her father's appearance at the door of her room. What do you think God must have felt toward Rachel every time this defenseless little girl was physically and emotionally wounded?"

The couple was silent for several moments. Then they began sharing their reflections. "God must have felt loving compassion for little Rachel. He probably hurt deeply for her. Her pain must have caused him great sorrow."

Then I said, "If God feels such loving compassion and sorrow for Rachel—and I believe he does—do you think it would be all right if you did?"

Silence again. The pastor seemed to be processing the concept through his theological training. He finally concluded that it was sound.

"The next time Rachel comes in," I continued, "instead of focusing on her need to forgive, try comforting her lovingly for what she has gone through. Say something like, 'As we think about the abuse you suffered, we just want you to know that we really hurt for you. It saddens us that you went through all that.' Simply share your love and comfort and see what happens."

The couple agreed. Several weeks later I received a note from them. It read, "It worked! We shared comfort with Rachel like you suggested, and something wonderful began to happen. She seemed so deeply affected by our sadness and love for her that she is now dealing with the issue of forgiving her father. It's a miracle!"

The expression used most often to describe Christ's emotional life was that he was moved with compassion.

Did Rachel need to forgive her father? Yes. Were this pastor and his wife wrong to urge Rachel to forgive as she had been forgiven by God? Absolutely not. Forgiveness was essential to Rachel's spiritual health and growth. Then why had this couple's ministry to her been, at least in part, ineffective? Because it lacked the full impact of Great Commandment love. Rachel needed someone to challenge her to obey the Scriptures with regard to her father. But she also needed someone to minister to her God's heart of compassion for the pain she had suffered. She needed someone to hurt for her just as God hurt for her and to minister God's love and comfort. When this couple simply expressed godly sorrow for her, she was comforted. Once someone began to meet her deep need for compassion and comfort, Rachel was better able to deal with her need to forgive.

That's what I mean by relevant ministry. The pastor and his wife were diligent in their beliefs and behavior about forgiveness. They exercised Great Commission fervor as they urged Rachel to obey Scripture. They were doing the right thing, but it was not sufficient. They were speaking the truth, but it lacked love. Once their demonstration of Great Commandment love matched their Great Commission fervency, things began to happen for Rachel. That's relevance!

DOES GOD REALLY HURT WHEN WE HURT?

"But wait," you say. "Isn't it a bit overstated to suggest that simply feeling sad with someone demonstrates God's love? And does God really feel sad for people? Does our pain really cause God to hurt?" Some find it difficult to believe that God grieves or feels pain, thinking it portrays him as emotionally unstable. They cringe at the idea that the pain and problems of mere humans affect God in ways that make him seem less than in full control. But isn't a large part of the gospel message about a God who vulnerably enters into the pain of humankind in order to declare his love? Wasn't God's loving act of redemption prompted by his grief and sorrow over our loss of relationship with him and the sad state of our sinfulness?

Scripture confirms it. In Genesis 6:6 we find that God's heart was "filled with pain" over wickedness. God said of wayward Ephraim, "My heart is turned over within Me, all My compassions are kindled" (Hosea 11:8, NASB). The expression used most often to describe Christ's emotional life was that he was moved with compassion.[1] Isn't this vulnerable sharing of his human creation's pain part of what it means to be the God of love? As Dietrich Bonhoeffer wrote at the point of his death, "Only the suffering God can help."

Remember the scene in John 11 following the death of Lazarus? Jesus arrived to find Mary and others weeping. "When Jesus therefore saw her weeping, and the Jews who came with her, also weeping, He was deeply moved in spirit, and was troubled. . . . Jesus wept" (John 11:33-35, NASB). What did the Savior's visible grief and tears communicate? They testified of his love, as revealed in verse 36: "The Jews were saying, 'Behold how He loved him!'" Jesus wept, and even the skeptics perceived it as an expression of his loving compassion!

When we share in the pain of another through heartfelt grief and perhaps even tears, we communicate the Father's love for that person and become channels for the healing power of his comfort. It is this Great Commandment compassion that compels us to reach out to the real needs of people and participate in God's solution. And it is Great Commandment compassion that prepares needy hearts to receive the ministry of Great Commission truth. As the familiar saying goes, people don't care how much we know until they know how much we care. This was the case with Rachel. When those ministering to her shared God's comfort with her, she was more ready to respond to God's truth about forgiveness.

Why have so many churches failed to see—and put into practice—the importance of expressing compassion to hurting people? Why have we so often emphasized the Great Commission without emphasizing the equally vital Great Commandment? I believe one significant reason for the imbalance stems from a basic misunderstanding of human need. In order to correct this misunderstanding, we must revisit and reevaluate the first human crisis.

CRISIS IN PARADISE

Where would you turn in the Bible to find the first human crisis? We have asked this question of thousands of ministry leaders attending our conferences. Roughly 30 percent point to the conflict between Cain and Abel in Genesis 4. Most of the remaining 70 percent suggest that the first human crisis was the temptation and fall of Adam and Eve in Genesis 3. While both of these events are significant human crises, neither is the first. To find the first human crisis you must turn to Genesis 2.

In Genesis 2:18, God utters these words: "It is not good." This is the first reference to the sobering words "not good." Up to this point in Earth's history, everything in creation was good.[2] Now when *people* state that something is not good, it may not be a big deal. But when *God* shows up on the scene and declares something to be "not good," you have a crisis—a *very* big deal.

So what could possibly be "not good" about the Garden of Eden?

Adam lived in a perfect world. There was no crime, no traffic, no pollution, no disease, no war. It was a totally crisis-free environment. Most notably, the Fall had not yet occurred, so Adam was sinless, innocent in heart and mind. This is all good.

Adam also possessed everything he could possibly need or want. The Garden and everything in it—with the exception of one unique tree—were his to use and enjoy.[3] Adam had it all. He never suffered want from a low bank balance, an empty pantry, or an investment loss. In Genesis 2, Adam was living a dream existence. He was in a perfect world and owned everything. What could be "not good"?

Adam had an exalted position. He had an excellent job with no competition for advancement. He was CEO over "the fish of the sea and the birds of the air, over the livestock, over all the earth, and over all the creatures that move along the ground" (Genesis 1:26). He had no problems with job insecurity, jealousy or envy with coworkers, or pressure to perform. Careerwise, he was at the top of the ladder. At this point he was the only person *on* the ladder, but at least he was at the top! Where is the crisis? What could be missing?

Adam enjoyed an intimate relationship with God. Above all the earthly benefits and blessings in the Garden, Adam walked and talked in perfect, uninterrupted fellowship with his Creator. Sin had not yet come between them. Can you imagine the thrill of communing with God face-to-face? You and I might talk about our daily "quiet time" with God. Adam could boast about literally being *with* God every day. Yet something was still "not good." What could possibly be wrong in such an ideal setting?

Created Perfect but Needy

You know the rest of the statement from Genesis 2:18: "It is not good for the man to be alone." God's startling announcement suggests that all the material and spiritual benefits Adam enjoyed did not provide a relevant solution for one particular need. Something vital was missing.

Adam was created with *physical needs.* God met those needs in advance, and it was good. Adam was created with a *spiritual need.* God met that need in advance, and it was good. Adam was created with a *need for human relationships,* but he was alone in the Garden, and it was *not* good. There it is, the first human crisis: Adam, needy for human relationship by God's design, was alone.

"Wait a minute," you may argue. "Adam wasn't alone. God was there. God and man enjoyed intimate fellowship. They walked and talked in the cool of the day. Didn't God meet Adam's relational needs?"

We are biblically incorrect when we assert that God is *all* we need.

Yes, God is the ultimate source for meeting all our needs. We understand both biblically and experientially the need for God. Nothing else—not possessions, not position, not success, not another person—can fill the void that seventeenth-century French physicist Blaise Pascal referred to as the "God-shaped vacuum" within every soul. God and God alone can bring peace and order to the human heart. We know it, we feel it, we live it, and we preach it. Stated simply, people need God.

But we are biblically incorrect when we assert that God is *all* we need. This is precisely why we need a new perspective on human needs and God's provision for those needs. In reality, God provides for our needs through a variety of intermediaries.

For example, consider how God meets our need for physical nourishment. God was not duty bound to create us with a need to eat grain, fruits, vegetables, etc., to survive. God is sovereign and omnipotent. He could have arranged for us to receive our nourishment directly from him without eating, like some kind of heavenly IV drip. But in his wisdom and design, we are nourished by gathering, preparing, and eating the various foods God has created for our use. To be healthy, we need God *and* food.

No man is an island.

JOHN DONNE

Nor was God forced to create us to need sleep for restoring our strength. Had he so chosen, God could have equipped us to receive perpetual energy drawn directly from him. But instead, he meets the need for physical restoration through the process of nightly sleep and rest from labor. In order to meet our need for physical strength, we need God *and* sleep. The fact that God provides for our physical needs through these intermediate sources in no way diminishes that he is the ultimate provider.

Similarly, God did not have to create Adam with a need for a relationship with another like him. The King of the universe could have simply declared to humankind, "I am all you need. Our intimate, personal relationship is sufficient for all your relational needs." Yet, according to Genesis 2, our sovereign God created us with relational needs and chose to meet some of those needs through other people, just as he meets our physical needs through intermediate means. Therefore, we have a need for both God *and* other people.

We Need God and One Another

Two very significant implications for life and ministry derive from the truth that God created us to need each other.

First, none of us can rightfully say, "All I need is God." To do so is to reject other people as a channel of God's loving provision. Adam lived in perfection with a deeply personal knowledge of God. If anyone had grounds to think his intimate relationship with the Creator was all he needed, Adam sure did. "It's you and me, God," he could have said. "You created the world, and I take care of it. Our relationship couldn't get any better. Together we can handle anything, right?"

But God disagreed. "Adam, our relationship is primary," he might have said, "and I will be your most intimate friend. But I also desire to bless you through human relationships, persons with whom you will experience the joy of giving and receiving to meet relational needs. For you and many of your descendants, some relational needs will be met by a spouse and other family members. For those who do not marry, I will provide close single friendships. And one day I will establish my church, where loving relationships will abound."

Meeting some of our relational needs through others was God's original plan in the Garden of Eden, and it remains his plan today. Claiming that we only need God discounts his purpose for human relationships.

Meeting our relational needs through others was God's original plan.

Some people point to Philippians 4:13: "I can do everything through him who gives me strength." They contend that if God was all Paul needed, he is all we need. They equate a holy sense of self-reliance with spiritual maturity. "As long as I walk in constant fellowship with God, as long as I love God completely and exercise enough faith, I don't need anyone else."

But that's not what Paul conveyed to the Philippians. The apostle's expectations and faith were clearly and rightly focused upon Christ, but he follows with verse 14: "Yet it was good of you to share in my troubles." His message is clear: "I can do everything through Christ, and he has chosen to involve you!" Paul, the spiritual giant of the early church, recognized that God lovingly involved others to meet his material, relational, and emotional needs.

I am reminded of Paul's declaration concerning the way each of us functions within Christ's body. One part of the body can't say to another part, "I don't need you."[4] The truth is, I need you, and it's OK for you to need me! When we deny our need for each other, we risk being identified with the lukewarm Laodicean church, who said in proud self-reliance, "I . . . do not need a thing" (Revelation 3:17). The rest of the verse reveals God's appraisal of fiercely self-reliant people: "You are wretched, pitiful, poor, blind and naked." By God's design, we need him and others.

A dimension of "oneness" is missing if the love relationship is limited to communion between God and man. To make "oneness" complete, the same self-giving love must flow in person-to-person relationships.

DAVID L. MCKENNA, *The Communicator's Commentary*

The second implication is closely related to the first. Just as we cannot claim, "All *I* need is God," we cannot truthfully convey the message "*You* only need God." To do so is to communicate a message of condemnation: "You should be able to take care of yourself without needing other people. If you still have needs, you don't have enough of Christ. If you were more consistent in your quiet time, if you had more faith, if you loved God with all your heart, soul, and mind, you would not be needy." As important and necessary as faith and quiet times and loving God are, God has chosen to involve people in meeting the needs of other people.

The "you only need God" message is crippling ministry after ministry today. This message is irrelevant to the real needs of people because it represents only half of the Great Commandment. We may have the loving-God part right, but love for God is incomplete without love for our neighbors. Dismissing our need for one another is the equivalent of saying to a starving beggar, "Go, I wish you well; keep warm and well fed" (James 2:16). To the single adult, it may sound like this: "You shouldn't be lonely because Jesus is a friend that sticks closer than a brother." Or we might communicate to a faithful ministry worker, "Your need to be appreciated is nothing more than pride. God sees your labors, and his reward should be enough." Or we might say to the Rachels in our life, "You just need to forgive and forget your abuse and move on with your life."

Love for God is incomplete without love for our neighbors.

I wonder what some people might have said to Jesus if they had been with him in the Garden of Gethsemane along with Peter, James, and John. Agonizing under the weight of rejection and impending crucifixion, the Savior turns to his disciples and says, "My soul is overwhelmed with sorrow to the point of death. Stay here and keep watch with me" (Matthew 26:38). I am concerned that he might hear some say, "Why do you need *us,* Jesus? Don't you know that you have your Father?"

Did Jesus have his Father? Of course he did. He and his Father were one! But at that moment the despised, rejected man of sorrows asked his closest friends on earth to be there for him, to support him, to pray with him. If the divine Son of God in the fullness of his humanity needed the Father *and* human relationships, how much more do we and the people around us need both the Father and his love through others. Commenting on Mark's Gospel, Ivor Powell wrote, "True religion not only reach[es] the heart of God, it also reach[es] out to the needs of men and women."[5]

TWO COMMANDS IN ONE

Come with me back to the scene as Jesus issues the Great Commandment. I can see the Pharisees and Sadducees gathered around Jesus and his disciples. A lawyer has just posed the question, "Which is the most important commandment in the law of Moses?" (Matthew 22:36, NLT). Jesus' reply will establish that love is what he and his disciples are all about. He is about to reinforce our fundamental need for God and one another.

I can imagine the disciples' expectations as they hear the question. Peter elbows John and says, "Hey, this is important. The Master is about to tell us his ministry priority." I can see John waving the other disciples into a huddle. "OK, fellows, listen up," he begins. "We're about to get our marching orders here. Jesus is going to establish the one commandment that will become our top preaching, teaching, and ministry priority." They all turn to their Master and listen intently as Jesus replies, "You must love the Lord your God with all your heart, all your soul, and all your mind. This is the first and greatest commandment" (Matthew 22:37-38, NLT).

Imagine what might have happened if Jesus had stopped there. I can see Peter turning back to the other disciples and saying something like, "OK, that's it. Our job is to preach a full and complete sell-out to God. We are to love him and him alone. So let's go out and tell the world, 'You only need God.'"

"Let us make man in our image, after our likeness" . . . was an expression of the will of God not only to reveal himself as a fellowship, but to make that life of fellowship open to the moral creatures made in his image and so fitted to enjoy it.

New Bible Dictionary

Of course, Jesus didn't stop after the command to love God. He went on to say, "A second is equally important: 'Love your neighbor as yourself.' All the other commandments and all the demands of the prophets are based on these two commandments" (Matthew 22:39-40, NLT). Jesus later reminded his followers, "By this all men will know that you are my disciples, if you love one another" (John 13:35). Love for God and love for others were inseparable in his teaching.

Imagine Peter turning to the other disciples now. "Did you hear that?" he exclaims. "The greatest commandment is actually two commandments in one! We are to love God with everything we have, and we are to love our neighbor as we love ourselves. So we also have to teach, preach, and live a message that demonstrates the importance of loving intimacy with God *and* others!"

There is no question that the disciples eventually understood Jesus' response that day. The Savior's Great Commandment discourse is recorded by all four Gospel writers. The words of the apostle John demonstrate that he was committed to teaching Christ's Great Commandment: "This is the message you heard from the beginning: We should love one another" (1 John 3:11); "We know that we have passed from death to life, because we love our brothers" (v. 14); "He has given us this command: Whoever loves God must also love his brother" (1 John 4:21). Both Paul and James also referred to fulfilling the whole law by expressing love for our neighbor.[6]

We are created with a capacity to love and be loved by God and others.

It is clear from Christ's teachings and life that we need one another. In his unsearchable wisdom, God opted to meet our relational needs through a love relationship with both himself *and* other human beings. By divine order, we are created with a capacity to love and be loved by God and others. If either of these dimensions is missing, we are not fulfilling the Great Commandment, and the result is not good!

Second Corinthians 1:3-4 further illustrates the need for both vertical and horizontal relationships: "The God of all comfort . . . comforts us in all our troubles, so that we can comfort those in any trouble with the comfort we ourselves have received from God." There is a comfort only God can give. But there is a measure of his comfort that God at times desires to give to others through us—and to give to us through others.

It is not that God's comfort is insufficient or ineffective. He is the "Father of compassion and the God of all comfort" (2 Corinthians 1:3). He hurts with us and comforts us at a level only he can touch. But he has chosen to share the ministry of meeting relational needs with us as we love our neighbors. If we fail, for example, to "comfort those in any trouble with the comfort we ourselves have received," people suffer a degree of relational aloneness that we are designed and called to fill. When this happens, our ministry of the truth to them is, at least in part, irrelevant.

THE MANY FACES OF ALONENESS

The voice on the other end of the telephone line was breaking with emotion. "David, I can't believe it. I feel sad, betrayed, and angry, all at the same time."

Ron was a leader in a prominent church. Chuck, a key elder in the church—and Ron's lifelong friend—had just left his wife and run away with another woman. Through his tears, Ron related a deep sense of betrayal. "What went wrong?" he asked. "Our church taught moral purity. I personally warned the men I discipled about temptation and compromise. I have tried to be a good example to them in my own marriage. Now this. Of all the men in our discipleship group, I never expected Chuck to be the one to fall. Why didn't it work?"

Let's pause to think about Ron's question, "Why didn't it work?" He was declaring the Word of God, making an effort at accountability, establishing a model of faithful marriage. If all these good things were happening, what didn't work for Chuck, allowing him to fall into sin?

"Ron," I said, "I don't know anything about your friend Chuck. I don't know the problems he may have had with his wife. I don't know the compromising circumstances he may have allowed with the other woman or the temptations he faced. But I can tell you one thing: Underneath all the symptoms and the obvious sinful behavior there was likely a huge reservoir of aloneness in Chuck's life. Apparently, he came to church week after week, dealing with his temptations alone. Even in an environment of accountability, he likely struggled with his guilt alone. Tragically, any of us can at times choose sin. But it seems that when a growing sense of aloneness is present, people are much more vulnerable to compromise."

Relational aloneness can be described as a sense of inner disconnectedness, emotional isolation, or relational alienation. This results when we do not experience and share Great Commandment love, that deep, intimate relationship with God and meaningful others. Chuck's adulterous behavior was likely an attempt to fill valid relational needs but in a tragic, sinful way. God designed to meet Chuck's needs through his relationship with Christ and through his wife, his family, and other believers in the body of Christ. God ordained the divine relationships of marriage, family, and the church to be a part of his plan to meet our relational needs. Just as surely as Adam and Eve chose to disobey in Genesis 3, Chuck chose an illegitimate relationship instead of God's abundant provision of relational love.

WRONG BEHAVIOR AND UNMET NEEDS

The caller was obviously stressed out. "David, my two sons are about to kill each other. I'm talking major sibling rivalry between my twelve-year-old and my ten-year-old. Rick and Jeremy are basically good boys. They are Christians, and they enjoy attending kids' activities at church. But at home they constantly yell at each other and try to hurt each other. Even when we're driving to church, I hear from the back seat, 'Daddy, he's breathing my air!' I don't know what to do with them."

Alan had called me for advice. Those of us in Christian ministry get these kinds of calls, don't we? Parents come to us perplexed about kids like Rick and Jeremy who don't get along. We counsel couples who argue and fight and cut each other with words and attitudes. We referee board members who tussle over budgets and the color of the new sanctuary carpet. And at any given time, people in the congregation may be criticizing one another, gossiping about one another, ignoring one another, or in other ways offending one another. Dealing with conflict in the church moved one pastor to quip wryly, "The ministry is great—except for the people."

My response to Alan that day took the form of a question: "How long has it been since you spent a block of quality time with Rick, your twelve-year-old? When was the last time he had your undivided attention, doing something with you *he* wanted to do?"

Alan was silent. Apparently he had no answer.

I asked another question. "How long has it been since you set aside time for having fun with Jeremy, your ten-year-old?"

Again he was silent.

When a growing sense of aloneness is present, people are much more vulnerable to compromise.

"Alan, what I'm about to suggest comes from many years of *not* practicing this with my own son. But when I finally began, it improved our relationship immensely. As soon as you hang up the phone, take Rick aside and say something like, 'This Saturday, you and I are going to spend the morning together. We'll do anything you want to do. Start thinking about some fun things you want to do, and we'll do them together.'" Then I urged him to make the same commitment to Jeremy for the next Saturday morning. "Invest some quality time with each of your sons doing what they want to do. Don't even talk about the problem during your special times with them. Just have fun, and see if the rivalry changes. Then call me back in a few weeks."

Alan didn't call back. But about four months later I ran into him at a meeting. He approached me with a smile. "It worked, David. I've been spending time with Rick and Jeremy individually, and they're getting along better than ever. They even apologized to each other. The arguing and antagonism is going away. And I really enjoy being with my sons again."

Was Rick's and Jeremy's behavior toward each other sinful? Yes, but simply hearing their dad tell them to stop doing wrong and start doing right was insufficient. Their sinful behavior was exacerbated by a powerfully motivating need: aloneness. They missed their dad. Alan had been so busy he failed to communicate his love to those closest to him. Rick and Jeremy were apparently starving for attention, and in addition to acting out their sinfulness, they were acting out their aloneness by fighting with each other. And by so doing, they did get a form of Dad's attention!

But as the boys' deep need for their dad's loving attention was met, they were better able to act on what they knew was right. And if further discipline was needed, their father's discipline would model the heavenly Father's, who "disciplines those he loves" (Hebrews 12:6). Love first, then discipline. That's a picture of applying a relationally relevant message to a glaring need. That's Great Commandment ministry in action.

We are talking here about applying the whole biblical message of loving God and one another to the real needs of people. When our message applies to spiritual needs while overlooking relational needs, it does not fully apply to the situation at hand. It is irrelevant, extraneous. Why? We are delivering only part of the answer. And we do so because we misunderstand the human need for relationship, claiming that people only need God. In reality, we need both God and others.

MEETING REAL NEEDS WITH A COMPLETE SOLUTION

As we explore the restoration of Great Commandment love to the twenty-first century church, imagine the difference in the impact of these two messages—"we only need God" versus "we need God and one another." Which sounds more relevant to real human need? Is it possible that the insufficient "you only need God" message is a significant contributor to the 91 percent whose responses to a survey indicated that the church was insensitive to their needs?[7] Could it be that the "we all need God and one another" message is more relevant to the needs at hand?

New Birth Missionary Church near Atlanta, Georgia, is a living example of how quickly and effectively this relevant message can be applied. The church became concerned about the rising crime rate among the youth in the area. As church leaders considered the problem, they acknowledged that the young people were not just delinquents; they were kids with deep, unmet relational needs. They had not experienced an abundance of Great Commandment love. New Birth decided to help at the level of deepest need.

The church worked out an arrangement with law enforcement authorities to assign youth offenders to church families. These families, trained to identify the relational needs of the young people, began to minister to their aloneness by loving them as their special "neighbors." Classes were also offered to equip neighborhood parents in Great Commandment love as their children began to function more appropriately at home. Together, church and families provided an abundance of loving attention, comfort, and care for these love-starved youth. As the wayward kids experienced loving care and came to consider their own personal relationship with Christ, their deepest relational needs were being met.

Imagine the difference in the impact of these two messages: "we only need God" versus "we need God and one another."

To date, hundreds of juvenile delinquents and their parents have been ministered to by the families of New Birth Missionary Church. Many have made personal commitments to Christ. An astounding 90 percent of the kids cared for in this way have not been arrested again! And this Great Commandment church is a growing church. As a result of its commitment to meet people at the point of their need, New Birth is one of the fastest growing churches in America, welcoming some seven thousand people on a typical Sunday. Over thirty thousand people attend the church's annual Easter service in Atlanta's Georgia Dome.

An essential step to becoming a relevant ministry in today's culture is acknowledging that people need both God and one another. Once needs are identified, love can be applied to meet those needs.

But what does Great Commandment love actually look like in ministry? How does Great Commandment love identify and meet the real needs of people? The next chapter will begin to equip you to identify those needs.

CHAPTER THREE

Great Commandment Love Identifies Needs

ANDY was big, burly, and mean, kind of like an NFL linebacker—except Andy didn't play football. He was just a very big, very angry forty-year-old man. Though he was a Christian, Andy had a history of violence that often got him into big trouble. In the past, when he flew into one of his frequent rages, Andy was likely to throw furniture across the room, drive his fist through a wall, or punch somebody's lights out. A dozen years prior to his visit with me, he had spent time in jail for physically abusing his wife and kids. This man had been like a hand grenade with the pin pulled, ready to go off at the slightest provocation.

During another time of marital separation caused by Andy's violent anger, his pastor and church elders had confronted Andy's sinful behavior. Church discipline in accordance with Matthew 18:15-20 was initiated. Even though Andy was beginning to respond to the Lord's discipline, his wife and the church leadership felt that still more help was needed.

Clint, Andy's pastor, called me. "David, I'm at the end of my wits with Andy. We have prayed together on numerous occasions about his anger. I sense his genuine desire to change and find freedom. He has made much progress, but both he and I are fearful of the future. I have counseled him from Scripture, and he is involved in a men's accountability group. But I still sense a reservoir of rage just below the surface. Nothing seems to help. I'm afraid that one of these days soon

Andy might hurt someone again. Will you please talk to him?" I said I would if Clint came along. He agreed.

When the two men walked in, Andy was noticeably irritated because Clint had insisted that he come. I sat down with this six-foot three-inch, 230-pound stick of dynamite and began to talk. "Andy, your pastor has filled me in on your background, and I have read about some of the things you have done. I rejoice with you in your recent confessions and appreciate your desire to find freedom from your anger. But I want to tell you something else I know about you. I know that underneath the anger and violence and rage that have ruled your life for so many years, you are really hurting."

Andy's face softened, as if the anger was being drained from him. I continued, "In fact, when I think about the magnitude of abuse that has poured out of your life, I'm convinced that there is an enormous amount of pain and hurt and fear inside you. That pain has probably been festering there a long time. And you have been dealing with it all alone."

God wants to minister healing to you at the point of your pain.

When I said the word "alone," tears came to Andy's eyes.

I said, "You know the pain is in there, don't you, Andy?"

He nodded in agreement.

"Andy, just like God brought you to a point of confession over your sinful rage, he also wants to minister healing to you at the point of your pain. Would you like to begin ridding yourself of the pain and hurt and fear that have haunted you all these years?"

He nodded, and the tears started to roll down his cheeks.

"You know that your pastor loves you, don't you, Andy?"

He indicated that he did.

"Then I'm going to slip out of the room for a few minutes. The

Bible states that God is the God of all comfort, and at times he desires to share with us some of his comfort through others. If you are willing, I'd like you to move over beside Clint and just begin telling him about your hurt, and let your pastor hurt with you. Would you be willing to do that?"

Andy said he would.

I prayed with them briefly and then left the room. I was gone for about twenty minutes while Andy wept and poured out three decades of deep hurt. When I returned, Clint and big, tough Andy were on their knees embracing. They had just finished praying together.

At Clint's encouragement Andy told me part of his story. Running home one night because he was late, nine-year-old Andy took a shortcut through the park. Some men stepped out of the darkness and grabbed him. The men sexually abused the terrified boy, then let him go.

When Andy finally got home, he was filled with shame and self-condemnation. Feeling that the abuse was his own fault, he took his punishment for being late and never told his parents about the incident in the park. For thirty years Andy had carried his pain and shame alone, blaming himself for the humiliating abuse he had suffered. "None of it would have happened," he had told himself repeatedly, "if I had not been late."

It was "not good" for Andy to carry his pain and shame alone, as evidenced by the violence and abuse that had boiled out of him since childhood. Andy had suffered through this relational and emotional crisis for thirty years, alone and without comfort. His sinful rage was inexcusable, and yet in a brief encounter with God's comfort, additional victory and freedom had been realized. Andy rose from his knees that day with a great burden lifted and a new perspective on his life as a Christian.

There was still much healing ahead. This was only one step in his journey of healing, but it was a very important step. His wife later offered her tear-filled comfort, and Andy experienced even deeper sorrow over how he had hurt her and his children. The Great Physician had begun a good work in Andy and his family, and he would faithfully complete it.

LOVE MEETS VALID NEEDS

What was it about Pastor Clint's ministry in those short minutes that brought additional blessing and freedom to Andy's life? He had previously done everything he could think of to help him get over his violent temper. He had led him in prayer many times. He had encouraged him to meditate on the Word of God. He had provided an accountability group of godly men to support Andy. What made the difference during their short time together in my office?

That day Clint began to meet a need in Andy that other efforts to help him, as good and necessary as they were, had not met. Andy needed someone to love him selflessly as the second half of the Great Commandment directs. He needed someone to be a channel of God's healing comfort on a horizontal level. In those few minutes in my office, God loved Andy through Clint and began to meet his need for comfort. Andy knew that God loved him all along, but it was the demonstration of God's love through Clint's comfort that brought additional healing to his deep inner pain.

Great Commandment love says,
"We need God *and* one another."

Clint and other church leaders had already challenged Andy with the first half of the Great Commandment. Their scriptural challenge had encouraged Andy's confession of sin, accountability to change, and intimate walk with God. These steps were necessary, but God also desired to minister to Andy's hurt through other people. As we have already said, a ministry that communicates "you only need God" is not fully relevant. Andy's healing was more fully encouraged when Clint—and later others—implemented the second half of the Great Commandment by loving him as they loved themselves. It is this demonstration of God's love that brings relevance.[1]

Identifying Valid Needs

Pastor Clint and others fulfilled the Great Commandment in Andy's life by bringing him to God *and* by meeting his human need for comfort. Great Commandment love says, "We need God *and* one another." It is relevant in human lives because it seeks to meet both spiritual needs and valid relational needs, thus removing the aloneness that God calls "not good."

But how do we identify valid relational needs? In short, by identifying in Scripture how God has demonstrated his love toward us and how we are to love others in return. Wherever you find God demonstrating his love for his human creation, you will also find a valid relational need that he desires to meet, at least in part, through us.

In 2 Corinthians 1:3-4, God is described as "the God of all comfort, who comforts us in all our troubles." This passage establishes that human beings have a need for comfort in times of trouble, because God would not comfort us unless we needed it. But he doesn't stop there. We are to "comfort those in any trouble with the comfort we ourselves have received from God" (v. 4). Notice the pattern. The passage establishes our need for comfort in troubled times, declares that God is the ultimate source of the comfort we need, and calls us to lovingly share his comfort with those who need it.

The teaching of our Lord and of the Apostle Paul continually centers around "I," yet there is no egotism about it—everything in the Bible is related to man, to his salvation, to his sanctification, to his keeping.

OSWALD CHAMBERS, *My Utmost for His Highest*

Another example is found in Romans 15:7: "Accept one another, then, just as Christ accepted you." The passage establishes our need for acceptance, declares that God is the ultimate source of the acceptance we need, and calls us to meet the need for acceptance in others.

In Romans 15:5 we find "the God who gives . . . encouragement," and 1 Thessalonians 5:11 adds, "Therefore encourage one another." These passages establish our need for encouragement, reveal God as the source of encouragement, and command us to lovingly share encouragement with others.

Twenty-four times in the New Testament, believers are instructed to "greet one another." The word "greet" means more than just saying hello. It relates to deeply knowing and expressing caring concern. Since we are urged to express care to one another, we must have a need for this kind of care. So we must express caring concern for others just as God cares for us. In these passages God seems to be saying, "Just as my Son took the initiative to enter into your world, to know you deeply, and to care for you with loving concern, you must do the same to your friends and the friendless."

A valid need is one that God has met in our lives and admonishes us to meet in the lives of others.

A valid need is one that God has met in our lives and admonishes us to meet in the lives of others through the expression of Great Commandment love. As we love God and freely receive from him, we are to freely give to others.[2] God is Jehovah-jireh, our provider. He has promised to meet all our needs,[3] and he has chosen to do so through our families, friends, and church communities as we love God and allow him to share his life through us. That's what Great Commandment love does: It meets valid relational needs from the resources God freely supplies.

TEN VITAL RELATIONAL NEEDS

Most of us can explain what love is. Passages like 1 Corinthians 13 define love as patient, kind, humble, forgiving, protective, persevering, etc. But where do we learn what love says and does in specific situations?

I believe we discover love's practical, caring dimensions in Bible passages that reveal relational needs we are to meet through God's limitless provision. The examples in previous paragraphs are a start. But dozens of passages in Scripture establish valid needs from God's perspective and call us to join him in the ministry of meeting those needs.

Consider the "one anothers" of the New Testament, for example: accept one another, encourage one another, be affectionate to one another, bear one another's burdens, and so on. Each reveals an area of human relational need where Great Commandment love may be applied in practical, caring ways.

In the following pages we will explore ten relational needs that appear to be among the most significant in Scripture. This list of needs is by no means comprehensive, but it will provide an excellent starting point for meeting the needs of others out of the abundance of God's love for us. When we grow in sharing Great Commandment love sensitively and sacrificially, our ministries will become increasingly relevant to the real needs of people.

In the chapters that follow we will describe in detail what Great Commandment ministry looks like as we meet the needs listed below. For now, we will simply identify and define ten specific needs from Scripture.

Dozens of passages in Scripture establish valid needs and call us to help meet those needs.

COMFORT

Giving Strength and Hope; Easing the Grief or Pain; Hurting with; Consoling[4]

The God of all comfort, who comforts us in all our troubles, so that we can comfort those in any trouble. (2 Corinthians 1:3-4)

THE HUMAN need for comfort is one of the most critical and perhaps most misunderstood needs in the church today. This is why we deal with this particular need in detail throughout this book. Since we live in a culture riddled with pain, it is vital that we learn and practice the loving ministry of comforting troubled people.

Everyone suffers physical and emotional pain in life. Medical treatment can bring relief to a physical injury or illness. But the emotional hurt from abuse, the death of a loved one, a business failure, or a broken marriage or friendship requires a different type of treatment. Romans 12:15 admonishes us to "mourn with those who mourn." In the Sermon on the Mount, Jesus said, "Blessed are those who mourn, for they will be comforted" (Matthew 5:4). Meeting the need for comfort in someone struggling with inner pain requires a Great Commandment heart expressing words and acts of compassion and comfort.

The ministry of comfort is not about trying to "fix" people.

The ministry of comfort is not about trying to "fix" people, correct them, or motivate them with a pep talk. Such efforts may help at times, but they do not bring comfort. The God of comfort gives hope and strength and eases pain in a hurting person when we compassionately mourn that hurt with them. Andy was comforted when Clint listened to him and shared in the pain of his past. The ministry of comfort from Clint, Andy's wife, and others played a critical role in Andy's continued freedom.

Today Andy and his wife are lay leaders in their church, leading a team of couples who help other couples and families struggling with the pain of their past.

ATTENTION (CARE)

Taking Thought of Another and Conveying Appropriate Interest and Concern; Entering Another's World

The members [of the body] should have the same care for one another. (1 Corinthians 12:25, NASB*)*

WHEN YOU were a child, who entered your world and showed you attention? Perhaps it was a parent who faithfully attended your soccer games or spent long hours with you assembling science projects. Perhaps it was a grandparent who got down on the floor with you to play with blocks or dolls. It may have been a teacher, a coach, a youth minister, or a pastor who generously gave to you his or her time, attention, and care. Do you remember how it stirred your heart that someone cared enough to know you and get involved in your world?

Everyone needs attention to some degree. Great Commandment love is expressed when we meet this valid need for attention in others. Jesus met our deepest need for attention by leaving his home in heaven and entering our world. He became like us in order to relate to us and allow us to relate to him. Paul urged believers to "have the same care for one another" (1 Corinthians 12:25, NASB). Having freely received God's personal and loving attention, we are able to freely give our attention to others.

ACCEPTANCE

Deliberate and Ready Reception with a Favorable Response; Receiving Willingly; Regarding as Good and Proper[5]

Accept one another, then, just as Christ accepted you, in order to bring praise to God. (Romans 15:7)

WE ALL have a deep relational need for others to accept us for who we are, "warts and all." When Paul admonished us to accept one another, he established Christ as our model. How did Christ accept us? Completely, by dying for us while we were yet in sin.[6] How was it that Christ was able to accept us? Because it is his nature to love the unlovable. His loving acceptance is able to distinguish who we are from what we have done. Even in our sin, we are the objects of his love. Since God has accepted us so freely in Christ, we are to share this same love by freely accepting others.

APPRECIATION

Recognizing with Gratitude;[7] Communicating with Words and Gestures Personal Gratefulness for Another Person; Praising

I praise you. (1 Corinthians 11:2)

EVERYONE NEEDS to hear and sense the praise and gratitude of others. Paul expressed appreciation to the Corinthian believers by writing, "I praise you for remembering me in everything and for holding to the teachings" (1 Corinthians 11:2). God seems to model his affirmation of us by calling us his children, saints, joint-heirs, and his own people.[8] He has made us new in Christ and then affirms his new work in us. In a similar way, God can love others through us as we share in a ministry of affirmation and praise.

SUPPORT

Coming Alongside and Gently Helping to Carry a Problem or Struggle; Assisting; Providing For

Carry each other's burdens, and in this way you will fulfill the law of Christ. (Galatians 6:2)

PEOPLE OFTEN feel more needy and alone in times of high stress than at any other time in their lives. Trying to balance a hectic schedule of work, family obligations, home upkeep, ministry responsibilities, committee meetings, and so on is stressful enough. Add a surprise layoff or major move, conflicts with neighbors or coworkers, a serious illness, a death in the family, relational disappointments, or a marriage, family, or financial crisis, and you have a high-stress situation. People under these conditions often feel alone, friendless, and lost.

God has given us the responsibility to provide support for those in need when times are tough. God supported us at the point of our greatest need by lifting our burden of sin and guilt. Just as God has sent the *paraclete*—the "one called alongside"—who provides daily support by comforting, guiding, and interceding for us, we are to do the same for others.

ENCOURAGEMENT

Urging Forward and Positively Persuading toward a Goal; Inspiring with Courage, Spirit, or Hope; Stimulating[9]

Therefore encourage one another and build each other up. (1 Thessalonians 5:11)

DISCOURAGEMENT IS a common human affliction. It can set in when we lose sight of a goal or when we lose hope through disappointment, frustration, rejection, or failure. Discouragement can set in when life just seems to be more than we can bear. God created us to lift the spirits of the discouraged, to inspire one another in dark times, and to give hope and courage when all seems lost. The writer of Hebrews challenges us to "consider how to stimulate one another to love and good deeds . . . encouraging one another" (Hebrews 10:24-25, NASB).

AFFECTION

Communicating Care and Closeness through Physical Touch and Affirming Words

Having thus a fond affection for you, we were well-pleased to impart to you not only the gospel of God but also our own lives. (1 Thessalonians 2:8 NASB*)*

DURING THE nine months before birth, a child is enveloped by human touch in his mother's womb. From the moment of birth we reach out for the warm embrace of a mother's arms. From infancy through childhood and into adulthood the God-created need for affection does not disappear. Touching somehow reconnects us with one another, makes us feel close, and removes our aloneness. No wonder Scripture instructs us to "greet one another with a holy kiss (Romans 16:16), encouraging appropriate, physical affection among believers. Paul's affection for those at Thessalonica was also communicated through tender, affirming words: "You had become so dear to us" (1 Thessalonians 2:8).

Great Commandment love may be expressed through the affectionate care of a father and a mother, the affectionate words of a dear friend, or the affectionate touch of a loving spouse.

RESPECT

Valuing and Regarding Highly; Conveying Great Worth; Esteeming; Honoring

Show proper respect to everyone. (1 Peter 2:17)

SCRIPTURE IS specific in its command to give honor and respect to others. We express Great Commandment love when we respect and honor our parents, the aged, and governing rulers.[10] But we are also to "give preference to one another in honor" (Romans 12:10, NASB) and show honor to those who are due honor.[11] We communicate respect as we value another's ideas and opinions and as we affirm another's strengths and gifts. We also show respect for others by respecting their privacy, property, and time.

SECURITY

Freedom from Harm, Danger, and Fear; Putting beyond Hazard of Losing, Want, or Deprivation;[12] Confidence of "Harmony" in Relationships

Perfect love drives out fear. (1 John 4:18)

WE EXPERIENCE security when we feel safe and sense that we will be provided for and cared for. A love relationship with God provides ultimate security. God promises to provide for us and protect us as we live in relationship with him. But God desires that we provide security and safety in our human relationships.

Loved ones may feel *satisfied* when their needs are *currently* being met. But they feel *secure* when they have confidence that their *future* needs will be met. For example, your children are satisfied after you provide a good meal for them. But they are secure when they know your love includes a commitment to meet their future physical needs and to be there for them tomorrow, next week, and next month. Your spouse may be satisfied with a comfortable home and nice clothes. But he or she will feel secure when your love prompts you to adequately prepare for the future, particularly through a commitment to spiritual growth and marital harmony. A friend may be satisfied when you help her pray through an important decision, but she is secure when she senses your commitment to deep and lasting friendship.

We build security in relationships when we say through our lives, "I am committed to be here for you and, as God allows and provides, to meet your needs both now and in the future."

APPROVAL

Affirming as Satisfactory; Giving Formal Sanction to; Expressing a Favorable Opinion; Approving Of[13]

Anyone who serves Christ in this way is pleasing to God and approved by men." (Romans 14:18)

GOD SEEMS to have created us with the need to hear him say, as he did about Jesus, "This is My beloved Son, in whom I am well-pleased" (Matthew 3:17, NASB). But we also have a need for others to express their love with words and actions that communicate, "I am pleased with you." Approval should focus more on people's worth to their Creator than on what they accomplish; not so much on what they achieve as why they achieved it. Approval places value on the qualities that enable success—qualities like determination, persistence, creativity, reliability, attention to detail, etc. Expressing love through approval requires that we really *know* a person. It is not enough just to know *about* him or her.

When we fail to share approval with others, they may become

"weary in well doing." But when we demonstrate loving and genuine approval, God seems to use it to motivate others to right living and faithful stewardship.

WHEN NEEDS GO UNMET

God created us with these basic relational needs. He is the ultimate source for meeting each need, but in his Great Commandment he calls us into partnership with him to meet the needs of our "neighbors" at home, at church, at work, and beyond. How important is it that we respond to his call by expressing Great Commandment love? It is critical for the spiritual, emotional, and relational health of our loved ones, friends, and coworkers. When we fail to express God's love to others in practical, need-meeting ways, needs go unmet. And this "love void" can set in motion a complex and painful chain reaction in hurting people. For example:

- When people fail to receive needed *comfort* for their emotional hurts, inner healing and spiritual growth are often hindered.
- When people are not granted sufficient *attention,* they may lose their sense of being important to others.
- When people do not receive *acceptance,* they may have difficulty grasping their worth in the Father's eyes.
- When people are not properly *appreciated,* they may struggle with feelings of insignificance.
- When people do not receive our *support,* they may feel overwhelmed and hopeless.
- When people are not *encouraged,* they may grow weary and give up.
- When people do not receive sufficient *affection,* they may feel unloved and unlovable.
- When people do not receive our *respect,* they may feel ignored and unimportant.
- When people do not sense *security* in a relationship, they may be paralyzed by fear and distrust.
- When people do not receive our *approval,* their sense of value may be diminished.

Most tragically, each of these breakdowns in human relationship may hinder an individual's openness to the heavenly Father and his love. Herein lies the great potential for the twenty-first-century church. As we clearly express God's Great Commandment love to those experiencing emptiness, rejection, pain, and loneliness, they become fields ready for harvest.

MESSAGE OF HOPE OR CONDEMNATION?

Several years ago I met a woman named Sandy, who was a psychiatric patient. She had been admitted to the hospital after attempting suicide. During several visits with her, I learned the woman's tragic story.

A year earlier, Sandy's husband had been killed in a head-on collision with a drunk driver, leaving her with three children under the age of six. Sandy was understandably devastated by the loss. But over a period of months she determinedly worked through her denial, her anger at God, and her bitterness toward the drunk driver. She finally began dealing with the enormity of her grief. When depressed or angry, Sandy was able to admit her feelings and deal with them. She came through the first nine months of her pain very well, all things considered.

God has ordained marriage, family, and the church to meet valid relational needs.

Finally Sandy found the courage to get involved in the singles ministry of her church. The church family had ministered to her often after the tragic accident. Well-intentioned people continued at times to ask how she was doing. In the past, she had often answered, "I'm just numb" or "I'm depressed." After processing much of her pain, she began to answer the question differently. Sandy said very honestly, "I just feel very lonely.

But the responses she often received were less than comforting:

"How can you be lonely? Don't you know you have God?"

"Lonely? That's not good. Maybe you need to see the pastor."

"A Christian doesn't need to feel lonely."

Self-doubt quickly set in. *I still feel lonely,* Sandy admitted to herself. *Why doesn't God take away my loneliness? There must be something wrong with me.*

Within three months, the message of condemnation heaped on top of her devastating loss prompted Sandy to try to take her own life. Her glaring need and deep pain had been met by something less than Great Commandment love, and we almost lost her.

God has ordained the divine relationships of marriage, family, and the church as circles of safety where love is expressed to meet valid relational needs. His desire for every marriage, family, and single adult friendship is a deep, loving intimacy with himself and others. People like Sandy, Rachel, and Andy represent hundreds of thousands of people attending our churches every week with unmet needs for comfort, support, encouragement, affection, approval, etc. And they represent countless millions of unchurched people who hunger for a relevant expression of the Father's love in their lives.

When the truth of God's Word is made alive in us, prompting us to love our neighbors by meeting their needs, relevant ministry takes place. As God's people freely share with others out of the abundance of his encouragement, acceptance, affection, comfort, etc., the twenty-first-century church truly becomes "Christ's ambassadors, as though God were making his appeal through us" (2 Corinthians 5:20).

The good news is that we can learn to better express Great Commandment love in all our relationships. The key to unleashing relevant ministry is what I often call *experiencing God's Word.* Scripture provides specific instructions for applying Great Commandment love to relational needs. Therefore, if we are to effectively express God's love in our homes, friendships, churches, workplaces, and neighborhoods, we must learn how to be biblically relevant—applying Scripture to human hearts and relationships as well as to the mind.

CHAPTER FOUR

Great Commandment Love Meets Needs As People Experience Scripture

THE prayer meeting had lasted for ten days straight, and Peter's knees were probably sore from kneeling. Just before ascending into heaven, Jesus had commanded his followers, "Do not leave Jerusalem, but wait for the gift my Father promised. . . . You will receive power when the Holy Spirit comes on you; and you will be my witnesses in Jerusalem, and in all Judea and Samaria, and to the ends of the earth" (Acts 1:4-8). Christ's words reminded Peter of the prophecy of Joel: "I will pour out my Spirit on all people" (Joel 2:28). So Peter, the disciples, and other believers, about 120 in all, had expectantly stayed, prayed, and waited.

After they had waited ten days, I can imagine that some in the upper room were getting antsy. Would anything really happen? Or was Jesus' promise a mere platitude to boost their spirits at his departure? But knowing that Jesus' words were to be both heard *and* experienced, Peter may have tried to steady the others. "We heard the Master say that he would send the Holy Spirit, so I intend to wait until I experience—"

A startling sound exploded around them. The noise may have taken Peter back to that stormy day on the lake—the day he thought he was going to drown. It seemed that the howling gale that had threatened to swamp the boat had now returned, as if to blow the house down around them. The roar was accompanied not by a torrent of water but a flood of fire baptizing all in the room.

Though filled with wonder and a tinge of fear, Peter did not panic. He likely understood that the words of the Master were being fulfilled in their midst. Since the disciples acted obediently on Christ's command to wait, God had met their need for the Spirit's indwelling power.

"This Is That Which Was Spoken. . . ."

The events of the next several hours swept by in a blur. Along with the roar of wind and the flash of fire came a supernatural ability to speak languages the followers of Jesus had never learned. They burst from the upper room and proclaimed the wonders of God in the streets to foreigners visiting Jerusalem for the Feast of Pentecost. A crowd of thousands gathered in amazement, asking, "What does this mean?" (Acts 2:12).

I can see Peter standing before the crowd. Pointing to the disciples who are witnessing by the power of the Holy Spirit, he says, "This—" he taps repeatedly on an Old Testament scroll unfurled to Joel's prophecy—"is that which was spoken by the prophet Joel" (Acts 2:16, KJV).

I can hear Peter continue. "People of Jerusalem, what you are seeing here today is what Joel 2:28-32 is supposed to look like—God's Spirit being poured out on all people. For centuries we have read and discussed Joel's prophecy, and now the followers of Jesus Christ are actually experiencing those Scripture passages!" Peter went on to preach a convicting sermon, three thousand people were converted, and the church began its relevant and powerful impact on the first-century world.

HEAR, RECEIVE, AND EXPERIENCE THE WORD

How often have we yearned to recapture the dynamic relevance of the first-century church? Haven't we prayed for people to be gripped by love for their neighbors, compassion for the lost, and boldness for witnessing? Don't we long to lead the congregations we serve to experience the dramatic growth of that first-century congregation? After two thousand years, the church in the book of Acts remains in many ways the high-water mark for all of us in ministry.

What made the early church dynamic and relevant? More important, what elements from the Acts church need to be restored to our ministries if we are to realize the vibrant health and growth of the early church?

One significant aspect of first-century church ministry was an emphasis on loving God and others. Consistent with Christ's Great Commandment emphasis, we note the early believers "continually devoting themselves to the apostles' teaching and to fellowship, to the breaking of bread and to prayer" (Acts 2:42, NASB). As noted previously, restoring Great Commandment love both vertically (with God) and horizontally (with our neighbors) is critical to relevant ministry in our day.

This new church ministered to one another. They loved each other, confessed their sins to one another, served one another and carried each other's burdens. It is difficult to imagine them "congregating," sitting in rows, looking at the back of one another's heads.

MICHAEL MACK, *The Synergy Church*

Another critical ingredient in the early church's success was its emphasis on the application of truth. They taught that the truth of God's Word was to be experienced in attitudes and actions. The apostle John admonished, "Dear children, let us not love with words or tongue but with actions and in truth" (1 John 3:18). Truth was meant to be believed *and* lived out.

Certainly we must take a firm stand for truth. We must proclaim that Scripture is the authoritative, absolute truth of God. Yet we must go further. We can be Bible-believing, Bible-teaching churches and still be irrelevant to the needs of people if we misapply God's Word by appealing only to the rational mind.

God's Word is to be believed and embraced as absolute truth. But truth is also to be experienced emotionally and relationally. The Bible is not only a book we are to believe intellectually; it is also truth we are to act upon and experience in our lives.

When we believe *and* experience scriptural truth in our relationships with God and others, we put Great Commandment love into action. And that's what a hurting world needs to see—a model of God's Word in action, a body of believers experiencing God's Book, loving God, and loving one another. That's relevance.

As Jesus walked with Peter and the other disciples beside the Sea of Galilee, he encouraged them to experience biblical truth by relating the parable of the sower, seed, and soils. He explained that we are to "hear the word, accept it, and produce a crop" (Mark 4:20). Hear, receive, and experience are three vital levels of involvement with God's Word. Hearing is important, but when the Word is not received and experienced, it can be stolen away by Satan or choked out by the worries of this life. Receiving the Word is also important, but if we fail to live out the Word, the troubles of life can cause it to wither and fall away.

After Jesus delivered the parable to the multitudes, the disciples came to him privately to ask him about it (see v. 10). They wanted to *know* more, so Jesus explained the parable of the sower to them. I can imagine the arrogance some of the disciples might have felt, realizing they were now better informed than the multitudes.

"I know what the seed represents; do you?"

"Let me fill you in on who the sower is."

Tragically, this is where much of our preaching, teaching, and leadership development ends. We have the mistaken idea that greater knowledge equals greater maturity; that the more people know from the Bible, the better prepared they are to live the Christian life and lead others.

The disciples now *knew* more about the parable of the sower, but had they actually *experienced* it yet? Not at all. But the day wasn't over, and Jesus intended to make this parable vitally relevant to his men.

In Mark 4:35, Jesus (the sower) sowed the seed: "Let us go over to the other side."

As they pushed off onto the Sea of Galilee, tribulation, Satan, and the cares of this life were there in the storm to steal the Word. The disciples were terrified. Everything they *knew* about who the sower is and what the seed represents would no longer help them. Lost in the screaming wind and pounding waves was the truth Jesus meant for them to experience: When the Master says "Let us go over to the other side," no storm will be able to prevent their safe arrival. Instead of trusting in Christ and his Word, the well-informed disciples cowered in fear. They failed to *experience* the Word that day, and their lack of faith was exposed.

The Word of God becomes relevant only when it is heard, received, *and* experienced. If our ministries are to be relevant to real needs, people must be challenged to both know and experience the living Word.

The Word of God becomes relevant only when it is heard, received, *and* experienced.

We are talking about a way of presenting Scripture that is different from the one many of us are familiar with. I call it *biblical relevance.* The new wine of biblical relevance will challenge the old wineskins of ministry. Sermons that prompt people to experience biblical truth will sound different from traditional sermons. Ministry to children and youth may need to be restructured in order to allow them to experience biblical truth. The entire ministry of the church may be radically affected.

The difference may be similar to what occurred in Jerusalem twenty centuries ago. On the Day of Pentecost, "that"—ancient words on a scroll—became "this"—relevant, visible ministry to the multitudes—as God made his Word come alive through his people.

Biblical relevance occurs when people discover what God's Word looks like by hearing it, receiving it, and experiencing it.

EXPERIENCING BIBLICAL TRUTH FIRSTHAND

What does biblical relevance look like in your life and ministry? As you begin to experience God's Word yourself, you will be better equipped to minister Great Commandment love to your spouse, children, friends, coworkers, fellow church members, and others. When biblical truth is experienced at the point of specific relational needs, God's love flourishes and people are blessed. The following pages give practical guidelines for how God's Word can be lived out in loving ministry to meet the ten relational needs introduced in the previous chapter.

Biblical instructions for meeting each individual need discussed here are not limited to just one passage of Scripture. There are many passages admonishing us to provide security, comfort, attention, acceptance, and so on in our relationships. But for the sake of brevity, we will limit our discussion to one Scripture passage for each of these needs.

Meeting the Need for Security by Experiencing 1 John 4:18:

Perfect love drives out fear.

COME WITH me as we look in on a service being conducted in a Great Commandment church. Imagine that this may be what a relevant twenty-first-century church looks like. What you are about to witness may seem implausible or unrealistic. You may wonder if this kind of service is practical in your church. Let me assure you that this type of service is happening in many churches in this country and around the world.

As we enter the church hall for an evening service, the congregation is clustered in small family groups: moms and dads with their children, single adults—and teens unaccompanied by parents—gathered in groups of three or four, or participating as "extended family," temporary "aunts" and "uncles" in the family groups. The minister has just completed his teaching on Christ's perfect love and is leading the congregation in reciting together 1 John 4:18: "Perfect love drives out fear."

Now he prepares to lead the congregation to make application of the passage by experiencing its truth. He places a slide on the overhead projector, and the following assignment floods the screen: "Take turns verbalizing your love and commitment to each member of your group. Be specific and sincere."

Family groups throughout the room become actively involved in quiet conversation. We approach one family—a husband and wife in their late thirties, a teenage daughter, and a ten-year-old son. We eavesdrop on their conversation. The husband is facing his wife and speaking. The kids are listening intently. We listen too.

"Marsha," he begins, "I want you to know how much it means to me that you create an atmosphere of openness and interaction in our home, encouraging us to share our day with each other."

Marsha smiles at her husband as he takes both her hands and looks deeply into her eyes. "Honey," he continues, "your love and commitment make me realize what a wonderful mother you are to our children and what a dear friend and lover you are to me."

Marsha's eyes well up with tears, but she says nothing as her husband continues to share. "And, darling," his voice cracks with emotion. "I want you to know that I am committed to you. I love you now, and I will always love you, no matter what happens in the future." He lifts both her hands to his lips and gently kisses them.

My conscience is captive to the Word of God. I cannot and will not recant anything, for to go against conscience is neither right nor safe. Here I stand. I can do no other. God help me.

MARTIN LUTHER

Their children, Nicole and Aaron, are wide eyed and silent.

Marsha is moved. She pauses a moment and then speaks. "Michael, you don't know how much it means to me to hear those words." She pauses again to wipe her eyes. "I see your commitment to me every day. You show it by providing for me and the kids. You work long hours, but you also work hard at being there for me when I need you. I really do love you, and I am committed to go through life with you as my husband and friend. I love you, Michael."

Michael's cheeks are also wet with tears. He pulls his wife to him in a tender embrace. Our eyes move to Nicole and Aaron, who are also moved with emotion. Soon the four of them are locked in a family embrace.

As each family group in the room finishes a prayer time together, the pastor concludes this part of the service by saying, "We are able to love one another like this only because we have first been loved by God, who is love. As we have received Christ's perfect love and then shared it with our spouses, parents, children, and friends, fear of divorce, family break-up, isolation, and aloneness is driven out. We have experienced together an aspect of God's truth from 1 John 4:18. His love indeed does cast out fear!"

This is what the experiential application of 1 John 4:18 might look like in a Great Commandment church. This family has experienced God's Word, and the need for security has been met. Children gain a measure of security from being loved by their parents. But they gain even more when they witness firsthand their parents' love for each other. When Michael and Marsha verbalized their commitment of love to each other in front of Nicole and Aaron, it helped diminish their fear of family break-up and met their need for security.

We are able to love one another only because we have first been loved by God.

Dick Day, marriage, family, and child counselor, states, "After talking to thousands of kids all over the country, I know that one of their greatest fears is that Dad is going to divorce Mom or vice versa. Every time I return from a speaking tour I am reinforced in the knowledge that one of the greatest heritages I can leave my children is my love for their mother."[1] Security for a child in our day, to a large degree, means freedom from the fear and danger of losing a parent to divorce.

Had the minister in this example merely defined the Greek words in 1 John 4:18 and explained what the passage means, Michael and his family would have gone away well informed, more knowledgeable. Had the minister included points of personal application, the family would have left understanding how the passage should relate to their lives.

But by inviting his congregation to experience perfect love in a practical, tangible way through a simple small-group exercise, Michael, Marsha, Nicole, and Aaron went home more secure and less fearful about their family relationship than when they came. What's more, they gained confirming testimony that God's Word works! That is a biblically relevant message. That is Great Commandment love meeting the real needs of people.

MEETING THE NEED FOR COMFORT BY EXPERIENCING ROMANS 12:15:

Mourn with those who mourn.

KEVIN WAS a fixer. For nearly thirty years of marriage, his response to all of Penny's problems was to fix them. When a household appliance broke, Kevin had it fixed in order to make Penny's work easier. If they faced a budget crisis, Kevin diligently worked the numbers and found the money, meeting Penny's need for financial security. Penny deeply appreciated her husband's commitment to provide for her. But there was one need in Penny's life that Kevin could not meet by fixing something.

Penny's childhood memories were a dark, painful gray. She had been physically and emotionally abused by a father who did not know how to express love. As a result, Penny's scrapbook of photos from her unhappy growing-up years portrayed her with a glum expression. Only one snapshot, taken at about age three, captured a glimmer of girlish excitement. Her father's abuse had stifled sweet little Penny and robbed her of a joyful childhood.

Penny's buried hurt resurfaced every time she and Kevin visited her parents. Driving home from these painful encounters, Penny was often depressed. True to his nature, Kevin moved in to fix it. "You don't have to feel this way," he would say sternly. "Don't let him jerk you around by your emotions. See your father for the emotionally hurting man that he is and forgive him." But the more he tried to fix the problem, the more Penny hurt. And the more Penny hurt, the more frustrated and inadequate Kevin felt about not being able to help her resolve her childhood pain.

Kevin and Penny attended one of our conferences for ministry couples. During an exercise in experiencing biblical truth, this pair had difficulty. Dismissing participants to their hotel rooms, I urged couples to share with each other a painful, disappointing, or sad memory—a death in the family, a financial disaster, a failed relationship, etc. Then I instructed them to experience Romans 12:15 by mourning those hurts with each other. I said it could be as simple as saying something like, "I'm saddened by what you experienced. I'm so sorry you had to go through that pain, because I love you."

But Kevin was apprehensive. He explained to me later, "To be honest, David, I just couldn't see how feeling sad with someone would be that much help. So I suggested to Penny that we put off the exercise until we went home after the conference. Then I assured her, 'I really do want to feel with you about your past. Because when I think of that picture of you as a happy, excited three-year-old, I really feel . . .' All of a sudden an overwhelming sense of sadness came over me for that little girl who had lost her excitement and joy. Tears welled up in my eyes. When I looked over at Penny, she was sobbing.

"I pulled Penny to my lap and wrapped my arms around her. I really began to feel her pain. I said, 'I'm so sorry you had to hurt like that.' Tears flooded my eyes. 'I'm so sorry for that little girl, for all that she suffered.' Then I could say no more. We sobbed in each other's arms for several minutes. For the first time in thirty years of marriage I had met my wife's need for comfort. I never knew what Penny needed from me, and Penny didn't even know exactly what she needed from me. But experiencing Romans 12:15 with my wife somehow enabled her to begin to release the pain and find additional freedom from the hurt."

A measure of Penny's aloneness was removed when she and Kevin experienced God's Word together.

Kevin had preached many sermons on confession, forgiveness, and love. He had appealed to Penny's mind and will: "Forgive your father. Release him from what he did. He can't hurt you anymore." Kevin had appealed to Penny spiritually: "Confess your sin of bitterness and receive God's love for your father." And while these biblical admonitions were true and needed, they were not sufficient.

We find freedom from guilt by confession of sin. We find freedom from anger by forgiving others. We find freedom from fear through the Father's perfect love. But we find freedom from hurt and pain by receiving comfort. Penny needed God's comfort applied to her heart through Kevin. When Kevin became the vehicle of some of God's comfort, he ministered to her a significant aspect of Great Commandment love—hurting with those who hurt.

We find freedom from hurt and pain by receiving comfort.

When Jesus said, "Blessed are they that mourn, for they shall be comforted" (Matthew 5:4, KJV), he spoke of comfort as God's remedy for the dark, disappointing moments of life we all experience.[2] In fact, the ministry of comfort is important even when the pain is the result of our own sin or failure. When people are properly comforted, they no longer face their pain alone. Here are a couple of guidelines for ministering comfort.

Separate comfort from counsel. When others suffer, too often we want to correct the problem ("The reason this happened to you is . . ."), teach a lesson ("The next time this happens you should . . ."), give a pep talk ("It will be all right. Put on a happy face!"), or give advice ("If I were you, I would . . ."). Hurt and disappointment are emotional needs that cannot be "fixed" through counsel or instruction. God's Word needs to be experienced in relationship with himself and others. Whatever else people need in their pain, they most certainly need comfort—someone to mourn with them, feel their pain, and just be there.

Learn the vocabulary of comfort. Use or adapt phrases like these to communicate comfort to someone who is hurting: "I'm so sorry that you are hurting"; "I hurt for you right now"; "I love you, and I want to pray for you right now"; "I'm standing with you in this"; "I'm committed to help you through this tough time"; "It saddens me that this happened to you." Words like these, along with an appropriate touch or embrace, will help ease the pain. When counsel or exhortation is also needed, minister the blessing of comfort first, and you will likely have a more receptive listener!

MEETING THE NEED FOR ATTENTION BY EXPERIENCING 1 CORINTHIANS 12:25:

Have the same care for one another. (NASB)

WHO IN your life enters your world in order to know you better and support you? You may have a colleague in ministry who serves as a caring confidant, sounding board, or prayer partner. Maybe your wife watches *Monday Night Football* with you or shows interest in another hobby. Perhaps your husband spends Saturday morning garage sale shopping with you because it is something you enjoy.

That's what attention looks like. Paul urged believers to "have the same care for one another" (1 Corinthians 12:25, NASB). The word "care" means being thoughtfully sensitive to share your loving concern and your attention with others. How can we show care for others as 1 Corinthians 12:25 instructs? Here are several suggestions for experiencing this truth.

Spend time with people. Time is a valuable commodity, so spending precious minutes with others is a significant expression of attention. Friendships are deepened when friends devote time to be together, not just to share common interests like movies or concerts, but also to "hang out," dream together, or share discouragements. Marriages are enriched when a husband turns off the ball game for unhurried conversation with his wife, or when a wife meets her husband for lunch in the middle of her hectic day. Parent-child relationships are strengthened when parents offer to spend an hour or two doing something the children enjoy.

Yield to another's agenda. I once helped a ministry family where the dad was greatly concerned over his three-year-old son's temper tantrums. It was easy to spot a significant aspect of the problem. This dad's idea of playing with little Johnny was to sit in the playroom and throw Velcro darts at the target while Johnny ran back and forth retrieving the darts for him. Johnny soon became bored with Daddy's game.

Giving attention means entering another person's world to follow his or her agenda instead of your own.

"Let's play puzzles and blocks on the floor," he begged.

But the father stayed in the chair tossing darts. It didn't take long until Johnny's frustration became impatience acted out in anger. Dad was spending time with Johnny, but it was Dad's agenda. No wonder Johnny was angry.

Giving attention means entering another person's world to follow his or her agenda instead of your own. Johnny's world was not chasing Velcro darts; it was down on the floor with the puzzles and blocks. In order to meet Johnny's need for attention, Dad needs to play what Johnny wants to play sometimes. In a marriage or friendship, individuals must take turns saying, "Tell me about your day" or "Let's do what you want to do tonight." Great Commandment love is experienced when individuals receive special, loving attention in their own world.

Listen with interest. People receive needed attention when we encourage them to talk about their lives, their goals, their feelings, and their plans—and then listen attentively with lots of eye contact. Attention-giving conversations work best when they occur away from distractions and interruptions. Ideally, everyone has at least one person who will listen with interest and caring concern: a spouse, a parent, a special friend. The need for attention is best met in relationships that are well balanced between sharing and listening.

MEETING THE NEED FOR ACCEPTANCE BY EXPERIENCING ROMANS 15:7:

Accept one another, then, just as Christ accepted you.

ACCEPTANCE CHALLENGES us to love others as God loves us. God's love is unmerited; it cannot be earned. So we are to lovingly accept one another without keeping score of who gives the most or who receives the most. God's love is unlimited; it will never run out. Acceptance overlooks an unpleasant trait in a parent, spouse, child, or friend even if they never change. After all, "Love covers over a multitude of sins" (1 Peter 4:8). Great Commandment love extends forgiveness toward those who offend us because unforgiveness short-circuits acceptance. Here are a few practical guidelines for experiencing Romans 15:7.

Accept people dealing with pain and disappointment. A woman in the church is divorced by her husband. The son of a couple in your neighborhood is arrested for drug possession. A colleague is removed from his position due to moral failure. Sadly, people in trouble or in grief are often avoided by others, who don't know what to say to them. Or they may receive additional pain from those who feel they need to give advice. Whatever else these people need in order to get through trying circumstances, they surely need loving acceptance. It might be as simple as saying, "I can only begin to imagine what you're going through, but I want you to know I care." A particular ministry of acceptance is needed when dealing with those in sin. Just as Christ ministered to Zacchaeus, to the woman caught in adultery, and to many others, acceptance plays a critical role in becoming known as "a friend of sinners."

Accept people who are different from you. People who look, talk, dress, act, or live differently may feel overlooked or unimportant to you. They have an acute need for the acceptance you can share through God's love. Take the initiative to get acquainted and show your acceptance.

Accept people struggling in a new environment. When people move to a new city, school, church, or job, the need to feel welcomed and accepted in that environment is high. You can serve as God's place of refuge and safety in the face of an unfamiliar environment.

MEETING THE NEED FOR APPRECIATION BY EXPERIENCING 1 CORINTHIANS 11:2:

I praise you for remembering me in everything.

VERBALIZING PRAISE and loving appreciation deepens relationships. Scripture challenges us to speak words that minister "grace to those who hear" (Ephesians 4:29, NASB). Here are a few suggestions for helping others experience biblical appreciation.

Praise others verbally and publicly. Verbalize your appreciation for family members, friends, lay leaders, and coworkers both privately and in front of others. Express gratitude to your spouse for what he or she does for you, especially the everyday things that are sometimes taken for granted. Let your children hear your appreciation for your spouse so they will learn to voice their praise. You might say something like, "Kids, I want you to know that you have a very special mom. I'm glad she's my wife and my best friend."

Focus on right behavior, not wrong behavior. Some people act as if they are self-appointed captains in the "sin patrol." They feel duty bound to catch their friends, spouse, kids, and fellow church members doing wrong and set them straight. Yes, people need to be lovingly and tactfully confronted when their behavior is hurtful or wrong. But at times God's love may prompt us to praise and appreciate right behavior, trusting God's Spirit to overcome the negative as the positive is strengthened through praise-filled encouragement.

Give tokens of appreciation along with your words. A special gift, a thoughtfully composed letter, or an appropriate greeting card says, "I appreciate you" and helps confirm and sustain your spoken words. Tokens of appreciation such as plaques, pictures, ribbons, mementos, etc., communicate praise for the person and his or her character, and they serve as visual reminders to continue in "love and good deeds" (Hebrews 10:24).

MEETING THE NEED FOR SUPPORT BY EXPERIENCING GALATIANS 6:2:

Carry each other's burdens.

UNLIKE ADVICE or suggestions, support cannot be offered from a distance. True support implies getting under the load with another person, coming alongside to share in the journey. Here are some practical ways to help people experience Galatians 6:2.

Be alert to periods of high stress in others. When people seem agitated, depressed, withdrawn, or stressed out, they may be carrying their burden alone and in need of support. Unless you go beyond surface conversation to ask how people are really doing, you may not know who needs support. Learn to ask questions that open the door for others to share their burdens: "How is it going at work?" "What is causing the greatest stress in your life right now?" "Is there anything I could pray with you about?" Support is often communicated simply by declaring your availability: "I just want you to know that I'm committed to be here for you and go through this with you."

Support is often communicated simply by declaring your availability.

Offer prayer support. When people share a burden with you, support them with your prayers. Add their special needs to your prayer list and send an occasional note simply communicating, "The Lord put you on my heart today, and I prayed for you." If appropriate, take the hurting person aside and pray together on the spot. When you take time to pray for people in their presence, they sense support immediately.

MEETING THE NEED FOR ENCOURAGEMENT BY EXPERIENCING 1 THESSALONIANS 5:11:

Encourage one another and build each other up.

LET'S FACE it: Living the Christian life in a world of tribulation can wear us out and tear us down. Ministers and laypersons alike need ongoing encouragement to offset the temptation to throw in the towel. Here are a few ways to help people experience 1 Thessalonians 5:11.

Communicate encouraging words. Send an encouraging letter, note, or card to someone who is "in the battle" or discouraged. Some churches take "Encourage one another" literally by making blank encouragement cards available at each worship service. Those in attendance may write an encouraging note to someone during the service and place it in a designated place. The church office staff supplies the mailing address and the postage.

Help people set and achieve goals. Discouragement can set in when people fail to set goals or lose sight of their goals. You may encourage someone by communicating, "What can I do to help you accomplish your goals this week?" or "If it's OK with you, I'd like to join you in that goal. We may both benefit by working on it together."

Let people know of God's encouragement in your life. At appropriate times, share candidly about times of discouragement, pain, trial, and defeat in your life, followed by Scripture truths that sustained and encouraged you. Your vulnerability helps remove aloneness. It prompts others to realize, "I'm not the only one who has been discouraged. Others like me have suffered and survived." And lovingly sharing with others the sustaining strength of Scripture provides hope.

MEETING THE NEED FOR AFFECTION BY EXPERIENCING ROMANS 16:16:

Greet one another with a holy kiss.

PAUL'S INSTRUCTION to share a "holy kiss" was a call to warm, caring displays of affection among believers. Although cultural norms may be different today, communicating affection to others within the bounds of propriety remains important. Just as the Master Teacher touched children and blessed them with affirming words,[3] we all benefit from verbalized love and affectionate touch. Here are two ways the principle found in Romans 16:16 can be implemented.

Display affection through appropriate physical touch. Children need the physical contact of being held, kissed, carried, and wrestled. Even teenagers desire affectionate touch—though they may not admit it!—as long as it does not embarrass them. Friends encourage one another with affectionate handshakes, hugs, and pats. In a marriage relationship, hugs, love pats, kisses, and body rubs have great need-meeting value in themselves, quite apart from sexual closeness.

Display affection through loving words. Try this some day and see what happens. Call your spouse, one of your children, or a good friend on the phone and say something like, "I was just thinking about how special you are to me and how much I appreciate you. So I just had to call and tell you. Have a great day. Bye." Planned, thoughtful messages like this communicate needed affection. If you have difficulty speaking words of affection, begin by sending cards or notes that convey your feelings.

MEETING THE NEED FOR RESPECT BY EXPERIENCING 1 PETER 2:17:

Show proper respect to everyone.

COMMUNICATING RESPECT for others, regardless of their behavior, beliefs, or differences, is a significant expression of Great Commandment love. Respect affirms that we regard individuals as persons of value, created in the likeness of God.[4] Furthermore, respecting the ideas, opinions, and perspectives of others, even when we do not agree with them, is an act of love. The ministry of respect, in fact, may open a door to share exhortation or reproof with others.

We can help people experience 1 Peter 2:17 in the following ways.

Consult the persons involved before making a decision. Marriage partners should discuss and decide together on business commitments, house guests, major financial expenditures, and parenting decisions. Parents might solicit their children's input on family vacations, household chores, and discipline measures. A Bible study leader might poll the group before deciding to change the meeting night. A friend might defer to another's idea concerning plans for a social gathering.

Respect the property, privacy, and preferences of others. If you borrow a friend's car, return it clean and maybe with a full tank. Knock before entering your child's room. If your spouse needs some time alone, honor that request. Respect a friend or coworker's schedule by being prompt for appointments.

Work at eliminating prejudices. Hold equal respect for all people, regardless of race, nationality, gender, theological persuasion, or socioeconomic level. The commonality of our need and capacity to relate to God and one another provides an important foundation upon which to exhibit a ministry of respect. Opportunities for further ministry can spring from this foundation of relational respect.

MEETING THE NEED FOR APPROVAL BY EXPERIENCING ROMANS 14:18:

Anyone who serves Christ in this way is pleasing to God and approved by men.

AT THE beginning of his public ministry, before he had performed one miracle or preached one sermon, Jesus heard his heavenly Father declare from heaven, "This is My beloved Son, in whom I am well-pleased" (Matthew 3:17, NASB). What impact did this audible statement of the Father's approval have upon Jesus? No doubt its affirming testimony in some way helped to empower his three-and-a-half-year ministry.

People around us also need to receive approval, not so much for what they do as for who they are. Here are some ways to help people experience Romans 14:18.

Frequently express approval to those you have been called to serve. The people you serve need to hear your words of approval more than your words of correction. Consider the many ways God blesses you through your spouse, your children, or your friends and take initiative to verbalize affirmation and approval. You may say something like, "I was just reminded today how much I am blessed by your diligence and dependability, knowing I can count on you for anything." Commend your children when they do a chore unasked, finish their homework on time, help a younger sibling with a task, etc. When an employee or coworker completes a difficult project, verbalize approval not only for the job done but for specific steps taken.

Express approval for character traits as well as for accomplishments. Josh McDowell says, "I appreciate my child's effort more than I appreciate my child's accomplishment, and I appreciate my child's worth as a human being even more than my child's effort."[5] We need to approve our children for doing right even if the outcome is disappointing. You may comment, "Your patience and respect of others was a great testimony in the soccer game today. It was much more important than the final score." We may also approve the generosity of the person who gives us a gift, even if the gift itself is not to our liking.

PROFOUNDLY SIMPLE, BUT NOT NECESSARILY EASY

I remember an occasion when I experienced God's Word with our son. A couple of summers ago, Teresa and I returned home from a trip to find twenty-year-old Eric very excited. He had gone to the gym that morning as usual, being very much into exercise, nutrition, and bodybuilding.

"I met a professional weight lifter at the gym today," Eric said, beaming. "Johnny gave me some great tips during my workout. He said if I met him at the gym early tomorrow, he would show me some more techniques. I can't wait."

Eric left the house at 5:00 A.M. the next morning to meet Johnny at the gym. As I was fixing my coffee at 6:00 A.M., I heard the garage door open. Eric walked in and dropped his gym bag on the floor.

"Dad, Johnny didn't show up."

I have never seen him look more dejected.

A dozen or more responses run through a parent's mind at a time like that. Most of them should just keep going on through! I could have said, "Well, Eric, it's not like you really knew this guy was dependable. It's not as bad as if you paid him money to be there. No need to get down over such a small thing." Or I could have been superspiritual: "Eric, you know God will bring some kind of good out of this. He wants to perfect your character."

As truthful as these responses may have been, they were not appropriate to Eric's need at the moment.[6] It may seem a bit overstated to say my son needed an expression of Great Commandment love over a missed appointment. But the truth is, Eric was hurting, and he needed some comfort. Like every parent, I have been guilty of rattling off a lecture when something much more relevant to the situation was needed. On this occasion, however, I sensed that God wanted to minister his love through me.

Being conformed to Christ's image is the daily disciplined process of loving God and living out his Word in our relationships.

I walked across the kitchen to face my son. "Eric, I'm really sad for you that Johnny didn't come. I hurt for you because I see how much this meant to you."

Then I hugged him. That's all.

No lecture, just comfort.

As we pulled apart, I knew I had done the right thing. Eric had a small tear in his eye. He said, "Thanks, Dad."

My response ministered to Eric's need, and he received comfort. We had experienced Romans 12:15 and Matthew 5:4 together:

"Mourn with those who mourn"; "Blessed are those who mourn, for they will be comforted."

Experiencing God's Word with others in order to express Great Commandment love and meet relational needs is profoundly simple. God has filled his written Word with instructions and examples for our attitudes, words, and actions. But the daily practice of experiencing his Word and helping others do the same is not necessarily easy. It requires spiritual discipline—staying in tune with God, allowing the Holy Spirit to minister to us and through us, saying no to the flesh, and living out our identity in Christ. When we experience his Word, we are in effect taking on Christ's loving character and acting out his nature. Being conformed to Christ's image is the daily disciplined process of loving God and living out his Word in our relationships.

Restoring the discipline of Great Commandment love to the body of Christ begins with spiritual renewal. We cannot hope to apply God's Word meaningfully to the deep needs of the human heart unless we are fully in tune with God's heart of love. Relevant ministry requires another vital step. Christian leaders at every level must get in touch with the very heart of God.

CHAPTER FIVE

Great Commandment Love Reflects the Heart of God

RICH Sterling is a gifted teacher of the Word at a rapidly growing suburban, middle-class congregation. Pastor Rich was barely two minutes into his sermon one Sunday morning when a side door near the front of the sanctuary opened. Every head swiveled to see a bedraggled "street person" step into the sanctuary. The man's matted hair and beard seemed to hide his face like a mask. Parishioners held a collective breath as the man shuffled to the vacant wing of pews nearest the platform and slumped down, as if defeated by life.

Pastor Rich glanced at the man but continued his sermon introduction without missing a beat. The eyes of the congregation flitted nervously between the pastor and the unkempt visitor. The air was thick with unasked questions: Who is this man and what does he want? How did he get past the ushers in the foyer? Is he drunk or stoned on drugs? Is he going to make a disturbance in the service? Has someone thought to call the police? Yet everyone sat motionless.

Everyone, that is, except sixteen-year-old Traci, a leader in the high school youth group. A few minutes after the man walked in, Traci got up from her place next to her friends in the wing opposite the vagrant's seat. As the pastor continued the message, Traci left the sanctuary, followed the foyer to the other side, and returned through the same door the man had entered.

As the congregation watched with wonder and trepidation, Traci walked to the man's pew and sat down near him. He stole a quick glance at her through his stringy hair. Traci flashed a warm smile as if to say, "Good morning, sir, and welcome to our service. You looked a little lonely sitting by yourself. I just came over here to show you how glad I am that you came today." Then she calmly turned her attention back to the sermon as if she did this every Sunday.

The congregation had barely settled down from Traci's actions when the unthinkable happened. Pastor Rich, who had been preaching about sharing Christ's love with others, turned to the visitor.

"What about you, sir?" he said, walking to the top step of the platform nearest his pew. The man looked up nervously, and everyone in the room held a deep breath.

"Yes, I'm talking to you," Rich continued. "You obviously have been through some tough times in your life. I wonder what the love of Christ means to you."

The pastor came down the platform steps to stand only a few feet from the man. He continued to speak pointedly and compassionately to him about Christ. The transient averted his eyes and sank lower into the pew. Meanwhile, the congregation watched in shock, and Traci maintained a vigil of silent friendship at the man's side.

After a few minutes, soft whispers and knowing smiles began to snake through the congregation. Several now realized that Pastor Rich had set them up. The man in matted hair and dirty clothes was not a real street person. He was a plant. The congregation was being treated to another of Rich's creative illustrated sermons.

Shortly the pastor broke off the act and introduced Del, the associate pastor, who was so well disguised that no one had recognized him. Del shuffled out the sanctuary in character, and Rich concluded his message on the importance of sharing the love of Christ with people, regardless of who they are.

But the most penetrating point of the message that Sunday came not from the pastor but from a sixteen-year-old girl. You see, Traci was not part of the act. Her response was real, from the heart. She simply saw a lonely, hurting man sitting across from her and did what she could to meet his need. She was the unwitting hero of Rich's poignant skit, and her unrehearsed part stood as an example of Great Commandment love in that church for years afterward.

THE GREAT REVERSAL

Suppose this event—not a skit, but for real—took place in a service attended by ministers and lay leaders. Imagine a sanctuary full of people wearing nice suits, dresses, and collars, and a downtrodden, dirty wino trudges in and sits down. The person could be another kind of misfit, such as a drug-addicted unmarried mother who is milking the welfare system to support her habit, her children, and her boyfriend. Or an avowed homosexual infected with AIDS. Whoever it is, for the sake of discussion the intruder's behavior is reprehensible to society in general and sinful according to the Word of God.

I would like to freeze-frame the scene and ask the group a question. Pointing to the surprise visitor, I would say to those in attendance, "What is this person's real need? What is the church's responsibility to this person?" Historically, the answers from ecclesiastical circles would stretch between two poles. While the following is a somewhat overly simplistic characterization of these views, it does strike at the heart of the message of these two positions.

Some people might quickly respond to my questions by saying, "He needs God" or "She needs to confess her sin and receive forgiveness" or "He needs to change his ways and obey the Word of God." This group might contend that the only problem is sin and that the responsibility of the church is to confront an individual's fallenness. This group would hold firmly to the first half of the Great Commandment, the challenge to love God.

Others might just as quickly answer, "This person needs unconditional acceptance" or "He needs to be placed in a shelter and be cared for" or "She needs an advocate to help her get back on her feet again." To this group, the real problem is human need and suffering. The responsibility of the church centers on relieving an individual's aloneness by holding firm to the second half of the Great Commandment, to love our neighbor as ourselves.

Why do we so often find Christians polarized on this issue? Is our first call to love others and alleviate human suffering or to direct them to love God in order to remedy the sin in their lives? Are we to take people by the hand and lead them to the shelter or to the altar?

Do we fit them with warm, clean clothes or with robes of righteousness?

Certain events that occurred at the dawn of the twentieth century provide an insight into these two divergent views of the Great Commandment. At that time, mounting urban problems, theological controversy, and rising rationalism prompted what some historians have called the "Great Reversal."[1] For several decades, the church had been at the forefront of social reform and movements geared to minister to human need. However, some leaders and churches involved in these reform movements began to embrace a theology that denied the authority and reliability of God's Word and even began to propagate the lie of human goodness instead of the truth of human fallenness.

Over time, two opposing camps formed within the Christian tradition. One group consisted of those who defended Scripture and revivalism with a focus on rational truth and spiritual needs. This group preached reconciliation to God and repudiated those who had abandoned the Bible. However, they were at times so concerned about humanity's fallenness that they tended to overlook the relational needs arising from human aloneness. Proclaiming the message "You need to love God," they often minimized or ignored the more complete message, "We all need to love God and one another."

Jesus was deeply concerned about the spiritual needs *and* relational needs of those he taught and served.

The second group emphasized human needs with a focus on social reform. Frequently denying the authority of Scripture and at times even the God behind the Scriptures, this camp proclaimed the lie of humanity's basic goodness while overlooking or denying fallenness.

The first group, the defenders of Scripture, would applaud Pastor

Rich's attempt to share the gospel with the street person in his congregation while possibly minimizing Traci's contribution of friendship. They might say, "An act of kindness, while admirable, never saved anyone. The deepest need of every human heart is for the gospel." The second group, the social reformers, would be more impressed with Traci's response in the scenario. They would insist, "What that girl did *is* the gospel."

Optimum ministry relevance is not possible when we lose sight of the true heart of the gospel, which fully embraces love for God *and* love for our neighbor. This is God's heart of love, as it is clearly portrayed in his Word. In order to regain proper balance and motivation for Great Commandment ministry, we must rightly discern and represent the heart of God.

JESUS MINISTERED TO HUMAN ALONENESS AS WELL AS HUMAN FALLENNESS

A significant loss of relevance occurs in personal and church ministry when we misrepresent the character of God, claiming that he is only concerned about human fallenness. In reality, God is concerned about both our fallenness and our aloneness. As early as the Garden of Eden, God made provision for Adam's aloneness (Genesis 2) as well as his fallenness (Genesis 3). Indeed, God ministered to Adam's aloneness before his fallenness was even an issue. Ever since the Fall, God has poured out his love to us at the point of our fallenness *and* our aloneness. Ministry at one pole or the other is insufficient. We must address both fallenness and aloneness if our ministries are to be relevant.

The clearest picture of God's twofold ministry is found in the life of Jesus Christ, his Son. Jesus' ministry was not one dimensional, limited only to addressing human fallenness. Throughout his earthly ministry, Jesus addressed both fallenness and aloneness in the lives of those he ministered to. He was deeply concerned about the spiritual needs as well as the relational needs of those he taught and served. Consider that:

- From childhood, Jesus cultivated relationships with his heavenly Father *and* with those around him. In Luke

2:41-49, the boy Jesus is found in the temple amazing the teachers with his understanding of the Scriptures. Then in verse 52 Luke writes, "Jesus grew . . . in favor with God and men." The Son of God was both spiritually and relationally involved.

Jesus demonstrated love and acceptance for the Samaritan woman before he challenged her to change her behavior.

- When Jesus called his disciples, relationship was clearly important to him. Mark records, "He appointed twelve—designating them apostles—that they might be with him and that he might send them out to preach and to have authority to drive out demons" (Mark 3:14-15). Notice that the disciples' first order of business was to "be with him." This passage suggests that mutual companionship and supportive relationship were fundamental to the mission Christ and the disciples would perform together.
- In John 4, Jesus demonstrated love and acceptance for the Samaritan woman before he challenged her to change her behavior. As a woman, she was viewed by most of that day as "inferior" to men. As an adulteress, she was an outcast even among women. Jesus broke social custom by initiating a conversation with her. By lovingly meeting her at the point of her need for attention and acceptance, Jesus gained opportunity to minister to her spiritual need, leading to repentance.
- Jesus dealt with the invalid at the pool of Bethesda, addressing him first at the point of his relational need. The seemingly unnecessary question, "Do you want to get well?" (John 5:6), invited the man to admit his helplessness. Had

he answered self-reliantly, "No problem, I'll get myself into the pool one of these years," I believe Jesus would have left him there unhealed. But when the man humbly admitted his aloneness with the words "I have no one to help me into the pool" (v. 7), Jesus ministered to him. On a subsequent occasion, Jesus addressed his fallenness: "Later Jesus found him at the temple and said to him, 'See, you are well again. Stop sinning'" (v. 14).

- Jesus ministered to the woman caught in adultery, who was relationally alienated and mired in sin. To the religious leaders, she was merely a pawn in their attempt to trap Jesus. They were ready to stone her to prove their point. To Jesus, she was a person in need of love and acceptance as well as a change of behavior. Imagine the double impact of his words "Neither do I condemn you. . . . Go now and leave your life of sin" (John 8:11). In one sentence he ministered to both her shame and her guilt.

THE ZACCHAEUS PRINCIPLE

Perhaps one of the most vivid examples of Jesus' Great Commandment ministry is found in his encounter with a tax collector. In fact, this encounter in Luke 19:1-10 so clearly pictures the impact of relevant ministry that I often refer to it as the "Zacchaeus Principle."

As an agent of the Roman government, Zacchaeus—a Jew—reached deep into Jewish purses for Roman taxes. Whatever else he could extort from the people, he likely kept for himself. The Jews typically regarded tax collectors with contempt, as deceitful traitors and thieves. His fellow citizens probably despised Zacchaeus, and he quite possibly felt rejected, guilty, fearful, and alone.

When Jesus looked up into the sycamore-fig tree, he knew all about the sinful behavior of the little man peering down at him. It is notable, however, that Christ did *not* say to him, "Zacchaeus, you lying, cheating thief, get down here right now and stop your sinful behavior." Rather, he said, "Zacchaeus, come down immediately. I must stay at your house today" (Luke 19:5). Jesus offered to enter the man's home and, as was the custom, eat out of the same dish with him. He could hardly do anything more accepting! Indeed, the Pharisees' big complaint was that Jesus actually ate with tax collectors and sinners.

Zacchaeus's immediate response demonstrated the impact of Jesus' offer: "He came down at once and welcomed him gladly" (v. 6). How thrilled he must have been that the popular, miracle-working rabbi wanted to be with him! I'm sure Zacchaeus experienced the same satisfying fulfillment we all experience when our spouse or a friend or even a stranger ministers to us at a time of feeling alone.

Jesus did not ignore the fact that Zacchaeus was a lying, cheating thief who needed to love and obey God with heart, soul, and mind. Jesus verbalized his concern for Zacchaeus's fallenness later in the conversation: "The Son of Man came to seek and to save what was lost" (v. 10). Jesus sought Zacchaeus at a relational level, taking time out to visit with this lonely, rejected, insecure man. As a result, Zacchaeus's spiritual needs were addressed very naturally in the context of this relationship. Luke 19:8-9 records, "Zacchaeus stood up and said to the Lord, 'Look, Lord! Here and now I give half of my possessions to the poor, and if I have cheated anybody out of anything, I will pay back four times the amount.' Jesus said to him, 'Today salvation has come to this house, because this man, too, is a son of Abraham.'"

Jesus looked beyond Zacchaeus's fault and saw his need.

What happened in Jesus' incredible encounter with Zacchaeus? Paraphrasing a popular song from several years back, Jesus looked beyond his fault and saw his need. And when the love of Christ touched Zacchaeus at the point of his need, that love constrained the sinner to confess his sin and make things right. In other words, Christ's love ministered to the man's deep need, and Zacchaeus responded by dealing with his fault.

If Jesus had simply rebuked Zacchaeus in the tree for his sinful behavior and gone on his way, would the results have been the same? Probably not. No doubt Zacchaeus had been rebuked regularly by the religious leaders of the day, who were not about to defile themselves by fraternizing with him. Jesus, however, discerned the tax collector's needs as well as his dishonesty. Like everyone else, Zacchaeus needed attention, acceptance, respect, etc., but he was seeking to meet those needs in sinful ways. Once he experienced Christ's loving acceptance, Zacchaeus was ready to receive the truth about his sinful ways. Jesus' life and message addressed both his need and his sin, both his aloneness and his fallenness. That's Great Commandment love in action. That's relevant ministry.

THE CONTEXT OF LOVE

A ministry couple in their middle thirties came for help some time back, concerned that they were about to lose both their marriage and their ministry. They sat down with as much space between them as they could arrange.

Dottie got right to the point. "David, I've heard that you fix husbands with problems, and mine needs fixing real bad. Travis is always complaining about money. He says things like, 'Don't you realize how expensive it is to live in this nice neighborhood? Don't you know how much it costs to send the kids to private school?' He nags at me to work full-time, but I want to be at home when the kids get out of school. His attitude is terrible. Can you do something with him?"

Travis sat there quietly. Before turning to him, I said to Dottie, "How do you feel about living in your neighborhood and being able to send your children to private school? How do you feel about being at home when the kids arrive from school?"

"I feel like Travis needs to stop complaining about it all the time," she snapped. "That's why I brought him to you."

It was easy to see that Travis's complaining and critical attitude and actions toward Dottie were wrong, obviously an expression of his fallenness. But equally clear was the fact that Dottie's "ministry" to his fallenness—trying to "fix" his nagging about money—was not relevant. Travis's sinful behavior was a problem, but Dottie had not looked beyond his fault to see his need. Neither had she allowed the Lord to deal with her part of the problem. So the problem persisted.

"What I mean, Dottie," I said, "is, how do you feel about having these nice things in your life? What kind of stirring in your heart do these blessings prompt?"

When she finally answered, her tone had softened. "Well, I'm grateful to live in such a beautiful neighborhood. I'm thrilled that our children can attend private school. And I appreciate the chance to be at home with them. My mother wasn't home for me when I was a girl, and I always wanted to be there for my children."

I reflected back to her the gratefulness and appreciation she had just expressed and then said, "I wonder if you have ever told your husband what you just told me." I glanced at Travis, and tears were starting to roll down his cheeks. He had never heard such affirming, appreciative words from Dottie concerning the life he had sought to provide.

"Dottie, if it's OK with you," I said, "I'm going to step out of the room for a few minutes. If you're open to it, I'd like you to consider slipping over beside Travis and maybe taking him by the hand. Perhaps you could look him in the eye and simply tell him about your gratefulness, appreciation, and excitement, just like you told me. Would that be all right?"

She said yes, so I left them alone for a few moments of experiencing Ephesians 4:29, sharing words that build up others according to their needs.

Ministry is relevant when we address people's fallenness within the context of love.

When I returned, the atmosphere in the room had completely changed. Travis and Dottie were sitting together, tearfully embracing. They had both apologized for their attitudes and had forgiven each other. In the months that followed, Dottie continued to be appreciative, and Travis's ranting about money ceased. It all started when Dottie rekindled a heart of love toward her husband, which God used to challenge him to deal with his fallenness.

Sound a bit too simple? Can a few words of love soften a hard heart so quickly? I have personally witnessed hundreds of similar incidents where a simple, loving expression disarms a critical heart and prompts a positive response. The constraining influence of Great Commandment love is practically irresistible!

Proclaiming the gospel message and loving our neighbor as ourselves are critically interrelated.

Ministry relevance occurs when we address people's fallenness within the context of love. Jesus said, "A new commandment I give to you, that you love one another, even as I have loved you, that you also love one another. By this all men will know that you are my disciples, if you have love for one another" (John 13:34-35, NASB). We are identified as followers of Christ by loving as Christ loved, not by religious activities and rule keeping.

Furthermore, Christian activity and rule keeping do not draw people to Christ. Dottie's message got through to Travis only when she began to share it through a heart of love. If we are to have relevant ministry, God's message through us must be proclaimed within the context of Great Commandment love.

Proclaiming the gospel message and loving our neighbor as ourselves are critically interrelated. They are like hydrogen and oxygen, which must combine to produce water. We cannot fulfill the Great Commission to "go and make disciples" without expressing genuine love for others as Christ loved us. And we cannot obey the Great Commandment and be biblically balanced without directing others toward Christ. Who we are—people who love God and others—must direct how we share his gospel with others. The church's mandate is to fulfill the Great Commission within the context of the Great Commandment. When we exercise Great Commission passion out of a Great Commandment heart, we become truly relevant.

SHARING THE GOSPEL AND OUR LIVES

When we fulfill the church's mission to make disciples within the context of sincere love for God and for others, ministry is relevant. For example, Paul harshly confronted the fallenness in some members of the Thessalonian church when he wrote, "If a man will not work, he shall not eat" (2 Thessalonians 3:10). Had the apostle's Great Commission fervor not been couched in love, how well would it have been received? Likely it would *not* have been received. But Paul had already expressed his Great Commandment heart to the Thessalonian believers: "We were gentle among you, like a mother caring for her little children. We loved you so much that we were delighted to share with you not only the gospel of God but our lives as well, because you had become so dear to us" (1 Thessalonians 2:7-8). Paul's rebuke was relevant because it was administered in Great Commandment love.

That's ministry relevance in a nutshell: "delighted to share with you not only the gospel but our lives as well." Does this statement reflect your personal ministry to others? Does it embody your church's ministry in the community? Are you communicating to others with equal clarity and fervor the truth of the Word of God *and* a heart of love for needy people?

Frederick, a senior pastor, was abruptly fired by his church. He was devastated by the sudden and unexpected turn of events. I visited with Frederick while doing some work with a denomination that was concerned about the high number of churches terminating their pastors.

"I have faithfully preached the Word and exhorted my people to righteous living," Frederick insisted, almost in tears. "What's wrong with that?"

During our visit he came to see that in sharing the gospel with his congregation he had failed to share his life with them through nurture and care. Unsure of their minister's love for them, Frederick's flock had rejected both the message and the messenger!

On the whole, I'm afraid much of the church of the twentieth century has too often been Great Commission rich and Great Commandment poor. We have been proficient at sharing the gospel, but we have frequently failed at sharing our lives with people. As a result, our passionate proclamation of the truth is often irrelevant and ineffective at resolving the crises that plague our culture.

In his essential life, God is a fellowship. This is perhaps the supreme revelation of God given in the Scriptures: it is that God's life is eternally within himself a fellowship of three equal and distinct persons, Father, Son and Spirit, and that in his relationship to his moral creation God was extending to them the fellowship that was essentially his own.

New Bible Dictionary

Bread and Fish or Stones and Snakes?

The world has turned to us for bread and fish—relevant ministry to aloneness as well as fallenness—and has often received instead stones and snakes—ministry that focuses on faults while overlooking needs.[2] To be sure, sin must be addressed, but we must go further. Relational needs must also be addressed or spiritual needs will go unmet.

Today, our needy culture hungers for the loving nurture of individuals and churches offering the bread of comfort, security, and hope. For example, a composite of several studies would reveal that a sobering 80 to 85 percent of the adult population today grew up suffering some form of parental separation or abandonment, physical or sexual abuse at the hands of a parent, or parental addictive behavior.[3] These people need the gospel, but unless we also meet them at the point of their need for comfort and security, our gospel message will be irrelevant.

Our culture is asking the church for bread—help and healing from a painful past. Will we offer them a stone instead? Will we share the gospel with them but fail to share our lives with them? Will we speak to their fallenness but fail to speak to their aloneness? Will we tell them to love God but fail to truly love them as we love ourselves? If we ignore the crying relational needs of our neighbors, we cannot expect them to be attracted to the message of the gospel.

If we ignore the crying relational needs of our neighbors, we cannot expect them to be attracted to the message of the gospel.

However, when we lovingly share our lives with others and meet relational needs, people want to know, "Where did you get the love, the care, and the comfort you shared with me?"

Our response can be, "I'm glad you asked! Let me tell you about the God of love and comfort."

People are eager to hear about God when they realize he is the source of the love that has touched them at the point of their deepest relational needs.

When Love Increases, Divisions Decrease

What is so attractive about Great Commandment love? In a word, unity. When believers are committed to sharing their lives with one another in love, conflict and divisions decrease, and those believers experience scriptural oneness in the Spirit. This is precisely what Jesus prayed for: "May they [his followers] be brought to complete unity to let the world know that you sent me and have loved them even as you have loved me" (John 17:23). Loving unity sets us apart in a world where jealousy, hatred, and envy characterize many relationships.

Paul wrote, "God has so composed the body . . . that there should be no division in the body, but that the members should have the same care for one another" (1 Corinthians 12:24-25, NASB). I believe there is a principle here that greatly affects ministry relevance in the world. When loving care increases, division decreases. When the unity Christ prayed for increases, disunity, strife, bickering, and criticism decrease. And when the world sees a caring, unified body of believers, people will pour through our doors saying, "That's what I need."

This principle can be applied to marriage. When loving care increases between husband and wife, division decreases. Jack was the senior pastor of a large, multistaff church that was in the process of building a huge new complex. He was in the middle of everything—site selection, design committee, finance committee—as well as the day-to-day concerns of running a big church. Jack was a very busy man, but it was his busyness that prompted him and his wife, Maria, to fly in from another city to seek help. Jack's busyness was tearing their marriage apart.

I spent about four hours with them working through a number of issues. Jack tearfully confessed his overcommitment and promised to make Maria and the family a priority. Maria asked Jack's forgiveness for being critical and cold. The couple took several positive steps during our time together. We agreed on a follow-up visit in two weeks.

People are eager to hear about God when they realize he is the source of the love that has touched them at the point of their deepest relational needs.

When Jack and Maria returned, I asked each of them to share one positive thing that had happened in their lives since our last meeting. A beaming Maria told how Jack had cut back on his schedule in order to be home with her several evenings and help with some things on her agenda. He had even planned a special couple date together, arranging the baby-sitter and sending flowers! But Jack's response really surprised me. This pastor had been involved with scores of people in numerous activities over the past two weeks. He could have told about the sermons he had preached or ongoing plans for a multimillion-dollar facility.

Loving unity sets us apart in a world where jealousy, hatred, and envy characterize many relationships.

Instead, looking misty-eyed, Jack said, "The highlight for me occurred just after we left you two weeks ago. As we were driving back to the airport in our rental car, Maria slid over beside me, put her arm around my shoulders, and gave me a gentle squeeze. I felt closer to her at that moment than I have in years. It made me want to spend more time at home."

Maria needed her husband's attention. Jack needed his wife's affection. When they increased loving care for one another by meeting those needs, the rift between them began to heal. I have found that when a husband and wife are not getting along, it can almost always be traced to a lack of loving care in some area. In some way, God's abundance is not being "freely received" and then "freely given." Someone's relational needs are not being met, sometimes out of lack of understanding and often out of unhealed hurts from the past. But when loving care increases, the divisions diminish and can even disappear—just as God's Word says.

The principle also applies to parenting, as Alan's experience with his two young sons, Rick and Jeremy, demonstrated. As you recall, the two boys were constantly at each other's throats. When Alan increased loving care for his sons by spending quality time with each of them, the sibling rivalry all but dissolved. When brothers and sisters are fighting with each other or with their parents, check to see where loving care is weak or missing. Increase care for your children by meeting their relational needs, and the squabbling between them will often diminish. If discipline is required, you will be able to administer it with a clear conscience, knowing it is bathed in loving care.

The principle is also valid in churches. If staff members are critical of one another or envious of another member's status or budget, increase loving care for one another. If board members nearly come to blows over the color of a new carpet or which songbooks to buy for the pews, they need increased loving care. If church members backbite or criticize or ignore each other or gossip about each other, they need to learn how to better share love with one another. When members focus on meeting relational needs, care increases in the church. And when loving care increases, divisions decrease.

How do we begin to develop Great Commission passion within the context of Great Commandment love? We start by returning to the source of the mandate. In order to increase loving care for others, we must increase our loving care for the heavenly Father. In order to understand the pain in the heart of a spouse, a child, a friend, or an unbeliever, we must get in touch with the heartfelt pain of the Man of Sorrows.

We will not know how to minister to our loved ones or a single mother addicted to drugs or to a man who doesn't know how to be a father to his kids or to a child who grieves his parents' divorce until we experience how God's heart aches for those individuals. We need a deeper sense of what it means to love God with all our heart, soul, and mind. The next chapter will better prepare you to be a relevant Christian by helping you get in touch with the very heart of God.

CHAPTER SIX

Great Commandment Love Springs from Knowing God Intimately

BROKEN relationships. Divorce. Sexual abuse. Death of a loved one. Loss of a job. Depression. Loneliness. Fear. Heartache. The pain experienced by people inside and outside the church runs deep and wide. Delivering a truly relevant message that meets the needs of this hurting generation may seem to be an overwhelming task. So let me quickly assure you: Expressing the relevancy of Christ's Great Commandment love is not primarily something you crank up and make happen. Rather, it is the result of better understanding human needs, properly applying the truth of God's Word to those needs, and accurately representing God's character in our relationships with people. We're not talking about *doing* more for God but about *knowing* God and his Word intimately, allowing the Holy Spirit to impart his likeness and love through us to others.

We sometimes overlook a certain simplicity to imparting Christ's love to others. I believe this is a part of what Paul meant when he wrote, "I am afraid [that] . . . your minds [may somehow] be led astray from the simplicity . . . of devotion to Christ" (2 Corinthians 11:3, NASB). It is not more activity, programming, or busyness that will meet the real needs of people. It is not more propositional truth, no matter how good and right it is, that will meet the real needs of people. It is not more Hebrew and Greek study or more thorough exegesis that will meet the real needs of people. As significant as these ingredients are, the "not good" of human aloneness is removed only through deep, intimate relationships with God and others.

We're talking about *knowing* God and his Word intimately, allowing the Holy Spirit to impart his likeness and love through us to others.

Meeting the real needs of people is an issue of the human heart, not the rational mind. Propositional truth, scriptural precepts, and textual exegesis are only a means to an end. These fundamental ingredients are intended to *lead* us into intimate relationship with God and others, not to *provide* it. We are not called to a program or a system. We are called to "sincere and pure devotion to Christ," an intimate relationship with the one who wants to meet all of our needs[1] and to involve us in ministry to the needs of others.

This truth gripped me personally several years ago. I had preached one Sunday morning in a church away from home. The theme of my sermon that day was Philippians 3:8-10: "I consider everything a loss compared to the surpassing greatness of knowing Christ Jesus my Lord. . . . I want to know Christ and the power of his resurrection and the fellowship of sharing in his sufferings." I was intrigued by the concept of entering into fellowship with Christ's sufferings. I assumed it referred to the crosses we must bear for being Christians. But to be honest, I really had no idea what it meant.

In my message that Sunday I had also shared a number of passages describing Christ's suffering from the Last Supper to Gethsemane to Calvary. Driving the rental car back to the airport following the service, I began to think about those passages and the rejection, humiliation, and pain Jesus suffered. Unexpected tears began to fill my eyes.

Soon I was weeping so profusely that I could no longer drive safely. I had to pull to the side of the road and stop the car. I wept openly, without explanation, for several minutes.

As I wept, I tried to figure out what the emotional outburst was all about. I asked myself, *Why are you crying?*

Before I could contemplate the answer, another question confronted me. *Who are you crying for?*

The answer came almost as quickly. *I think I'm crying for Jesus. I think I'm feeling sad for the pain he must have felt. Maybe I'm entering into fellowship with his suffering.*

I had never cried for Jesus before. I had never participated in his suffering as I did that day. I had studied the topic. I had exegeted the passages and preached on them. But that day beside the highway, it was as if God said, "David, you know a lot about my Son's suffering. Would it be OK if I helped you experience these verses in order to deepen your love for me and others?"

From that point on, I began to know Christ and experience the fellowship of his suffering in a brand-new way. That roadside encounter dramatically changed my life and ministry. It unlocked to my understanding the motivation behind loving others and the core of relevant ministry. Mercifully, it opened my heart to the very heart of God.

> **Meeting the real needs of people is an issue of the human heart, not the rational mind.**

GOD'S HEART: THE CORE OF RELEVANT MINISTRY

It is easy to slip into the mind-set of caring for others by routine. We can approach the call to love others just like any other Christian duty: jot it on the calendar or "to do" list, perform the task as scheduled, move on to the next item. For example, a church member's company goes belly-up, triggering financial disaster and emotional upheaval in the family. The chairperson of the appropriate committee calls, delivers a few encouraging words, and then arranges for a food shower. Having put the machinery of caring in gear, is she also moved with Christ's compassion for this hurting family?

Only as we grow in our love for God are we able to express his love to others.

The senior minister steps to the pulpit to deliver the morning message. Having invested hours in studious preparation, he utilizes current events, commentaries, and even the comics to drive the truth home. Does the congregation go away merely informed and challenged by the pastor? Or do they leave also sensing Christ's compassion—through the minister—for their needs?

Where does the motivation come from to genuinely love others as we meet relational needs in the people around us? I'm not talking about the directives in Scripture to meet needs: comfort one another; encourage one another; accept one another; bear one another's burdens. Those are certainly clear enough. Rather, I'm talking about the impetus to carry out these commands with love and compassion, moving beyond the letter to the spirit of the Word.

Jesus told his disciples, "If you love Me, you will keep My commandments" (John 14:15, NASB). Motivation for obedience is rooted in an intimate love relationship with Christ, the headwaters of the Great Commandment love that must flow through us to quench the thirst of others. I believe we experience this love when we enter into deeper intimacy with God's heart and allow Christ's constraining love to fill and empower our activities.

I was deeply touched by this source of motivation on the day I cried for Jesus—finally, after many years of task-oriented ministry. As I began to experience the fellowship of his sufferings, God seemed to tenderize my heart to care more deeply for others.

appears clouded with gloom. Perspiration streams from his brow and drips from his hair and beard. I can almost hear him saying in a quavering voice. "I must . . . I must go . . . just a little farther." He looks past us to Peter, James, and John, his closest and dearest friends on earth. Imagine his imploring words, "Come with me, my friends. I need you now. I really need you."

Leaving the others behind, Jesus and the inner three continue trudging up the darkened garden hillside. We follow them. The Master's body appears to convulse from the mounting grief. His low moans turn to sustained cries of the deepest pain. Jesus can hardly get his next words out. His voice seems strained with emotion. "My soul is overwhelmed with sorrow to the point of death. Stay here and keep watch with me" (Matthew 26:38).

He leaves us behind and staggers farther up the knoll, bracing himself on tree stumps and boulders. Loud cries of travail roll from him. There he writhes and sobs and prays.

Meanwhile at a distance from the Savior, we huddle with the three to watch. Soon Peter, James, and John fall asleep.

The Son of God faces the darkest hour in the history of creation. The one who knew no sin would soon become sin for his disciples—for you and me. He has vulnerably sought the prayerful support of Peter, James, and John. These men love the Master dearly. They have left their careers to follow him. They have walked with him, sat at his feet, and leaned on his breast. But now they seem oblivious to the Master's need.

Jesus returns to the place where we are watching the heartrending drama. Imagine as he looks down at his dearest friends, who are asleep. Tears, soil, and blood streak his face and stain his cloak. He moves past us and wakes the men. Let yourself sense the pain-filled loneliness and grief of the Savior's heart as he asks, "Could you men not keep watch with me for one hour?" (Matthew 26:40).

See the pain of disappointment in his eyes as he returns to his place of agonizing prayer.

Amazingly, the scene plays out again and then again. Three times the Master shares his pain and need with his closest friends, and three times they let him down. Do you care for him in his pain? Can you hurt with him? Can you fellowship with his suffering?

Now Judas and the soldiers appear on the scene. We are close enough to see Jesus betrayed with a sign of affection from Judas. Do you feel the sting in that kiss? A scuffle breaks out with the soldiers, and the disciples flee into the night to save their own lives. How does it affect Jesus to be abandoned by those he loves?

Peter follows in the shadows at a safe distance. But then he is discovered in the temple courtyard and accused of being one of Christ's disciples. He curses and swears vehemently, "I don't know this man" (Mark 14:71).

Jesus looks directly at him. The pain in his gaze is no longer that of abandonment but of betrayal. Can you hurt for this one who is both despised and rejected as Peter disavows their friendship? Can you hurt for him?

Allow yourself to fellowship with the suffering of Jesus. Sorrow for him. Grieve his loss, his rejection, his betrayal. As you do, you are in fellowship with the broken heart of God.

It is that same brokenness that a few days earlier caused Jesus to lament, "O Jerusalem, Jerusalem, the city that kills the prophets and stones God's messengers! How often I have wanted to gather your children together as a hen protects her chicks beneath her wings, but you wouldn't let me" (Matthew 23:37, NLT).

Allow yourself to fellowship with the suffering of Jesus.

Can you feel his grief for a lost world more deeply? Can you sense a greater measure of his compassion? Are you touched by his longing to forgive sin and remove aloneness through reconciled relationship?

Why not pause right now and tell God about the sadness of your heart. Share with Christ the compassion that God's Word has stirred within you. Thank him for trusting you with a few sacred moments of fellowship with him.

For me, this meditation gives new meaning to Christ's exhortation to the Pharisees, "Go and learn what this means, 'I desire compassion, and not sacrifice'" (Matthew 9:13, NASB). It is love for Christ, not rules and commands, that motivates Great Commandment love. Having experienced a measure of fellowship with Christ's rejection by his disciples, I feel more compassionate toward others who are forsaken, rejected, ignored, and alone. Having been moved to tears at the insensitivity his bickering followers showed Jesus, my heart is more tender toward those who are overlooked by others.

It is love for Christ, not rules and commands, that motivates Great Commandment love.

Something else happens in my heart when I enter into the fellowship of Christ's sorrow. I experience a deeper sense of repentance. Having more intimately shared in the pain of his rejection and betrayal, I don't want to add to his grief with my continued sin. His love constrains me to walk uprightly with him. I feel a measure of what he has suffered. I love him too much to add to his pain. It's just like Jesus said: If you love me, you will walk in obedience. Walking intimately with him motivates us to righteous living and compassionate caring.

Oblivious to Needs

How could the disciples have been so dense, so heartless toward the Master? They loved him. They did not want him to leave. They did not want to hurt him, nor did they intend to fail him. Why were they so insensitive to his need for their prayerful support, comfort, and encouragement?

We used the word earlier: oblivious. For all the time they had spent with Christ, these men did not know how to relate to him deeply, intimately. They knew much about the Father from what Jesus had taught them, but it was mostly in their heads and not in their hearts. They had yet to be touched by the depths of love from the Father's heart. Consequently, their ministry to the suffering Savior was irrelevant. Instead of providing needed support for the Master, Peter hacked away with his sword trying to fix things, and then he fled. Instead of consoling Jesus with words of comfort, the outspoken disciple denied him with bitter curses.

You may say, "It's hard to imagine a person so close to Jesus being so thickheaded and hard-hearted."

I would have agreed with you up until that day I cried in the rental car on the way to the airport. I claimed to be close to Christ at that point in my life. I had been exposed to considerable theological truth and training. I had been a minister of the gospel for several years. But I was in many ways oblivious to God's heart. I had not entered into fellowship with the sufferings of Christ. I had not experienced the full impact of his constraining love. As a result, I was ineffective at imparting compassion to others, particularly those dearest to me.

What impact did my insensitivity have on my closest relationships? The answer came as quite a shock to me a few years before my intimate encounter with Christ beside the highway. I had considered my marriage to Teresa to be as good as that of any other Christian leader. My busy schedule kept us apart much of the time, but that was to be expected of someone called to ministry. A little dispute flared up between us now and then, but we seemed to handle it as well as most couples. Our marriage wasn't perfect, but I thought we were doing as well as could be expected.

Then one night I found out the true story. During a vulnerable moment, I asked my wife, "Teresa, do you love me?"

Now keep in mind that we were in Christian leadership. We provided premarital and marital counseling in our church. We would soon be teaching together at retreats and conferences on biblical principles for a strong marriage. We were supposed to know what makes a marriage work. That's why I was so ill prepared for Teresa's shocking answer.

In the pages that follow, I want to tell you a little of Teresa's and my journey and explain how the Great Commandment Principle had a dramatic impact on our marriage, family, and ministry in the twenty years since that crisis.

Why do I share our experience? Because in our interaction with thousands across the country we have discovered that our story is not unique. Everywhere we go we meet pastors, youth workers, Christian educators, parachurch leaders, and influential church members who struggle with prioritizing ministry and family. We meet men and women who readily identify when I confess to not really being sensitive to the needs of my wife, children, and others. We meet single men and women who are fearful of relationships, feeling inadequate and alone.

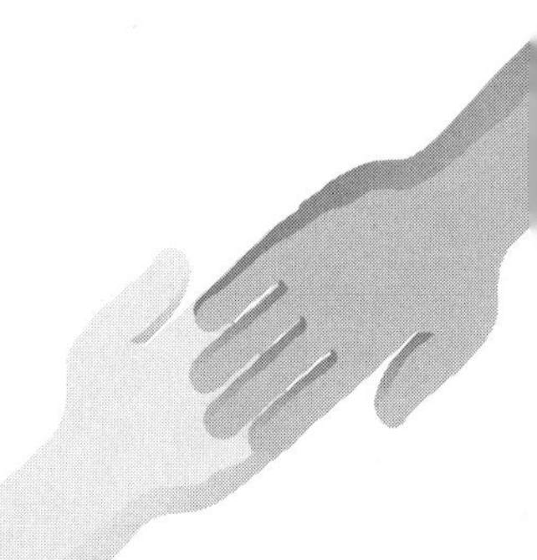

One of the greatest challenges that Jesus faced was to reorient the disciples' "me first" mind-set.

LYNNE AND BILL HYBELS, *Rediscovering the Church*

As we share how the Great Commandment Principle transformed our lives, I trust it will help you see how deepening your own relationships is actually God's means of increasing your ministry effectiveness.

PART TWO

Expressing Love

DAVID FERGUSON
with Teresa Ferguson

CHAPTER SEVEN

Where Great Commandment Love Begins

IT HAD been another stressful-yet-fulfilling day juggling a secular job and a demanding part-time ministry to students. My schedule had been packed with typical activities: an early morning discipleship group, a number of appointments throughout the day, paperwork, lunch with a church elder, several phone calls from students, and another round of tinkering with a faulty computer program. I left a pile of work on my desk at 6:00 P.M. to run home for a quick supper. Then I hurried off to the church for a counseling appointment and a committee meeting that would last until past ten.

As usual, Teresa and the children barely noticed that I had come and gone. They were accustomed to my brief appearances at home. But I prided myself on being diligent in both work and ministry, as evidenced by the long hours I put in.

By the time I got home late that night, Teresa was in bed but still awake. I slipped into bed beside her and turned out the light. We talked in generalities about the day. I described my accomplishments and she related how the kids had behaved—and misbehaved—at home.

At this point in our marriage, our conversations were rather superficial, as was the rest of our relationship. I was so busy with my job and running a growing student ministry, and she was so busy running the home, that we rarely connected deeply with each other. I silently lamented the fact that Teresa was not more committed to the ministry, which I sometimes interpreted as a lack of commitment to me as well. We were not enemies, yet there was a distance in our marriage that was unsettling to me.

Staring up at the ceiling in the darkness, I addressed the issue. "Teresa, I sense a dryness between us, like we live on opposite sides of a big desert. We are so involved in our own separate worlds of activity that we hardly notice each other. Is this the way it's always going to be with us?"

There was silence on Teresa's side of the bed, followed by a deep sigh. "I don't know, David."

Finally I found the courage to ask the question that had been haunting me for months. "Teresa, do you really love me?"

Silence again. When Teresa finally answered, I was not prepared for the directness of her response. "David, I don't feel anything for you. I'm just numb."

The words stung my heart. I didn't know what to say. I knew there was some distance between us, but she was talking about a complete lack of love.

Ever since becoming a Christian, I had been trying to strike a workable balance between my family, my work, and my ministry commitments. Up until that moment in the bedroom I thought I was doing a pretty good job. In the wake of Teresa's sobering statement, I was more confused than ever about love, relationships, and God's plan for ministry.

To be honest, I did not know the first thing about sharing God's love with those dearest to me. I was deeply committed to the ministry, for I would soon become a full-time associate pastor. But I also desired intimacy with a devoted wife and loving children. With Teresa's loveless words echoing painfully in my heart, it appeared that I might be on the verge of being denied both.

PRIORITIES IN CONFLICT

At the time, I thought the dry distance in our marriage was rare among ministry couples. But as Teresa and I interact with thousands of couples and single adults in Christian leadership every year, I realize that our painful struggle with priorities is not at all uncommon. Many Christians in ministry have misplaced priorities related to family relationships and ministry. According to the figures cited in chapter 1, not many succeed in reordering their priorities. Consider again the telltale findings:

- Eighty percent of ministers surveyed believe the ministry negatively affects their families.[1]
- Forty-one percent of married Christian leaders struggle with anger toward their spouse.[2]
- Seventy percent of ministry leaders have no one they consider to be a close friend.[3]
- Many feel overwhelmed by the demands of their job.[4]

We have also observed that countless single adults in Christian leadership minister to the multitudes while struggling with a deep fear of intimacy in their own personal relationships! These findings are staggering. Why does the divine call to minister to others produce such adverse results in the God-ordained relationships of marriage, family, and friendship?

Trying to balance family and ministry runs contrary to Great Commandment love.

I believe one major culprit is an insidious, destructive myth among today's Christian leaders: the idea that we can achieve balance between ministry and family demands. We assume that the call to family and the call to ministry are separate and distinct, competing against each other for our attention.

These two roles are like two china plates a juggler spins at the top of long sticks. When pressures at church mount, we urge our families to "just understand, adjust, and be patient" while we give all our time and energy to keep the ministry plate spinning. When pressures at home mount due to neglect, we give the wobbling family plate a few frantic spins by repenting and canceling a few commitments in hopes that God and the family are satisfied. But we cannot keep both of them spinning successfully. Sooner or later, one of them will fall.

Trying to balance family and ministry runs contrary to Great Commandment love. These seemingly conflicting roles are not like two fragile plates we must keep aloft and spinning. Family and ministry are two concentric circles surrounding an individual's personal relationship with God. Any public ministry God grants us should flow out of our love relationship with him and out of our loving ministry to family, friends, or other "nearest neighbors." In these nearest relationships we come to understand the practical aspects of Christian ministry. In them we learn both to live and to share God's concern for fallenness and aloneness. Living out the truth in our nearest relationships is the prerequisite for teaching the truth effectively in our ministry relationships.

Any public ministry God grants us should flow out of our love relationship with him and out of our loving ministry to family.

I have discovered that those who try to maintain this myth of balancing home and ministry too often end up elevating the need of human fallenness over the needs of human aloneness in their families and friendships. Consequently, the priority of relationships is pushed aside by the overwhelming demands of the ministry.

Being versus Doing

When Teresa told me that she felt nothing for me, that she was emotionally numb, I was painfully aware that something was miss-

WHERE TO BEGIN

If you identify in any way with the need to minister more from the Father's loving heart, you may be asking, "Where do I begin?" As a husband, father, wife, mother, or single adult, you want to know how to become more of a loving ambassador for Christ in your personal relationships. As a youth worker, Bible study leader, deacon, elder, pastor, or parachurch leader, you want to know the action steps for expressing Great Commandment love more consistently and effectively in the areas of your ministry.

Fostering a heart of Great Commandment love is not a matter of *doing* something; it's a matter of *being* where love is. Just as the disciples remained obediently in Jerusalem for the promise of the Father, so we must abide in the heart of God in order to love as he loves. The Great Commandment love we need in order to meet the relational needs of spouse, children, and others comes from the heart of God. The apostle John wrote, "God is love, and the one who abides in love abides in God, and God abides in him. By this, love is perfected with us" (1 John 4:16-17, NASB). We cannot love as God loves unless we abide where that love is: in the very heart of God.

Wait in Jerusalem

They stood there with their eyes lifted toward the clouds, straining for a last glimpse of the Master. Suddenly two angels appeared. "Men of Galilee, why are you standing here staring at the sky? Jesus has been taken away from you into heaven. And someday, just as you saw him go, he will return!" (Acts 1:11, NLT).

The disciples made their way back to Jerusa-

To love at all is to be vulnerable. Love anything and your heart will certainly be wrung and possibly broken. If you want to make sure of keeping it intact, you must give your heart to no one—wrap it carefully round with hobbies and little luxuries; avoid entanglements; lock it up safe in the casket or coffin of your selfishness. But in that casket—safe, dark, motionless, airless—it will change. It will not be broken; it will become unbreakable, impenetrable, irredeemable.

C. S. LEWIS

lem to the upper room. They no doubt recalled the Master's clear mandate to go and make disciples. The Great Commission to preach the gospel was still ringing in their ears, and I can imagine the disciples' eagerness to get on with the task. This small band of followers had experienced the Savior's fellowship, witnessed the undeniable reality of his resurrection, and watched him ascend into heaven. The Good News of the gospel had been committed to them. They possessed the message of hope for a desperate world. Surely they must tackle the task at hand. Surely they must follow in their Master's footsteps and be about the Father's business.

But just before he left them, Jesus in essence said, "Wait in Jerusalem until you receive what you need before you try to do what I instructed you to do."[5] The two concepts must have sobered them. First Jesus said, "Go"; then he said, "Wait." The clear implication was that before effective ministry *for* God could take place in Jerusalem, Judea, and Samaria, the disciples had to spend time *with* God. Effectiveness on the horizontal plane of ministry to others was dependent on the depth of the vertical encounter with God. So they waited.

Perhaps during those days in the upper room the disciples remembered how Jesus modeled this principle in his own life and ministry. It was his pattern to live out in his relationships with others what he drew from his intimate walk with his Father. They may have remembered his words: "The Son can do nothing of Himself, unless it is something He sees the Father doing. . . . For the Father loves the Son, and shows Him all things" (John 5:19-20, NASB). They may have recalled that Jesus began his ministry-filled days by rising before dawn to spend time with his Father.[6]

As they waited before God and contemplated the Savior's ministry, perhaps the 120 believers more fully understood that their relevance to a needy world was dependent on their relationship with God. The truth of their dependence on God was crystallizing in their hearts, truth that John and Paul would later put into words:

- Let us love one another, for love is from God. (1 John 4:7, NASB)
- The . . . God of all comfort; who comforts us . . . so that we

Ever since the fall of Adam and Eve, the human family has been alienated and separated from God. But God, whose heart is rich with love and compassion, went to incomprehensible lengths to restore the fellowship interrupted by sin. Reconciliation could take place only if a remedy for sin was made possible. So Jesus Christ willingly took on a robe of flesh, suffered the relational pain of humiliation and rejection, died a criminal's death, and, in becoming sin, experienced the aching void of separation from his Father. And he did it for you and me. In order to make provision for both our fallenness and our aloneness, God Almighty personally suffered the separation caused by our sin.

He who knew no sin became sin in order to remove our sin. He who knew no aloneness experienced aloneness in order to remove our aloneness.

Does this insight help you enter the compassionate heart of God? Do you sense more poignantly how God hurts when you are alone, when your spouse, children, or dearest friends are alone, when the members of your congregation, Bible study class, or leadership team are alone? Does this clearer view into God's heart of compassion motivate you to minister to those he has placed in your life? Could the Creator's declaration—"not good"—become a source of constraining love that prompts you to co-labor with him in removing the aloneness in others?

Let us linger awhile in God's heart. Come with me back to Golgotha's hill. Jesus Christ, God's only Son, has been nailed to a rugged cross. Stand with me and watch the crowd. What are the people doing? The soldiers are gambling for Jesus' garments as blood flows from pierced brow, hands, and feet. The priests, scribes, and elders are taunting him. Can you hear their vile, self-righteous epithets? The Savior's mother and her comforters stand nearby weeping. But on the cross, the Son of Man is alone. No one can comfort him or support him now except his Father.

Suddenly, darkness falls over the land and lingers for three hours. We watch Jesus writhe in pain. We hear short, ragged gasps as he struggles to breathe. Finally, we see him lift his bloody head toward the blackened heavens and cry out in agony, "My God, my God, why have you forsaken me?" We shudder at the realization. Even the Father has turned away from the sin-burdened Savior. We watch helplessly as the Son of God cries out and struggles and dies utterly alone.

Can you imagine the ache in the abandoned Savior's heart in those last moments? Can you imagine that same ache in the heart of the Father, who had to turn away? God the Son was so passionately concerned about your fallenness and aloneness that he became sin and suffered agonizing aloneness. Are you gripped by the glorious irony? He who knew no sin became sin in order to remove our sin. He who knew no aloneness experienced aloneness in order to remove our aloneness. This is the compassionate heart of God. This is the fountainhead of relevant ministry. It is here at Calvary that we experience the only source of true love, and it has been expressed toward you and me!

As I write these words with tears streaming down my face, I am in awe of his grace. But these are not tears of sorrow. They are tears of gratitude for his love and mercy toward me. Can you rejoice with me in a God who has so passionately and selflessly acted to remove our fallenness and aloneness? Will you allow your heart to overflow with thanksgiving for his unbounded grace? Have you captured a sense of God's love and passion for those who are spiritually and relationally alone? Are you freshly motivated to enter into partnership with him in the ministry of removing the aloneness of those around you? Can you sense him inviting you to love him intimately with all your heart, soul, and mind and then love others as you love yourself?

Put the book aside for a few moments and express your gratitude to God. Allow your eyes to see as he sees. Allow your heart to become one with his. Thank him. Praise him. Worship him. Be still and know him. Quietly spend time with the God who is love.

CHAPTER EIGHT
God's Priority for Ministry

SEVERAL years before Teresa's penetrating statement "I don't feel anything for you, I'm just numb," I was aware of the growing distance between us. At the time, I held a full-time job in Texas state government and served part-time on our church staff as director of a booming student ministry. Ministry was my passion, and my family suffered as a result.

While I was in desperate need of reordering my priorities, I seemed powerless to do anything about it. But God in his bountiful mercy continued to provide wake-up calls that challenged me on two fronts. First, he apprehended me in a rental car on the way to the airport, as I described earlier. Experiencing the fellowship of Christ's sufferings that day dramatically awakened me to the heart of God. Prior to that I had misrepresented God's heart in my ministry and my relationships, assuming that he was only concerned about human fallenness.

Second, God brought me face-to-face with a destructive self-reliant attitude. I lived as if I did not need others, and I treated others as if they should not need me. I had been relating and ministering to others from a misunderstanding of human need, claiming that we need only God. Those suffering the greatest pain from my misplaced priorities were the people dearest to me: my wife, Teresa, and our three children.

I want to share with you how God lovingly challenged my self-reliance and began to reorder my priorities. But first, a little background on Teresa and me will help you understand why our relationship was in dire need of Great Commandment love.

A Desert of Distance

Teresa and I were both sixteen years old and still in high school when we got married, and neither of us was a Christian at the time. The whirlwind romance began with our first date. We went out for a Coke; then I took Teresa with me to the county jail to visit a crazy buddy of mine. This guy's goal in life was to see the inside of every jail in the state of Texas—as an inmate! Perhaps I wanted to impress my new girlfriend by showing her that I hung out with people who had clear goals in life.

Despite a less than romantic beginning, Teresa and I fell in love. Six months later, we faced our parents with a rebellious ultimatum: "We have decided to get married. If you don't give your permission, we will elope to Kansas, where marriage at our age is legal." Our parents shed tears at our wedding, but they were not tears of joy.

We spent our wedding night in a local motel. Early the next morning while Teresa was still asleep, a friend of mine knocked on the door of our room. Stanley and I were pool-shooting buddies, and he wanted me to go shoot pool with him. The fact that I was on my honeymoon didn't seem to matter to Stanley, and it didn't make much difference to me. I loved shooting pool, so I got dressed, and we left for the pool hall. It never entered my mind to tell Teresa, who was still asleep when I walked out the door.

Teresa tells what happened next: "When I woke up and found David and his car gone, I didn't know what to think. Had I displeased him already? Had he changed his mind about being married to me? I was only sixteen years old, and I felt confused and abandoned. So I left the motel and walked the several blocks home to my parents, crying and feeling very alone."

Somehow Teresa and I survived that rocky beginning. But I had communicated through my behavior that she was not the only thing in my life—and sometimes not even the most important thing. Without the tools to deal with such deep insensitivity and selfishness on my part, Teresa buried her pain, and we simply carried on with life. That honeymoon experience was in effect the first truckload of sand in what would grow to become the Ferguson Desert over the next fifteen years.

About the only thing we did right in those early years was to stay in school. After finishing high school, I enrolled at the University of

Texas to study nuclear physics. Education became my priority while Teresa filled her life with caring for our new baby daughter, Terri.

Out of her loneliness she and Terri began to attend a small neighborhood church. Through her persistence, Teresa finally convinced me to begin attending the little church. I was initially reluctant at the thought of adding religion to my life. But God used the caring concern of a few new Christian friends to lead me to Christ. Curiously, Teresa did not become a Christian at that time.

Along with my commitment came an urgency for spiritual things. Within a year, and admittedly long before I was ready, my zeal for God and my enthusiasm to reach others landed me in a part-time church staff position as director of a growing ministry to students. It wasn't long until every Friday night about twenty-five student leaders would crowd into our house for dinner. Later, all the students they were discipling would join us for a big Bible study—about one hundred students in all.

Teresa cooked the dinner for the leaders, but she did not share my emotional and spiritual fervor for ministry. In my attempt to encourage her to a deeper love for God, I'm sure I sounded more like a drill instructor than a caring husband. I wanted her to catch my vision for God and ministry, but the spiritual and emotional distance between us only widened.

"Becoming a Christian remedied my estrangement from God, but it did not make a significant difference in our marriage."

When our church began an aggressive street ministry, I was right in the middle of it. In fact, the man we brought in from California to train us in street ministry stayed in our home for about six months. It was during this time that Teresa trusted Christ as Savior, and I was thrilled about her decision.

Now she will surely identify with my passion for serving others and join me wholeheartedly in ministry, I thought hopefully. *The intimacy I have longed for in our relationship will finally become a reality.*

But I was wrong.

Teresa relates her perspective on her conversion. "Becoming a Christian remedied my estrangement from God, but it did not make a significant difference in our marriage. Before David became a Christian, he was always gone with his single friends—drinking and playing pool. After his conversion he was always gone with his Christian friends—doing 'the work of the ministry.' And I was left at home with our two girls, Terri and Robin, and our infant son, Eric. Even as a new believer, I subconsciously regarded the church and the ministry as my enemy, constantly taking my husband away from me. David was still a layman when someone commented to me, 'Wouldn't it be something if you turned out to be a pastor's wife someday?'

"I shot back quickly, 'Whatever I do, I don't ever want to be a pastor's wife.'"

Who Are Your Dearest Disciples?

One day our street evangelist houseguest pulled me aside for a man-to-man chat. "David, I have been observing your life over these past several months," he said. "You are very busy, but you are also very barren. Wouldn't it be tragic if your dearest disciples were not your wife and your three children?"

I bristled at my guest's directness, but I was also grieved by his observation about my relationship with Teresa and the kids—more correctly, *lack* of a relationship. He was right, of course. My dearest disciples at the time were the student leaders I was working with. But that was my calling, my ministry. *Teresa has just become a Christian,* I reasoned, *and it will take time for her to regard ministry as a high priority like I do. But once that happens, she and I will connect emotionally and all will be well.*

But the lingering thoughts of my "dearest disciples" haunted my mind and caused me to begin thinking about the true meaning of ministry, love, and relationships. Did the Lord want me to reconsider how I was expressing his love to Teresa, Terri, Robin, and Eric? Did he want me to consider my family a higher priority than my ministry?

Several years passed, and Teresa did get more involved in ministry. She grew spiritually and became involved in her own ministry, which reached thousands of women each year. Her insights into Scripture and its application to life were at times amazing to me. And while I was pleased at her increased involvement in ministry, Teresa and I still lacked a deep oneness in our marriage. By putting my ministry before our marriage, I left Teresa alone. By putting our children and her ministry before our marriage, Teresa left me alone. Although the church viewed us as the ideal ministry couple, we continued to silently endure the pain of being very alone.

I have had more trouble with myself than with any other man I have ever met!
DWIGHT L. MOODY

My time was consumed by Bible study groups, all-night prayer meetings, and aggressive street evangelism. I had little time for wife and family during those years. Teresa was left with the responsibility of attending to our two daughters and young son. Occasionally, she would lament her lack of a loving husband and devoted father for our daughters. But my attitude was, "Teresa, you don't need more of me to have a fulfilling life; you need more of God."

One day, in my frustration to conform Teresa to my ministry-intensive lifestyle, I confronted her in the kitchen and issued an ultimatum: "Teresa, if you don't come along with me, I'm going on without you." Then I walked away.

Teresa explains her reaction to my statement. "David's pointed words pierced me like a lance. He left me standing in the middle of the kitchen wondering exactly what he meant. Was he talking about leaving me *physically* through separation or divorce? Was he talking about giving up on me *spiritually* and *emotionally?* He could not have known the terrible pain those words caused me. And it only got worse.

"As David continued to lose himself in ministry, he *did* leave me every way except physically. I was alone and floundering while my husband filled his life with his top priority: the ministry. As a result, I became increasingly aloof and independent. I tried to play the 'ministry wife' role, but the more he pulled away into the ministry, the more I buried myself in activities at home with our children."

"Wouldn't it be tragic if your dearest disciples were not your [spouse] and your children?"

The Barrier of Self-Reliance

An old gospel song we used to sing summarized my life during those years. The lyrics are, "He's all I need; he's all I need; Jesus is all I need." My skewed theological perspective at the time convinced me that all I needed for a successful marriage and fruitful ministry was God in my life. Consequently, my stubborn, self-reliant attitude communicated to my wife, "All I need is God, so I don't need you." This attitude ministered condemnation to Teresa as I communicated a second, equally painful message, "All you need is God, so what is wrong with you that you think you need me?"

The Christian ministry may be the most self-reliant profession of them all. We cling doggedly to Romans 8:31: "If God is for us, who can be against us?" But we get into trouble when we erroneously interpret that verse to mean, "As long as I have God, I don't need anyone else." While our hopes and expectations should be directed in faith toward God and him alone, we must allow our sovereign God to provide as he wills. And he often involves others as his ambassadors. When we misunderstand human need, claiming that we need only God, we unwittingly foster unhealthy and unbiblical self-reliance.

Self-reliance is often followed closely by a condemning message that communicates, "All you need is God, so it's *not* OK to need me."

Teresa suffered tremendous self-doubt induced by the painful messages of my self-reliance. She often thought, *Maybe if I were more spiritual or sensed a deeper call to ministry, I wouldn't need David's love, acceptance, comfort, and encouragement so much. If I just had more faith, I wouldn't miss him so much when he is away doing ministry.*

In reality, God desired to minister to Teresa's need for love, acceptance, comfort, and encouragement through me. But my self-reliant attitude was a barrier to his plan.

Have you ever communicated in some way to the people you serve, "If you were more committed spiritually, you wouldn't be so needy of other people"? Or have you found yourself wondering, *When are some of my people going to grow up so they don't need so much of my personal time and attention?* Or how often has the attitude of self-reliance caused you to think or even say to someone you care about, "If you were more committed to God and the ministry, you wouldn't need me so much?"

When we misunderstand human need, claiming that we need only God, we unwittingly foster unhealthy and unbiblical self-reliance.

This was the attitude that directed my behavior. And the more I denied my needs and asserted my self-reliance, the more I distanced myself from Teresa. The more I condemned her neediness and lack of spiritual fervor, the more I pushed her away from me.

I expected Teresa to deal with her needs in a self-reliant manner just as I did, and I chided her for not being spiritually independent. The more involved I became in the ministry, the more uncomfortable she became living in the goldfish bowl of congregational scrutiny.

Teresa explains, "As a fairly new Christian, I was still deciding what I believed and battling false guilt and self-condemnation over how insecure I felt in the ministry. Someone once made the thoughtless remark, 'I would never have believed you were David's wife, since you're not as spiritual as he is.' But by this time I had developed a bubble of self-protection against the pain in my marriage and the church. I became extremely self-reliant in my own world in order to shut out the pain I experienced in my relationship with David and other Christians. I had mastered the skill of not feeling, not hurting. This was how I developed the numbness I later expressed when David asked, 'Teresa, do you really love me?'"

By falsely equating self-reliance with spiritual maturity, my love grew increasingly cold in my relationships with others. If those nearest to me were to become my dearest disciples, humility would have to replace my self-reliance.

Breaking through the Barrier of Self-Reliance

Sadly, it is fairly common for people in Christian ministry to exercise self-reliance when dealing with their own deep relational and emotional needs. This attitude keeps us from receiving God's love through the very people God sends to meet our needs. Breaking this unhealthy pattern requires God's work of humility and faith. It is humbling to admit we have needs we cannot meet on our own. This work of humble dependence on God, sometimes accompanied by brokenness, must precede the blessing of his abundant grace.[1]

Many of the ministry leaders Teresa and I share with suffer silently from unmet relational and emotional needs. Husband and wife hunker down in separate foxholes of self-reliance, expecting God to meet needs in their lives that he desires to meet through their partner.

Multitudes of single Christian leaders also live out the all-too-common misunderstanding that we need only God, when in reality we need both God *and* one another. Self-reliance is an unbiblical way to deal with our God-created neediness, and it strikes a deadly blow to meaningful relationships among thousands of Christian leaders.

I remember clearly the day God began to break through my self-reliance. It was a typically overloaded midweek day: a counseling session, a meeting on the new building program, finalizing details for Sunday service, preparation for teaching the adult Bible study, and gathering my notes for preaching the midweek service. It was five o'clock, and I was more than a little behind schedule.

Into my office walked Gabe, a Nigerian graduate student I had been helping with a citizenship application. Gabe had stopped in to check on my progress. When I saw him, I immediately tensed up and became irritated. *I don't have time for this,* I thought. *If another person needs one more thing from me today, I'll scream!*

Gabe must have sensed my tension, as he inquired about his application very politely and respectfully. His sensitivity softened my heart. I remember thinking to myself, *David, why are you trying to do all these things on your own? You won't admit that you need other people, and you are very alone.* I thought of Christ's agony in the Garden of Gethsemane and how he sought prayer and support from his three closest disciples. I was struck with the thought, *If Christ needed prayer, so do I. If Christ asked for help, so can I.*

After a long silence, I said to Gabe, "To be honest with you, I haven't checked on your application this week. And at this moment I feel overwhelmed with everything I have to do in the next few hours." Gabe nodded, and I went on. "This may sound like a strange request, Gabe, but would you pray for me?"

A broad smile lit up his face. He walked over to me and laid his hands on my shoulders. He prayed first in his native language, then in broken English. He asked God to strengthen and encourage me. He then thanked God for how Teresa and I had ministered to him and his family after they had experienced such religious persecution in Nigeria.

My eyes began to fill with tears. God was doing more than encouraging me through Gabe's prayer. He was affirming to me his pleasure that I would seek and receive help from Gabe. Like Peter before Christ in the upper room, I had resisted others' washing *my* feet. As Gabe ministered to me, I saw Christ's humility, and I was humbled.

Receiving God's love through Gabe that afternoon prompted deep gratefulness and renewed joy in my life. It sustained me the rest of the evening. God had begun to help me break free of my proud self-reliance. Since that day, even though I still struggle with self-reliance,

I have been learning to freely receive from others God's provision for my relational needs. As I have done so, Christ's constraining love in me has grown deeper, allowing me to freely give to others.

God intends to minister some of his love for others through me.

I drove home that night blessed by the new insights I had received and grateful for Gabe's care. My mind flooded with Scriptures that had greater meaning to me after what I had experienced. I thought of Paul's metaphor of the body in 1 Corinthians 12:21: "The eye cannot say to the hand, 'I have no need of you'" (NASB). It occurred to me that I had literally experienced that verse by admitting my need to Gabe and asking for prayer. I thought of Paul's words in 2 Corinthians 1:3-4: "The . . . God of all comfort . . . comforts us in all our affliction so that we may be able to comfort those who are in any affliction" (NASB). I realized that I might have totally missed God's comfort in my life had I failed to be open to Gabe's ministry.

It was beginning to sink in. People around me needed God. They needed his love in the form of care, comfort, and acceptance. But God intended to minister some of his love for others through me, just as he had loved me through Gabe. Teresa needed an intimate and obedient walk with God, but she needed God's ministry of love through me! This was how she would become my "dearest disciple."

One final Scripture verse gripped my heart as I turned into the driveway: "We are . . . Christ's ambassadors, as though God were making his appeal through us" (2 Corinthians 5:20). I was to be Christ's ambassador in my relationships, especially to those nearest to me. His love expressed through me would draw others to him. I was beginning to understand Great Commandment ministry.

MINISTERING FROM GOD'S HEART, SEEING THROUGH HIS EYES

The truth was getting through to me: I needed God *and* others; the people around me needed God *and* me. But I still clung to the myth that I could balance the demands of ministry with my responsibility to family and close friends. *Is it always wrong to sacrifice time and commitment to my family in order to fulfill an aspect of Christian ministry?* I pondered. *How do I meet the relational needs of my family and friends while doing the important work of the ministry?*

My problem was my focus. I was intent on striking a proper balance when I really needed a complete paradigm shift. Instead of focusing on the priority of ministry, I should have been focusing on the priority of God. In other words, the central question about priorities is not, "How can I balance ministry with family responsibilities?" Rather, the key question is, "How do I capture the heart of God, who will in turn direct my ministry to make disciples, beginning with those nearest to me?"

God challenged me that my "Jerusalem" was my home.

Up to this point in my life I considered the responsibilities of ministry and family as separate obligations in need of careful balance. Now I sensed God challenging me to "wait in Jerusalem" until I was empowered with his compassionate heart of love. Then, moving out through concentric circles of ministry, I was to express his love to others according to the pattern in Acts 1:8. Christ's challenge to witness in this verse was obviously geographic—"Jerusalem, and in all Judea and Samaria, and even to the remotest part of the earth" (NASB). Yet God challenged me that my "Jerusalem" was my home.

I was confronted with this question: If I do not share Great Commandment love and ministry with my nearest and dearest disciples—my wife and children, how can I effectively love and minister in "Judea," "Samaria," and beyond—other areas of Christian ministry to which I am called?

I had no answer. I knew God's paradigm was sound. I needed a paradigm shift. And it all started with capturing the heart of God, seeing people through his eyes. I determined to move beyond knowing *about* God to deepen my heart-to-heart relationship *with* God.

As I purposed to capture God's heart, I began to see my wife and children in a whole new light, as evidenced one night when Teresa and I hosted a Bible study in our home. On this particular evening we were discussing how our concept of God is often shaped during childhood experiences. I asked everyone to share an early memory about their father. We went around the circle sharing memories; then it was Teresa's turn. She told a story I had never heard before. Here it is, in her words.

"With six children in our home, sometimes my parents didn't seem to have enough attention to meet all our needs. To complicate matters, three of my siblings were hearing impaired, requiring special attention. So as a five-year-old, I remember craving my daddy's attention and being disappointed when he had so little left for me. Every evening just before Daddy arrived home from work, I got very anxious. I remember thinking, 'Maybe Daddy will play with me when he gets home tonight.' But he rarely did, and I often went to bed in tears.

"One Saturday morning I woke up early, realizing that Daddy didn't have to go to work that day. My brothers and sisters were not awake yet, so I wandered through the quiet house looking for my daddy. He was not inside, so I went outside, first to the front yard, then around the back. I spied him on top of the house getting ready to reroof the house. As usual, he didn't notice me watching him. I remember going to the ladder and climbing it rung by rung to the roof—a very scary activity for a five-year-old. But I looked past the fear because this was my chance for Daddy's attention. I just wanted to be with him."

As Teresa shared her touching story, something profound began to happen in me. Similar to my experience of participating in the fellowship of Christ's sufferings in the rental car, I began to experience a top priority, we are subsequently called to share Great Commandment love with others around us. Remember Jeff, who counseled distraught Wendy with a pep talk and a Bible verse, and Mark, who responded to Fred's problem by giving him an armload of books? Are we just as quick to offer a "spiritual" solution to people in pain or to try to fix their problems while ignoring their relational need for comfort, support, etc.? If so, people may walk away impressed with our knowledge of Scripture and good advice, but they may also walk away alone if we fail to share the full expression of God's love with those in need.

Are you as concerned about people's aloneness as you are about their fallenness?

Remember Sara, who focused on fault-finding and exhortation when her daughter Marcia suffered relational pain? Are we inclined to approach people in crisis with questions like, "What did you do wrong?" or "What should you have done differently?" instead of imparting encouragement and support? If so, those who look to us for love may walk away with an acute awareness of their failures, but they will also walk away alone, untouched by the fullness of his love.

Imagine what Great Commandment ministry could look like to someone like Wendy, needing comfort. In addition to the hopeful and certain promise of Romans 8:28, what if Jeff had also shared with Wendy from his heart, something like this: "I can only imagine how painful these last two days have been for you, Wendy. It saddens me as I know it must sadden your heavenly Father to see you hurting so. Hopefully, in your pain you can still sense the special blessing of others caring for you. Most important, God cares for you, and he can be trusted with your pain and your future."

In addition to his helpful parenting suggestions, what if Mark had shared with Fred from his heart. "I appreciate your coming to me with your struggle concerning J. R. God may have prompted you to come to me because Marge and I have been where you are. We also experienced the sleepless nights, the fear of what we would find out next about our son and his behavior. We have experienced the shame and embarrassment.

"I really hurt for you at this time, Fred. But remember, you're not alone. Marge and I are here for you. We want to be of comfort and encouragement to you. Let me pray with you for God's special wisdom, comfort, and strength."

Sara's ministry to her daughter Marcia would have been more relevant to the girl's need had she begun by offering reassurance and comfort from her heart. She could have said something like, "Marcia, come here and let me hold you. I'm so sorry you were hurt by the unkind words of your classmates. Just let me hold you and hurt with you. You are such a special young lady, and it makes me sad when others hurt you with their words. You are a lovely, caring person with a tender heart, and I love you so very much."

As you reflect on your ministry to others, does it express the compassionate heart of God? Are you as concerned about people's aloneness as you are about their fallenness? Are your dearest disciples among your nearest relationships? Do you sense God revealing any barrenness in your relationships and ministry to others?

Take a few moments to prayerfully consider how God might want to reorder your priorities. The next chapter will provide specific guidelines to help you do just that. But for now, may I suggest that you find a quiet place to be alone with God? Allow him to search your heart and your motives. You need not be afraid of disclosure with God, who is rich in mercy.[3] He knows you better than you know yourself, and he loves you beyond comprehension.

Pray the prayer of King David: "Search me, O God, and know my heart; test me and know my anxious thoughts. See if there is any offensive way in me, and lead me in the way everlasting" (Psalm 139:23-24). Open your heart to God. Ask him to reveal any self-reliance in you. He wants to express his love in and through you to a needy world, beginning with your Jerusalem.

row. But that day God shared with me some of the same sorrow he must have experienced as he heard his sinless Son cry out, "My God, my God, why have you forsaken me?" The tears I shed that day were prompted by the Father's sorrow over his Son's dying this selfish sinner's death.

For the first time in my life I was deeply grieved over my self-centeredness. I felt heart-wrenching guilt over the pain my selfishness had brought to Jesus Christ, the Lamb of God, who was slain on my account. And I grieved deeply over the desert of neglect and hurt my selfishness had caused Teresa for over fifteen years. My misplaced priorities had shut her out and alienated her from the loving husband she needed. I saw her alone and hurting. Great sorrow for Teresa rose in my heart, and I sensed her pain as never before. I wept over how I had failed to express God's love to her. Just as promised, godly sorrow was producing repentance.[2]

My heart turned to my three precious children. I sensed their longing for a daddy's attention, approval, acceptance, and protection. God had touched my heart, and I yearned to meet the needs I had neglected for so many years. The Father had opened my eyes to the pain and aloneness my loved ones experienced. I sensed his forgiveness, and with it came gratitude and renewed hope. The tears streaming down my face were no longer tears of sorrow, but tears of joy—the joy of his promised cleansing and forgiveness. I was truly experiencing 1 John 1:9.

UNDERSTANDING THE PAIN PROMPTS CONFESSION AND HEALING

The impact of this time of brokenness in my church office was immediate. I went home to Teresa in the middle of the day and tearfully confessed not only my selfish behavior in the driveway that morning but a pattern of self-centeredness that had painfully stolen from her my attention and care for more than fifteen years. A ministry of healing in our marriage began that day as the promise of James 5:16 was experienced: "Confess your sins to each other and pray for each other so that you may be healed." God's love was being rekindled in my Jerusalem.

On Wednesday evening, I stood before the congregation and confessed my part in wounding many of them through my selfishness. God was helping me reorder my priorities and restore love in my relationships and ministry.

If we do not grasp the magnitude of the pain we cause, repentance is hindered.

My years of neglect had caused serious damage to Teresa's emotions. I had a good deal of confessing to do, and an integral element of my confession was the experiential understanding of the pain I had inflicted on her heart. I believe a major problem with much of the conflict in our relationships is that we are blind to the pain we cause one another. We hear a burst of angry words or see the tears of sorrow, so we know something is wrong. We respond to the outward expression by simply saying, "I'm sorry." But if we do not grasp the magnitude of the pain we cause, God's work of repentance is hindered, and we are likely to repeat the offense.

This is why it was years before the pain I caused Teresa on our honeymoon was fully healed. As you recall, I left Teresa sleeping in the motel room after our wedding night while I went off to shoot pool with my buddy. Teresa walked home to her parents that morning feeling confused, alone, betrayed, unloved, and abandoned. This was major pain for her. For all she knew, I had left for California on a whim with my buddies, an irresponsible stunt I had pulled on my parents about a year earlier. Suddenly I was gone again, and Teresa had no way of knowing whether she would ever see me again.

When I finally showed up at her parents' house and found her crying, I knew I had blown it. I said something like, "I shouldn't have done that. Now let's go." I displayed about as much depth of understanding for her pain and sympathy as I would ordering a pizza. I kind of confessed my offense, and she kind of forgave me. And that's where the issue lay buried for the next fifteen years. My numbness to the magnitude of Teresa's pain contributed to a lack of intimacy from day one of our marriage.

After I became a Christian, I addressed the issue again. I think I said something like, "That was *really* wrong of me to go off shooting pool that morning. Please forgive me." Still, I had not connected with the depth of her pain, so the issue was buried again for several more years without being fully healed.

When I experienced 1 John 1:9 that Monday morning in my office, godly sorrow worked true repentance. I knew that Teresa's honeymoon pain was still an unresolved issue between us. And so, more than fifteen years after the event, I sat down with her, desiring to experience 1 Peter 3:7 by showing respect and consideration for my wife and her need for healing.

Feeling a significant amount of anxiety, I said, "Teresa, I want you to tell me about the pain you felt that morning at the motel. Take as long as you need; I want to listen. I want to understand how deeply I hurt you that day."

When you approach your loved ones like that, you are in effect taking off all your protective armor and handing them a loaded gun. You are opening yourself up to truth and honesty that may be painful to hear. But exposing the depth of the pain is critical to resolving the issue and healing the pain.

Teresa talked for almost a half hour—which seemed to me like four hours. God's work in her heart allowed her to express her feelings with "I" messages instead of accusative "you" messages.

"When I woke up all alone," she said, "I felt so betrayed and afraid. I sensed such deep rejection that I began to question my importance to you or to anyone."

As she described in detail the betrayal, fear, uncertainty, and hurt she felt, my heart broke for her. I saw that confused sixteen-year-old girl walking home to her parents feeling used, abused, and abandoned. I sensed God's heart breaking for his beloved child whom I had wounded through my self-centeredness.

Teresa and I wept that day as we mourned her pain together. With new understanding and a contrite heart, broken now to the depth of her pain, I said, "Teresa, I am so sad for the pain I caused you. It hurts me deeply that you hurt like that. Will you forgive me?" Her reply was powerfully reassuring: "I did that years ago, but it means so much to me that you care about my hurt." An old wound, washed in tears of true grief, was finally healed.

Great Commandment Love Prompts New Patterns of Behavior

Living consistently in tune with God's Great Commandment heart prompts new patterns of loving behavior in "Jerusalem," our relationships with those nearest to us. It is not in our old nature to put others first and focus on meeting their needs in order to experience relational intimacy. But God's Word and the power of the Holy Spirit empower us to break unhealthy patterns and create new, godly patterns of behavior that are genuine expressions of Great Commandment love.

As I continued to experience biblical truth in my relationship with Teresa, healthy new patterns of loving behavior began to emerge in my life.

Loving patterns of behavior prompt a positive chain reaction in others.

About a week after I experienced 1 John 1:9 and confessed my self-centeredness to Teresa, I was downstairs pouring myself a cup of coffee. A brand-new thought entered my brain that morning: *Why don't you pour a cup for Teresa, too.* I had never entertained that thought before. I didn't know it was possible to carry two cups of coffee at the same time!

The idea didn't come from me; it was all from God, the result of

place in her life. Responding to unresolved issues in his own life, Doug had worked long hours to show that he could care for his wife. He had sought outside speaking engagements to earn extra money. He had spent everything he made and more trying to please Ruth and gain her primary affection. But she still regarded her father as the most important man in her life.

We must no longer look to our parents and siblings to meet relational needs God intends to meet through a spouse.

The order of events in Genesis 2:24 was crucial for Doug and Ruth: leave family of origin, cleave to one's spouse, become one flesh. Oneness in Doug and Ruth's marriage was hindered because Ruth still turned to her father instead of trusting God to work through her husband to fill her need for appreciation and approval.

As we talked, Doug mentioned that he and his wife would be visiting his in-laws for a few days, so I took him aside and challenged him with an assignment to help his wife take a positive step toward leaving her parents. I suggested that, during the visit, he state to his in-laws in Ruth's hearing how happy he was that he was her husband and that she was his wife. He did not understand why I gave him the assignment, but he agreed to do it.

The next time we got together, Doug was beaming as he shared with me what happened. At the close of the visit with Ruth's parents, Doug and Ruth were ready to walk out the door. The luggage was packed in the trunk of the car and the children were in the backseat. Doug stood beside Ruth, wrapped his arm around her shoulder, and faced her parents. "You know, Mom and Dad, I don't think I've ever told you this before, but you have a very, very special daughter. And I'm thrilled that she's *my* wife! I just want you to know that. Bye."

As Doug turned to walk out the door, Ruth looked at her father and then back at her husband. Then she broke into tears—happy tears, she later shared with us. Ruth was able to take a giant step toward leaving her parents when Doug's simple, loving statement met a significant need for acceptance and approval in her life. Once in the car, the couple took a giant step toward cleaving and becoming one.

"David, as we drove away, Ruth slid over beside me and put her arm around me," Doug related. "And she hasn't done that in over ten years."

Loving God and loving our spouse require breaking inappropriate ties to our family of origin. It is God's plan for intimacy, and his plan pays off!

Leaving Emotional Hurts from Your Family of Origin

It was my birthday, so we had invited our extended family over for barbecued steaks. On occasions like this, Teresa slips into a special gear that I humorously refer to as "whip and drive." She puts her mind to getting things organized and getting people fed in the most efficient way possible.

With Teresa humming along in whip-and-drive mode for my birthday dinner, I got the big idea that I could help. This was a break from tradition around our house because I don't cook. But that day I boldly swaggered into the kitchen where everybody was hanging out and announced, "I'll barbecue the steaks." And since I viewed gourmet homemade barbecue sauce as a "guy thing," I started messing around with the bowl of sauce on the counter, that was already mixed and ready to go.

When Ms. Efficiency saw what was happening, she came unglued. "David, what do you think you're doing?" Teresa barked in front of everyone. "Leave the barbecue sauce alone or you'll spoil it."

Her words could not have hurt more if she had jabbed me with a knife as she spoke them. "Then just forget it," I snapped defensively. I tossed the meat fork down and stomped out of the kitchen.

Not only had Teresa embarrassed me in front of our family, but her reaction to my interference had ripped a scab off a large emotional wound from my childhood. My father was a no-nonsense marine drill sergeant, and he seemed just as tough at home. If Dad couldn't make a quarter bounce off my sheets in the morning, I had to keep making the bed until he could. Even with good motives to see me disciplined and diligent, he was a hard man to please at times.

As a boy I yearned for the closeness and affection that Dad seemed unable to show. Whenever he worked on our car, I would go into the garage just to be near him. Sometimes he would bark an order like, "Son, give me the half-inch socket." The problem was, I wasn't all that familiar with tools. So in my effort to please I might hand Dad an open-end wrench instead. If it was the wrong tool—and it often was—he might throw it down, curse, and order me into the house. These occasions of rejection hurt me deeply. And every time Teresa criticized me in areas where I felt inadequate, the old, unhealed pain came back to haunt me again.

When Teresa realized she had hurt me, she quickly and compassionately responded. She explains, "When David tossed down the meat fork, whirled, and left the room, I realized how deeply I had wounded him. Aware of David's painful childhood, I knew I had thoughtlessly touched an old wound. At that point, the birthday party and all my preparations were unimportant. The steaks could burn to embers and our guests could starve, but I had to make things right with my husband.

"I went into the living room where David was hurting and put my face close to his. Touching his arm, I said with remorse, 'David, I realize how I have just hurt you. I deeply regret the pain I have caused you. It was so wrong of me. Will you forgive me?' David said yes, and we embraced. I was freshly aware that a moment's insensitivity can deeply hurt the one I love most. As a result of the painful birthday party encounter, I sought to be more in tune with God's heart of sensitivity, and I purposed to be more acutely aware of David's need for affection."

When Teresa rebuffed me in the kitchen on my birthday, she unwittingly exposed my painful unmet need for affection. When she questioned my ability to barbecue the steaks, it felt the same to me as being rebuked as a child and sent into the house in shame. The incident revealed to me an area where I had not left my parents emotionally. There was a part of me that was still longing for affection, and God used this incident to sensitize Teresa's heart to that need.

When a painful incident like this occurs in a relationship, at least three levels of response are needed. First, the immediate hurt must be dealt with. To her credit, Teresa did this by leaving her tasks to apologize and seek my forgiveness for the pain she had caused. Second, the underlying hurt must be healed. In the next section of this chapter I will explain that process and illustrate it with my own experience of healing after the birthday-party episode. And third, the root cause of that hurt must be addressed. Later in this chapter I will share with you how our gracious and loving God brought healing to my relationship with my father.

COMFORT: GOD'S HEALING REMEDY IN THE HEALING PROCESS

Emotional hurt during the growing-up years is inevitable. Just like a physical injury, emotional pain must be treated in order to heal. We may be tempted to say, "Forget it; it happened a long time ago. Let bygones be bygones."

True, the experience may be past, but the pain of resentment or fear or anger is an unhealed issue of the present. Consider, for example, the Christian single adult who repeatedly ends dating relationships because of a fear of relational intimacy. Far too often there is a connection between such a fear of intimacy and the childhood trauma of parental divorce.

Consider the pastor whose anger seems to boil just below the surface, reflected not only during moments of controversy, but even in his sermons. Seething anger is far too often connected to one's exposure to rage during the growing-up years.

Or consider the women's ministry leader who is vengeful toward any male authority figure who questions her leadership. The connection is all too common between such resentment and the tragedy of childhood sexual abuse.

Unresolved pain from our family of origin can exhibit and express itself in many unhealthy ways in our lives. After dealing with thousands of people in ministry I can tell you that neither oneness in marriage nor healthy relationships in general can be achieved unless and until the unresolved pain is healed.

Part of the leaving process that facilitates greater oneness in relationships involves ministering comfort when deep hurts from the past are exposed. Teresa lovingly walked through this part of the process with me, opening the door for more of God's healing in my life and for deeper intimacy in our relationship.

Identify the hurt. It is helpful to explore how reactions to current experiences may have identified some unhealed hurts and unmet needs from the past.

Teresa could not effectively mourn with me or comfort me until my underlying pain was identified. As we sat down together and I shared how her critical remarks seemed to touch a deep sense of rejection and inadequacy within me, I was able to identify an important unmet need related to the pain: "Teresa, so many times in my life I have not sensed loving affection, and it hurts me deeply."

Sometimes God desires to share some of his comfort through others.

Allow God to provide someone who will share the pain and provide comfort. Second Corinthians 1:3-4 indicates that sometimes God desires to share some of his comfort through others. If you are married, that someone will most likely be your spouse. If you are single, it may be your closest and most supportive single friend. Be alert to the person God has placed near you to minister comfort. For me, that person is my wife, Teresa.

"When David told me about his lack of affection," Teresa recalls, "I got a picture of young David crying into his pillow over his sense of rejection. I also considered how God must have felt as he looked down on that little boy and saw him hurting alone. Feeling God's hurt for David heightened my awareness of my husband's pain, and we wept together."

Teresa participated in my pain by asking herself, *How does the God who is love feel toward David in his pain?* Sharing in God's compassion for my pain helped Teresa tap into the God of all comfort, who comforts us so that we can comfort others.

Mourn with the hurting person by expressing the sadness and pain you feel. "Mourn with those who mourn" (Romans 12:15) may be one of the simplest yet most profound ministries of love found in Scripture. Teresa's response that day is a clear illustration. After she and I talked together, she held me in her arms and said something like, "It deeply saddens me that you experienced such rejection. I can only imagine the stab of hurt that must have pierced your heart that day in the garage and other times when you were rejected. I'm saddened that you have not received the affection you need."

As she held me and spoke, a fresh message of God's comfort touched my heart. The healing of both the immediate incident and the unhealed pain from the past had commenced.

It is God's ministry of comfort that brings blessing at the point of mourning.

In ministering God's comfort, Teresa did not try to counsel me, correct me, instruct me, psychoanalyze me, or give me advice. Nor did she try to explain why people at times act the way they do. Such efforts may help in some way, but they do not comfort. And it is God's ministry of comfort that brings blessing at the point of mourning. As we experience with our loved ones the biblical truth of Matthew 5:4, "Blessed are those who mourn, for they will be comforted," intimacy is deepened, aloneness is removed, and blessing is imparted.

The blessing of mourning and comforting each other's emotional hurts has become an ongoing discipline in our marriage. When

Teresa and I experience the inevitable disappointments, misunderstandings, and rejections in this life, we allow God to use them to bring us together through his comfort. We no longer keep disappointments to ourselves. We resist the self-reliant temptation to handle the pain alone. And we reject the thought that we are protecting each other by burying our own pain.

We are convinced that God wants to bless us abundantly with his comfort and then involve us in ministering that comfort to others. When comfort is ministered and healing occurs, intimacy with one another—and with God—is enriched and deepened.

A Fifty-Dollar Mistake, a Five-Hundred-Dollar Response

Teresa shares how she also left a painful childhood hurt so it would no longer hinder our marriage relationship.

> David and I had just concluded a pastors conference in Atlanta. We were on a tight schedule for our flight home, but we were also hungry. So David dropped me off at the terminal while he returned the rental car. He pulled some money out of his pocket—a few ones and a fifty-dollar bill—and handed it to me. After checking our bags at the curb and tipping the skycap, I went to the restaurant and ordered our lunch.
>
> When we finished our lunch, David asked me for the $50 so he could pay the bill. But when I reached into my pocket, the money was gone. Apparently I had dropped the big bill when I pulled the money out of my pocket to tip the skycap. When I realized the money was gone, my fifty-dollar mistake ballooned into a five-hundred-dollar tragedy in my mind. I began tearing myself down and berating myself, saying something like, "I am so stupid. I am so dumb. I can't believe I lost fifty dollars." But this time David quickly cut me off. He reached over and touched my hand, saying with compassion and understanding, "Sweetheart, it's OK."
>
> As he continued to comfort me and reassure me, I was suddenly aware of a deep pain that had gone unhealed. As I was growing up, our family lived in near poverty. Money was a big deal in our home because there usually wasn't enough to go

> around. I had considerable anxiety over money as a child, but one particular incident stood out.
>
> One day I was sent to the grocery store to get a few things, but on the way I lost the money. It was a childish mistake, and I felt terrible. I returned home and shared what had happened, deeply needing Mom's comfort and forgiveness. Instead, I was scolded severely and ordered back outside to look for the money alone.
>
> This lack of comfort left a wound that was suddenly exposed when I discovered that the fifty-dollar bill was gone.

When Teresa related that story from her childhood, she also identified an unmet need for approval. At first she turned on herself, which only made the pain worse and fueled a negative emotional reaction that had often been disruptive in our marriage. But as she identified the pain of her unmet need, I was able to minister comfort by mourning with her.

I said something like, "Teresa, it deeply saddens me to think of you as a young girl fearful to ask for what you needed and scolded often when you needed comfort. I'm very sorry you were hurt like that, because I love you. It saddens me to think of you hurting."

As we experienced Romans 12:15 together, the God of all comfort ministered an added dimension of healing to Teresa's heart. And God used what she shared that day in the airport to motivate me to look for additional ways to help meet her need for approval.

About a month later, Teresa was in another airport on her way to speak at a women's conference. Standing alone in front of a security checkpoint, she looked down to find a fifty-dollar bill lying at her feet. There was no one else around, so she picked up the money and—encouraged by the security guard—put it in her pocket. We believe God dropped that bill there just to express to Teresa how much he approves of her, loves her, and is attentive to her needs.

Leaving Father and Mother by Making Things Right

The process of leaving father and mother also includes taking advantage of specific opportunities to convey God's love to those who have played such significant roles in our lives. But remember, these steps often must be accompanied by the ministry and blessing of comfort. Remember Rachel, the woman who had been sexually abused by her father? Her well-meaning counselors were largely unsuccessful at getting her to forgive her father until they learned to minister comfort to her deep pain from the abuse. Once Rachel began to experience God's healing through the ministry of his comfort, she was freer to deal with the issue of forgiving her father.

Once emotional healing is underway, it is time to turn attention to the ministry of loving and forgiving those who have hurt us, principally our parents.

Loving Enough to Confess Your Wrongs and Apologize

A Great Commandment heart loves enough to confess any unhealed offenses to parents, siblings, and other family members and seek their forgiveness. I believe seeking the forgiveness of those we have hurt must precede the initiative to fully forgive them. It is nearly impossible to forgive another without a contrite heart that first deals with its own faults. Ephesians 4:32 speaks of forgiving others as we have been forgiven by God. The gratitude and wonder that spring from having been forgiven by God seem to empower us to forgive others.

It is nearly impossible to forgive another without a contrite heart that first deals with its own faults.

I was sharing this perspective with a minister friend recently, and he objected. "What if your parents emotionally and physically abused you? It's hard enough to forgive them for what they did, let alone apologize to them for something you might have done."

My minister friend was not viewing his parents from a Great Commandment heart. Jesus commanded us to love even our enemies and pray for those who persecute us: "If you love those who love you, what reward will you get?" (Matthew 5:46). We must begin to see those who may have hurt us through God's eyes and feel their hurt through his heart. As we do, it will not be difficult to discover the hurt we have caused in the past. When you perceive their hurt, move to confess your part in it and ask forgiveness.

Loving Enough to Forgive

A Great Commandment heart loves enough to forgive family members who may have hurt us in the past. Scripture is clear about the importance of forgiveness. Jesus told his disciples, "When you stand praying, if you hold anything against anyone, forgive him, so that your Father in heaven may forgive you your sins" (Mark 11:25). And immediately after he prayed what is referred to as the Lord's Prayer, Jesus said, "If you forgive men when they sin against you, your heavenly Father will also forgive you. But if you do not forgive men their sins, your Father will not forgive your sins" (Matthew 6:14-15).

God never tells us to do something without also empowering us to obey the command.

Forgiving others, no matter how badly they have hurt us, is a direct command from God. And he never tells us to do something without also empowering us to obey the command. Just as he provides the healing power of comfort for your hurts, he will also provide the liberating power of forgiveness toward those who hurt you.

In one sense, forgiveness completes the emotional healing process. Forgiveness is a beautiful gift from the God who has our best interests at heart. To refuse God's gift is to remain in bondage to the pain of the past. God wants us to forgive so we can put away our anger and experience the full healing that comes from his comfort.

Forgiveness is a beautiful gift from the God who has our best interests at heart.

Loving Your Parents Enough to Honor Them

Having confessed our faults and apologized to our parents for the pain we caused them, and having forgiven them for any pain they caused us, we must continue to express Great Commandment love by honoring them as our parents. "Honor your father and your mother," God commands (Exodus 20:12). We owe honor to our parents simply because they are our parents, regardless of how well or consistently they have fulfilled their God-assigned responsibilities to us.

We honor them when we acknowledge their strengths, their wisdom, and their character qualities in loving and consistent ways. But we also honor them when we come to accept them as "real" people, with weaknesses as well as strengths. This means we embrace them even though at times they may have been uninvolved in our lives, critical, distant, or unloving.

Soon after I became a Christian, I felt deep conviction over the disrespect and rebellion I had exhibited toward my parents. My subsequent brokenness and tear-filled confession had gone a long way toward healing our relationship. Great Commandment love enabled me to leave my father and mother so I could cleave more intimately to my wife. But I still related to my father more with a cordial concern than with the honoring love that is needed to break down barriers between fathers and sons.

Early in my ministry to students, I was often complimented for my sense of humor. I guess I came by it honestly, because my father had a wonderful sense of humor. He always made family trips fun and brought joy to the most boring situations. But I discounted compliments about my humor, saying things like, "Humor is unimportant to me because I want to be a serious student of the Word." In reality, my unhealed pain at that time hindered me from fully appreciating my father's strengths.

As the process of healing, forgiveness, and leaving-and-cleaving began in my life, I was free to embrace and appreciate my father's contributions to my life, including his marvelous sense of humor. As I freely received this gift, God began to use it in my ministry. It was a significant step for me in learning to honor my father despite the pain we had experienced in our relationship.

Then I started writing notes of appreciation to Dad and Mom. On the occasion of one of their special wedding anniversaries, I wrote what our friend Dennis Rainey, director of Family Life Ministry, calls "a tribute" to Mom and Dad![1] Whenever we got together with my parents, I shared memories of special blessings from our relationship. I made it my practice to praise my parents privately and publicly. I took the initiative to communicate my care, concern, and love for them regularly. I knew Great Commandment love was maturing in me. My parents were being honored, and surely God was pleased.

Then came a challenge from God I did not expect. God seemed to say, "Why not tell your dad about the kind of relationship you still want to enjoy with him?"

I responded, "God, you must be kidding. I'm a grown man. I have a wife, three kids, an intimate relationship with you, and a growing ministry. Why do I need a deeper relationship with Dad at this point?"

God seemed to answer my question with a question: "What hinders you from experiencing Ephesians 4:15—'speaking the truth in love'—with your dad?"

The answer was immediately apparent to me: fear. I was still afraid Dad would reject me. God seemed to say, "David, if you let me, I will drive out your fear with my perfect love."

After months of arguing with God, praying, and seeking counsel from Teresa and others, D day finally arrived. Blessed by Teresa's ministry of comfort, I was confident that, as I faced my fear, the truth would come out in love as I became vulnerable to Dad with humility and gentleness. Regardless of the outcome, I knew that God and Teresa were there for me.

A holiday family gathering brought Dad and me together. We were in my parents' backyard discussing the latest urban encroachments on the serenity of their lovely home. Developers were busy at work across his back fence, disturbing Dad's dog daily and covering his trees and shrubs with dust.

In what must have sounded like the most awkward conversation transition of all time, I blurted out, "Dad, I've been thinking. Now that I have my own kids, I realize that I haven't been as close to you as I would like, and I'm looking forward to changing that." Then I hugged him and ran into the house before he could say anything. The truth had been spoken in love, I had faced a measure of my fear, and I sensed God's pleasure.

Dad did not respond to my comment that day or for the next several months, even though we were in contact frequently. Then another holiday brought us together again. We were alone in the kitchen putting our plates into the dishwasher. This time it was Dad who spoke first, and from his first word I knew something special was about to happen.

He began by speaking my name in a calm, gentle voice: "David." That was very significant to me. For most of my life Dad called me Son. As a military man, he addressed people by their rank or title. My rank was "Son," just like that of my younger brother—which caused confusion in our family at times. But at the sound of my name spoken by my father, tears immediately came to my eyes.

Then I heard a tough drill sergeant's version of a contrite confession: "David, I've been thinking. I was rough as a cob on you growing up, but you turned out all right." For a marine, it was the most affirming compliment imaginable. Then, to top it off, he hugged me!

After our awkward embrace, the tender interlude was over. But our relationship had taken a giant step forward. From that day on, we began to develop common interests. Our conversations grew deeper and more personal. Contacting Dad and spending time with him became a pleasure for me, not a duty. We even laughed together about how he bounced quarters on my bedsheets! A genuine friendship developed between us. A father was honored; a son was blessed.

The blessing continued up until Dad's death. Plagued for years with bad health and a poor heart, he could have slipped away on any one of his pain-filled nights. But our good God allowed me to be in town when he did. I was between ministry trips when Mom's frightened call came. We rushed to their home and, as Teresa calmed Mom, I went to Dad's room and held him in my arms.

God gave us a few more special moments together to hold one another and exchange endearments. Several times we assured each other, "It's going to be OK." As I held Dad close, he spoke his last words: "It's going to be OK." Then he went to be with the Lord. Dad was right; it *was* OK. During the few years of our adult friendship, God had restored the years the locusts had eaten. We had expressed together an important measure of Great Commandment love.

Even after Dad's death, the blessing of honoring him continues. Some years back, the initial shipment of my first book arrived at our office. I had decided that I would sign and send the first case of books to family members and friends who had loved, supported, and accepted me as a rebel prodigal. I prepared a special copy for Teresa in gratitude for the miraculous grace and forgiveness she had exhibited. I signed books to Terri, Robin, and Eric with notes of thanks for accepting and loving a father "in process." I gave a special copy to Mom for the enduring faith that allowed her to see her son finally grow up.

As I picked up the next book to sign, tears began flowing down my cheeks before the words were framed in my thoughts: *I wish Dad were here.* I sensed the special presence of God's comfort in that moment. My next thought was the memory of Dad's touching words, spoken years earlier as we stood by the dishwasher: "David . . . you turned out all right." My tears that day were tears of joy. I was so grateful that God had healed our relationship and blessed me with Dad's deepened love and true friendship.

LEAVING FATHER AND MOTHER: TWO EXERCISES

Would it be OK if we turn from my journey of leaving parents and explore your relationship with your parents? I encourage you to work through the following exercises with your spouse, fiancé(e), or close single adult friend.

(Photocopy the exercises so that you can complete them separately and discuss your responses together.)

Rejoice with Those Who Rejoice

The following exercise is designed to help you reflect joyfully about a positive childhood experience. How were you loved by your parents as a child? What were your fondest memories of home life? I have found that focusing on the good we experienced in our family of origin better equips us to adequately deal with the not-so-good experiences. This exercise will lead you in experiencing the first part of Romans 12:15: "Rejoice with those who rejoice."

1. Think about a positive memory from your childhood, preferably before age twelve. You may think of an occasion when your parents or someone else made you feel loved, cared for, special, or appreciated. It may be your best birthday, praise from a teacher, a sports achievement, a memorable fishing trip, etc. Describe your positive, pleasant memory here.

____

____

____

____

____

2. Share your pleasant memory with each other. For example, your partner may say something like, "When I was about nine, I remember my Dad taking me fishing. We had gone a few times before, but we never caught anything. But this particular day was really special for two reasons: One, I caught my first fish, and two, Dad opened up, telling me about his childhood. I felt very close to him that day."

As your partner shares a memory with you, consider how he or she must have felt at that time and how you feel right now about his or her pleasant experience. You will likely think of words like happy, glad, pleased, joyful, etc. Then "rejoice with those who rejoice"! Express your good feelings about this pleasant memory by verbalizing how glad you are that he or she had this experience. You may say something as simple as, "That's wonderful! I'm glad you and your dad had such a meaningful fishing trip! I rejoice with you that your relationship was strengthened that day. I'm excited for you!"

That's all. Avoid getting into a discussion about the event or giving advice or telling a similar story from your past. Just rejoice with your partner!

3. Now switch roles and repeat the exercise so each person has an opportunity both to share a pleasant memory and to rejoice with a partner sharing a pleasant memory.

4. Reflect on the experience by answering the following questions: As my partner rejoiced with me, how did it make me feel? As I rejoiced with my partner, how did it make me feel? How does experiencing Romans 12:15 relate to removing aloneness and deepening intimacy? Share your answers with each other.

During this exercise, your partner may have shared a memory you never heard before. You now know more about each other than you did before. You not only discovered an example of how he or she received love during childhood, but the exchange also helped the two of you connect emotionally at a deeper level. Knowing each other better, you are better equipped to identify and meet each other's needs. As you continue to minister to each other in this way, the intimate oneness of your relationship is deepened.

Steps to Leaving Parents

1. Confess. As you reflect on your growing-up years and adult life, allow God to bring to your heart ways in which you may have hurt your parents or others in your family through rebellion, disrespect, insensitivity, rejection, ungratefulness, etc. Pray: *Heavenly Father, bring to my mind now areas I need to confess and seek forgiveness concerning:*

My father ____________________________________

____

My mother ___________________________________

____

Other family members (siblings, stepparents, grandparents, etc.)

____

____

Acknowledge your responsibility to God, experience his sorrow, then rejoice gratefully in his promised forgiveness.[2]

Describe your plans to experience James 5:16, "Confess your sins to each other," with each person listed above. (For example, will you make a personal visit, call on the phone, write a letter, etc.?)

____

____

____

____

2. Leave. We must no longer look to our family of origin to meet needs that God desires to meet through our adult relationships: spouse, fiancé(e), or close friends. Review the key intimacy needs we discussed in chapter 3: comfort, attention, acceptance, appreciation, support, encouragement, affection, respect, security, and approval. Consider ways you may still be looking to parents or other family members to meet these needs. Write your reflections below.

I still may be inappropriately seeking Dad's ________________.

I still may be inappropriately seeking Mom's ________________.

I still may be inappropriately seeking ________________ from ________________ (other family member).

After sharing this information with your partner, pray together. Ask God to bless you abundantly in these areas through your spouse, fiancé(e), or perhaps your mentoring relationships in the body of Christ. Then ask God to involve you in blessing your partner.

3. Comfort. Reflect again on the key intimacy needs discussed in chapter 3, giving particular attention to those needs that, to a significant degree, went unmet during your growing up years. Note the ways you may have been hurt as a result. Be as specific as possible, even citing a specific incident that caused you pain.

I believe I missed/needed more from my father. It hurt that

____

____.

I believe I missed/needed more from my mother. It hurt that

____

____.

I believe I missed/needed more from other family members. It hurt

That ____

____.

Once you have completed your reflections, share them with your partner. Mourn your loss and pain together, then share and receive God's comfort. Listen intently as your partner shares personal reflections, seeking to capture the Father's heart of compassion for him or her. How did God feel when your partner experienced this pain? Imagine Jesus being moved with compassion, wrapping his arms around your partner and hurting with him or her.

Participate in God's compassionate care. Resist the temptation to counsel, correct, instruct, or fix the problem. Simply be God's channel of his comfort.

4. Forgive. Forgiveness is an issue of stewardship. We choose to share with others the unmerited gift of God's forgiveness as we have received it from him. In reality, the forgiveness we share is not really ours; it is his. Will you share with your parents, siblings, and others

she nipped him, the more I felt sorry for him and spoiled him. We ended up totally polarized about how to raise this little guy.

The process of leaving father and mother is just as vital to your parenting as it is to your marriage relationship.

Ironically, at the same time, Teresa and I were expanding our ministry by teaching parenting conferences for church leaders. One day Teresa said, "David, we have to stop teaching these conferences because we don't know what we're doing."

She was right. Eric was "acting out" something terrible, and I did not yet realize that unresolved issues in my own life were provoking much of it. So for several years we gave up our parenting conferences to concentrate on raising our own children.

At the age of eight, Eric was going through all kinds of anxiety, fear, and panic because of our disunity over his behavior. His eating and sleeping habits were negatively affected. His stomach was tied up in knots. He refused at times to go to school and even tried running away from home.

Having learned about meeting needs in each other, Teresa and I went beyond trying to correct Eric's wrong behavior to discovering some of the causes behind it. In addition to administering appropriate and timely discipline, we also began to ask, "What does Eric need?" His anxious behavior told us he needed security. So we began to adjust our travel schedule to reduce our time away from him. When he complained about monsters in his room at night, we comforted him about his fears with compassionate reassurance and prayer instead of trying to explain them away rationally.

We began to enter his world, identify his needs, and experience God's Word with him at the point of those needs. The results were almost immediate. His sleeping and eating habits improved, and he began doing better in school. As his need for security was met, his anxiety was reduced. But the root of Eric's lack of security was yet to be addressed.

Many people at this point would have said that our family was struggling with a problem child. I'm so thankful God protected us from those people. In reality, our family was struggling with a problem *dad*. My unwillingness to step up and discipline Eric was behind many of his problems. But a paralyzing fear from the past was at the root of my reluctance.

Dead Plants and Toothpaste

The issue came to a head one spring day when Eric was ten. It was clean-up-the-yard day at the Ferguson house, and everyone had an assignment. Eric's job was to dig up some dead plants in the front flower bed while the rest of us worked in the backyard. At one point I went around to the front yard to check on him. One dead plant had been dug up, but Eric was nowhere to be seen. He had apparently hopped on his bike to go riding somewhere in the neighborhood.

Had Terri or Robin gone AWOL like that, I would have jumped in the car, tracked her down, disciplined her, and then stood over her until she completed her assignment. But this was Eric. So I quickly picked up the shovel and began digging up the dead plants, finishing his work for him. What's worse, I was not planning how I would discipline him when he got home. Instead, I remember thinking, *I had better hurry up and finish this job before Teresa catches me.*

In the counseling field, that's called pathological: enabling my son's irresponsible behavior while fearing my wife will catch me doing it! And that day it struck me how unhealthy my behavior was, for both me and Eric. So with trepidation I began to explore what might be lurking behind my pathology.

I came face-to-face with a fear from my childhood that still controlled my behavior. It had never come out with my daughters, but it was coming out with my son. The fear sounded something like this: "If I discipline Eric, if I tell him no, I'm afraid he might not like me. I'm afraid he might feel toward me how I felt at times toward my dad, the rigid, drill-instructor disciplinarian from my childhood." This fear seemingly rendered me powerless to be an effective father to my own son. The sad outcome of my unresolved fear was spilling out on Eric in the many problems he experienced.

I knew I had to address the problem. First, I apologized to Teresa for my inconsistency and lack of support for her parenting efforts with Eric. Then I poured out to her my recent, painful realization that what I had often missed in my relationship with my dad was being expressed in a fear of losing Eric's love. I grieved, particularly over how my behavior was hurting Eric. Teresa mourned with me and comforted me as we prayed together. The Holy Spirit began to prompt Teresa to "freely receive" God's affection and comfort, and to "freely give" it on to me.

If the pattern of my response sounds familiar, don't be surprised. It is the same pattern we recommend for dealing with emotional pain at any level of relationship: Identify the hurt, mourn the hurt, both with God and a trusted journey mate, receive some of God's comfort through that person, then move on to deal with wrong behavior. In this case, I had to break the unhealthy parenting pattern I had established with Eric.

Identify the hurt, mourn it with a trusted journey mate, receive God's comfort through that person, then move on to deal with wrong behavior.

I committed to join Teresa in meeting Eric's need for security through consistent discipline. I apologized to Eric for the hurt I caused him by not providing guidelines and rules for his behavior. I even told him about my fear that he would not like me if I corrected him. And I promised him that I would be more consistent at disciplining him. You can imagine how this commitment blessed him!

A few weeks later, I glimpsed God's grace at work as I purposed to follow through with my commitment. One morning as he was getting ready for school, Eric could not find the toothpaste in his bathroom. So he came into our bathroom and used the tube in our drawer. But instead of putting it away, Eric walked out leaving the tube on the sink with the cap off. Now, this may not seem like a big deal to you. But having rarely disciplined Eric for the first ten years of his life, it was a big deal to me. I forced myself to call after him, "Eric, you need to come back and put the toothpaste in the drawer where you found it."

Children are to be given to, never taken from.

Much to my relief, Eric returned, screwed the cap on the tube, and put it in the drawer. As he left the bathroom this time, my quick-witted little guy looked back over his shoulder with a big smile on his face and said, "By the way, Dad, I still like you."

That morning I recognized the handiwork of a good God. He allowed me to experience love from Eric and assured me that everything was going to be OK between my son and me. I hate to think what would have happened to him had I not dealt with my fear and the unmet need for affection from my past. Eric is now in his twenties, and the father-son bond between us has never been stronger.

CHERISHING CHILDREN BY MEETING THEIR NEEDS

As in all other relationships, we minister Great Commandment love to our children by identifying and meeting their relational needs. By doing so we model to our children the love of our need-meeting God. As a child's needs for affection, attention, comfort, approval, etc., are met and some of his aloneness is removed, the Holy Spirit will prompt him at some point to consider the source of such unmerited love.

Imagine a child wondering, "Where did Mom and Dad get the love they share so generously with me? How are they able to give me such acceptance and approval?" We can share with them that we love because the heavenly Father both loves us and loves through us. We meet some of their needs because the heavenly Father has abundantly met our needs. What child would not be encouraged afresh to love and serve a God who loves like that?

One caution in dealing with relational needs in the family: Be careful who is meeting whose needs. As gifts from the Lord, children are to be given to, never taken from. Sadly, many children in Christian homes are being subtly used to meet their parents' needs. Mothers turn to their children for comfort and attention when their husbands are not there to meet their needs. Dads attempt to relive their career, ministry, or sports exploits vicariously through their children. Strengthen your marriage by mutually giving from God's abundance to meet one another's needs; then you will be able to focus together on giving to your children, not taking from them.

The family is the first social unit, and it holds primacy over all man made communities, economic entities and governments.

A DECLARATION FROM THE WORLD CONGRESS ON FAMILIES PRAGUE, 22 MARCH 1997

The needs of children are often met differently from the needs of adults. For example, meeting your child's need for attention will require a different strategy than giving attention to your spouse or a friend. Meeting a child's need for attention means entering his or her world to do what interests the child. For example, you will not likely meet a six-year-old boy's need for attention by setting aside quality time to chat with him about the stock market. Rather, entering his world may mean playing ball with him for a half hour. Discovering the top needs of your children and the best ways to meet them requires astute observation and investigation on your part.

An Intimacy Heritage

With our children, Teresa and I have learned to *look for the needs behind the deeds.* What children say and do reveals the needs parents must meet by exercising Great Commandment love.

When one of our kids expressed with frustration, "I just can't do it," we knew encouragement and practical support were needed. Overhearing, "I don't fit in at school," prompted us to comfort wounds of rejection and supply reassuring prayer. "Mom and Dad, you're always too busy," was a wake-up call to reevaluate our schedules and supply needed attention.

When Teresa and I committed to meet our children's relational needs, this high priority affected our schedules. We dedicated and carefully protected one night each week as "family night" for fun and laughter with the kids. We cultivated common interests with each child. For Eric, entering his world meant getting involved with him and his bicycles as a boy and his customized trucks as a teen. Robin was into every imaginable sport, so we became her biggest fans. Terri's world revolved around a career of teaching and counseling at the time, so we became keenly interested in her ministry to children and youth. Teresa and I took the initiative to spend more time in each child's world and minister to each one's individual need.

We made a special effort to acknowledge and appreciate each child's unique character qualities—Terri's creativity and caring compassion, Robin's diligence and dependability, Eric's resourcefulness and flexibility. By getting to know each child deeply and expressing heartfelt care, we began to mirror the way God knows and cares for us.

By getting to know each child deeply and expressing heartfelt care, we began to mirror the way God knows and cares for us.

We purposed to leave our children an "intimacy heritage," as summarized in the statements about parents listed at the beginning of the chapter. Over the years we developed these statements as personal goals for our parenting and prayed diligently that God might make them true in our lives.

CHERISHING CHILDREN BY EXPERIENCING SCRIPTURE WITH THEM

Many Christian leaders understand how to teach and preach the Word but do not know how to experience the Word, especially with their kids. This was the case with Richard, the pastor of a growing church. Not long ago, Richard came to see Teresa and me at his wife's insistence. Millie had had it with Richard's schedule. The young pastor was putting in seventy to eighty hours a week, often leaving the house before their two small sons were awake and returning long after they had gone to bed.

God loved his Son for who he was, not for what he had done.

After we talked for a while, Richard said, "David, I know what to do at the church. I can preach and teach. I can chair a meeting and delegate projects. I can train people in visitation, evangelism, Christian education, greeting, and ushering. I feel very adequate in my ministry tasks. But I don't feel adequate at home. I see two little guys who need a loving, supportive father. And I don't know what a loving, supportive father looks like, so I just stay away."

That day we helped Richard begin to experience 1 Corinthians 12:25, which urges believers to care for one another. Richard's boys needed his caring attention. They needed their father to take a concerned interest in their daily lives, to enter their world and spend time doing what they wanted to do. I explained that Richard could find examples of caring attention in Scripture. I turned to Matthew 3:16-17 and read about the baptism of Jesus, calling attention to the Father's statement from heaven, "This is my Son, whom I love; with him I am well pleased." Richard acknowledged that he would never find a better model of parental care than that of the heavenly Father for his Son.

"Richard," I said, "the Father spoke these words before Jesus had preached one sermon or performed one miracle. He loved his Son for who he was, not for what he had done. Would it be all right if you shared your unqualified, loving attention and approval with your sons as God did with his Son?"

Richard said he could do that. I encouraged him to go home and spend some time with his two boys and at some point pull each of them aside separately and say something like, "I'm so proud to be your dad, and I'm so pleased that you're my son. I love you."

A few weeks later Richard came to see me. He was so excited. "I'm becoming a real father," he said. Richard was experiencing 1 Corinthians 12:25 and meeting his two sons' need for attention. God's Great Commandment love was being expressed in their relationship!

CHERISHING CHILDREN BY LIVING THE TRUTH IN FRONT OF THEM

It is one thing to commit yourself to love your children by meeting their relational needs. It is quite another thing for both parents to commit to loving each other by meeting each other's needs. One of the most important gifts we can give our children is the example of sacrificial love between parents. This point was emphasized to me in our own home several years ago.

It had always rather puzzled me that Teresa seemed almost paranoid about locking up the house at night. Locks and dead bolts are not something I usually think about. But before we headed off to bed, Teresa would methodically make the rounds, checking every door and window to assure that we were sealed in for the night. As I began to enter Teresa's world in order to meet her needs, I realized that her concern for locking us in every night revealed a high personal need for security. If I was going to minister to Teresa's need for security, I had to establish new patterns of behavior.

As a result, I committed myself to be more security conscious, because in her world, security was a high priority. Today, activities such as locking up at night and parking in well-lit areas are important to me because they are important to Teresa. This is what it looks like to enter your spouse's world and meet his or her needs. As your children witness this commitment in action, they learn volumes about exercising Great Commandment love in relationships.

Another incident in our lives alerted me that I still had much to learn about being an example of Great Commandment love for our three children. One Friday night we were out with some friends. It was time to go home, and both Teresa and I had our cars there. I had Eric with me and Teresa had the girls with her. All our married life my normal pattern was to jump in my car when I was ready to go and just leave. My rationale was, "Teresa is a big girl, and she knows how to get home. If something happens to her, she knows who to call."

But on this night a new idea entered my head: *Since security is a high priority for Teresa, why don't you wait and follow her home.* So instead of hotfooting it home ahead of her, I waited. Even though nothing had ever happened to her while driving alone, I realized I could help meet her need for security by following her home.

As Eric and I sat in the car waiting for Teresa and the girls to leave, he was puzzled. "Dad, what are we doing?"

"We're going to wait and follow Mama home," I answered.

If there were no other reason to commit to meeting needs in our marriage relationships, our children would be reason enough.

His next question revealed to me how foreign this new, selfless behavior must have seemed to him. He simply said, "Why?"

The Bible says that we are living epistles, known and read by everyone.[1] Up to this time, Eric had often read selfishness in my life, prompting him to wonder why I would wait to follow Teresa home. If there was no other reason to commit to meeting needs in our marriage relationships, our children, who are reading and imitating our behavior, would be reason enough.

CHERISHING CHILDREN BY HEALING THEIR HURTS BEFORE THEY LEAVE HOME

Reflecting on our own journey of leaving father and mother, Teresa and I began to consider a wondrous possibility. Could we initiate God's ministry of healing hurts in each of our children *before* they left home? Could we help them resolve many of their leave-father-and-mother issues, thus freeing them to cleave more intimately to a spouse, should God direct them into marriage? We sensed a resounding yes from God.

As we undertook this journey more than a decade ago, an even larger question loomed. Could the resolution of disappointments and the deepening of friendship between parents and children be missing elements in the youth and family ministries of most churches? Is it possible for church ministry to help facilitate the healing of inevitable family hurts *before* children leave their parents' home?

More than a decade of experience with hundreds of church leaders and families has convinced us not only of the possibility but of the crying necessity! The healing of inevitable family hurts seems to be a significant factor in young adults' either deepening their own Christian faith or rejecting their parents' values and ideals.

Healing Family Hurts Proactively

Over the years, Teresa and I learned to heal hurts by practicing confession and forgiveness with our children on the spot when tempers flared, when impatience was expressed, when harsh words were spoken, or when wrong priorities strained parent-child oneness. In addition to our as-the-problems-arise practice, we added annual family intimacy checkups to our calendar. Each year, usually between Christmas and New Year's Day, Teresa and I get away together for our own goal-setting retreat. During this time we prayerfully develop specific goals for our parental ministry to each child. For example, we framed goals like doing more life-skill work with Terri on her finances, spending more time with Robin decorating her bedroom, and providing more support for Eric in his latest hobby.

During these planning and prayer sessions, Teresa and I were often convicted of new areas where confession and healing were needed in our relationship with the kids. These annual checkups help keep accounts short, apologies current, and lines of parent-child communication open.

In time God added yet another dimension to our ministry of healing family hurts. Reflecting on our own childhood experiences, Teresa and I realized that our parents had at times disappointed us or hurt us unintentionally, without even being aware of it. When parents realize they have hurt a child, the healing promises of 1 John 1:9 and James 5:16 are in order. But what if parents are not aware of the hurt they caused? Who should take the initiative to explore such issues, the child or the parent?

The family is an intimate community of love and life.
VATICAN II

As we sought the Lord through study and prayer, the answer became obvious. If Christ's agape love shows us anything, it testifies of his loving initiative. We did not seek him; he sought us. As representatives of Christ in our home, Teresa and I clearly had to take the initiative to discover and deal with any hurt we had unknowingly caused our children.

On the heels of this discovery, we decided to utilize pivotal, crossroads events in our children's lives for heart-to-heart talks to clear the ledger of any unknown hurt. We had such a talk with Eric when he entered high school and again when he graduated. We did the same with Robin on her graduation from high school and college and during her preparation for marriage. Key talks with Terri occurred when she entered college, graduated, and approached marriage.

Vital to each conversation was our vulnerability. We said something like, "We have sought over the years to apologize and ask forgiveness when we have wronged you. We have sought to share comfort when you were disappointed by us or others. But we cannot possibly know about all the times when you have been hurt. Now that you are entering college (or other significant events), we deeply desire to hear about any ways you have been hurt or disappointed, by us or by others, so that confession or comforting can happen. Let's take a moment together to ask God to bring these hurts to mind so we can talk about them and experience his healing." We would not trade one of these touching experiences, because each time God blessed us with his healing presence.

During one discussion with Robin, she burst into tears over a hurt that was hidden to us. Having attended private school from preschool through high school, Robin was wounded by the numbers of her friends who left for public school each year while she remained. She had never before grieved her aloneness and experienced our comfort over that hurt. But that day she did. She also indicated her disappointment that we failed to ask her feelings about attending private school, particularly during the challenging high school years. Although she was greatly blessed through her private school experience, she needed to sense that her opinions and desires mattered. This talk helped us better understand Robin's key need to be respected and for her ideas, opinions, and perspectives to be valued.

One of the most insightful times for me was our first talk with Terri at age nineteen. She was quiet at first; then she began to share. "Do you remember when I graduated from high school last year? We had a great party, I received wonderful gifts, and everyone special to me was there. But I never told you how sad I was earlier in the day. I went to my last day of classes that morning then went on to my afternoon part-time job. But after work I had to drive myself to my own graduation ceremony alone. Dad, it would have meant so much to me if you had picked me up at work and taken me to graduation."

Deep sadness filled my heart over Terri's disappointment. She had been robbed of some of that day's specialness. Worse yet, I didn't know it! Terri was still mourning her disappointment, and no amount of facts, logic, or reason on my part could have ministered to her or pleased God. I reached over, took her hand, and shared gentle words of comfort. Who knows how long that hurt would have remained unhealed if Teresa and I had not taken the initiative to approach Terri.

More than a decade has passed since that visit with Terri, but the lesson I learned about Terri remains. On countless family and ministry trips since then, I have been faced with a decision: Shall we meet Terri at the airport for departure or shall we go five minutes out of our way to pick her up at home? Which would best express Great Commandment love to Terri?

One of the first times I asked myself that question, God challenged me with another question: "I gave myself up for you; what have you given up lately for Terri to express my love for her?" Going five minutes out of my way and climbing a flight of stairs with Terri's luggage seems painfully insignificant when compared with how Christ went out of his way from heaven to Calvary for me. Before she relocated to another city, Teresa and I made many, many five-minute trips out of our way to pick up and deliver Terri. God was pleased and Terri was blessed.

Children Are a Reward from the Lord

Great Commandment ministry to children is not without reward. The depth of our friendship and intimacy with each of our children is a source of blessing that has empowered our ministry to others. Countless times during the stress and overload of ministry God has enriched us and rekindled our zeal through one of our "rewards"—Terri, Robin, or Eric. During a stress-filled day at the office, I often focus on one of the many family pictures in my office. As I pause to remember a time of family blessing, God rekindles a heart of gratefulness for our children.

One Saturday afternoon Teresa and I were driving home from a week of ministering to Christian leadership couples in crisis. Our son, Eric, who was in his early twenties at the time, called on the mobile phone, and Teresa answered.

"Hi, Mom," he said. "What are you and Dad doing?"

"We're on our way home," she said.

"What are your plans tonight?" Eric pressed.

We were silent for several seconds. Exhausted from an intensive week of ministry and teaching, we had no plans, and we didn't want any plans. But Eric obviously had an agenda.

"No plans, Eric," Teresa said. "We're just going home."

Eric presented his request. He wanted to know if he and his girlfriend could come to our house and play games with us. We were silent again, then the blessing came: Our young adult son wanted to bring his girlfriend over to spend time with us. This kind of stress we can manage! The joy of the Lord was our strength that night as we treasured the relationship with our son.

Robin and her husband, Ike, bless us daily with their choice to work with us full-time in our ministry, enriching thousands of church leaders with their support and caring concern.

Terri, our oldest, recently brought into our lives the special blessing of Wayne, her new husband. Wayne had been widowed with two precious sons, Brad and Michael. We not only have a new son, we also have instant grandsons to multiply our blessing. Our reward from the Lord continues to grow.

CHERISHING YOUR CHILDREN: AN ASSESSMENT

You may not be able to leave your children a heritage of property or wealth, but you can leave them something of much greater value: an intimacy heritage. Allow the following exercise to help you better cherish your children as gifts from the Lord. Once you have completed the assessment, set aside some time to discuss it with your spouse or a trusted friend.

1. Listen for needs. Sensitive listening for needs is a critical element of compassionate parenting. Consider the statements below and identify the underlying need: attention, affection, appreciation, acceptance, approval, security, respect, support, encouragement, comfort. Then determine which of your children, if any, may at times make this type of statement.

	Need	Child's Name
"You're too busy!"	______________	________________
"Look what I did!"	______________	________________
"I just can't do it!"	______________	________________
"I'm really upset!"	______________	________________
"I never get to choose!"	______________	________________

2. Give priority to family. Occasions of uninterrupted family fun and togetherness provide a foundation for deeper relationships. Assess your time priorities and write about specific plans for your family.

Regular "family nights" together we could schedule:

____

____

____

Plans to enter into each child's world:

____

____

____

Common interests and hobbies we could develop as a family:

____

____

____

3. Affirm uniqueness. Each child is uniquely special. Communicating and affirming each child's uniqueness adds special blessing to the family. Consider each child's unique intimacy needs: attention, affection, appreciation, acceptance, approval, security, respect, support, encouragement, comfort.

Child's name	Needs	Plans to better meet this need
_______	_______	_______
_______	_______	_______

Consider each child's unique character qualities, such as sensitivity, diligence, dependability, creativity, compassion, flexibility, resourcefulness, etc.

Child's name	Qualities	Plans to share your appreciation (notes, private praise, gifts, etc.)

4. Heal hurts. Prayerfully consider ways you may have hurt each child with your insensitivity to needs, wrong priorities, angry outbursts, disrespect, lack of support or compassion, etc. Each hurt must be confessed, comforted, and healed.

Child's name	Specific hurts needing confession

Now plan a time with each child to vulnerably confess your wrong. Plan subsequent times to say something like, "Are there other ways you were hurt while growing up? Please share them with me now and in the future. I want to confess any role I played in them. And I want to comfort you even if I did not play a role in the hurt."

5. An intimacy heritage. Great blessing comes from imparting our lives[2] to our children. Review the list of statements at the beginning of this chapter that describe an intimacy heritage you may leave with your children. Identify at least one quality from this list you would like to see strengthened in your relationship with each child.

Child's name — Intimacy heritage quality to strengthen

A New Beginning to Relevant Ministry

Implementing Great Commandment ministry with your spouse, children, family of origin, and friends may be a fresh new beginning for you. Hopefully you have found much to rejoice in as you discovered God's abundant blessing in the previous chapters. You may also have uncovered some pain from your past, and you may have identified unhealthy behavior patterns to break. The process of restoring and maintaining intimacy in your relationships may at times seem tedious and slow. But don't be discouraged. You have embarked on a worthwhile journey that will take time and effort. But the rewards for you and your nearest ones are beyond description.

Here is another important point to remember: Relevant ministry to family members and friends does not require you to be a perfect expression of Great Commandment love. In fact, sharing your own ongoing journey—complete with your failures as well as your successes—will encourage others who still struggle in their relationships. You and your nearest ones have the opportunity to become models of Great Commandment love *in process.* Those to whom you minister need to see God's love happening in other relationships in order to apply it in their own lives.

Capturing God's Great Commandment heart, experiencing biblical truth, and meeting the relational needs of others all begins at home—in your Jerusalem and Judea. But there is also a world out there in desperate need of the relevant message of Great Commandment love.

Meeting the relational needs of others begins at home.

I want you to see what relevant ministry in today's culture could look like. The chapters that follow are designed to help you make specific application of Great Commandment ministry to your local church or parachurch ministry. We will identify key ingredients that promote relevance in a local ministry and show real-life examples of how it is being implemented.

We rejoice with you in anticipation of what God has in store for you, your "neighbors," and your ministry. As you apply the principles in these chapters, you will join a growing movement of Christian leaders destined to help lead the relevant church in the twenty-first century.

Relevant ministry does not require you to be perfect.

➢ *To further help you on your journey, we have developed an experiential video series and workbooks for people in ministry leadership. These resources will help you further apply the intimacy message in your relationships and ministry. Using this book along with the companion video series and workbooks, you can become a model of servant leadership to those you lead and serve. Further information on these and other helpful resources is listed and described in the appendix of this book.*

PART THREE

CHAPTER TWELVE

Restoring Great Commandment Ministry to the Church

PASTOR Ken Sanders normally preaches from behind a large oak pulpit on the platform. But today, instead of stepping to the pulpit, Ken descends the carpeted platform steps and stands in front of his congregation on ground level. He has neither Bible nor sermon notes in his hands. His eyes glance from face to face, greeting his beloved congregation. They return his unspoken greeting.

He begins in a conversational tone. "Our text today is Ephesians 4:31, which admonishes us to 'get rid of all bitterness, rage and anger.' Before I talk about the Greek words and their meaning, I want to share with you how God has been dealing with me through our text this week."

Several members of the congregation look puzzled. They are not accustomed to their pastor speaking about his life with such transparency.

Ken pauses, drops his head, and wanders a few steps to his right. He speaks haltingly. "It may surprise you to learn that . . . that I have a problem with . . . with anger." He lifts his head to resume eye contact, but he does so with difficulty. "I am a driven, task-oriented person, and when something or someone blocks my path to a goal, I can get pretty upset. If you don't believe me, ask Martha and Janet." Pastor Ken nods in the direction of his wife and college-age daughter sitting in the second pew on the side aisle. They smile at him approvingly.

Ken ambles across the front of the sanctuary as he speaks. Every eye is riveted on him. "For years I have excused my angry outbursts as an expression of my type A personality. But this week God arrested me with the first three words of Ephesians 4:31: 'Get rid of.' I sensed him saying to me, 'Ken, I never tell people to get rid of something they can't get rid of. You're not wired to respond to problems with such anger and rage. You are hurting the people you love by excusing your anger. I want to heal the pain that is fueling your anger and give you victory through my Spirit so you can get rid of it.'"

Pastor Ken drops his head again and stands silent and motionless for a full minute. When he lifts his head, his eyes glisten with tears. He continues, "So before I could share Ephesians 4:31 with you today, I had to experience it myself. Some healing had to take place so I could find additional freedom in this area of my life."

His voice breaking, Ken proceeds. "I grew up in a home that was characterized by anger, abuse, and fear. I'll never forget the day my dad came into the barn and told me, 'Your mother and I are getting a divorce. She's moving to Michigan, and you're staying here with me to work the farm.' At that moment my heart seemed to turn to ice. I didn't feel sad. I didn't feel mad. I didn't feel anything but an icy numbness."

Ken wipes a tear from the corner of his eye. "For forty years I buried my pain. I was torn away from the loving arms of my mother and robbed of the warmth of two parents who loved one another. That unresolved hurt has been with me all these years. Too often it has come out in angry outbursts aimed at my wife and daughter and at many of you here in the church."

Tears now trickle down Ken's cheeks. Scattered sniffles can be heard in the sanctuary, and a number of people reach for handkerchiefs and tissues.

The pastor continues. "This week, for the first time in my life, I allowed my deep inner pain to be comforted by my loving wife, Martha, and my sweet daughter, Janet. I was also deeply grieved over the bitterness that has gripped my heart for decades. But I was overwhelmed with gratefulness for God's forgiveness, and I was able to find freedom from my bitterness. I then sought Martha's and Janet's forgiveness for my hurtful anger, and they forgave me. Now I need to seek forgiveness from some of you."

Ken focuses his attention on a man sitting in the sixth row on the center aisle. The pastor says, "Allen, during the trustees meeting last week—"

"Just a moment, Pastor," interrupts Allen Dixon, chairman of the trustees, rising to his feet. "I need to do something before you go on."

Dixon steps into the aisle and makes his way toward the pastor. "I certainly forgive you," he says warmly. "But I also want to tell you how sad I am for the loss you suffered and the pain you have carried all these years."

The trustee embraces his pastor and tearfully shares words of comfort. Other church leaders step forward and join the caring, comforting huddle. Parishioners weep openly in their pews at the sight of such compassion.

By the time Ken Sanders steps behind the pulpit to preach, the congregation is leaning forward in anticipation. Ken's message from Ephesians 4:31 rings with relevance in light of his personal sharing. People eagerly welcome the Word, which has already been experienced by their transparent shepherd.

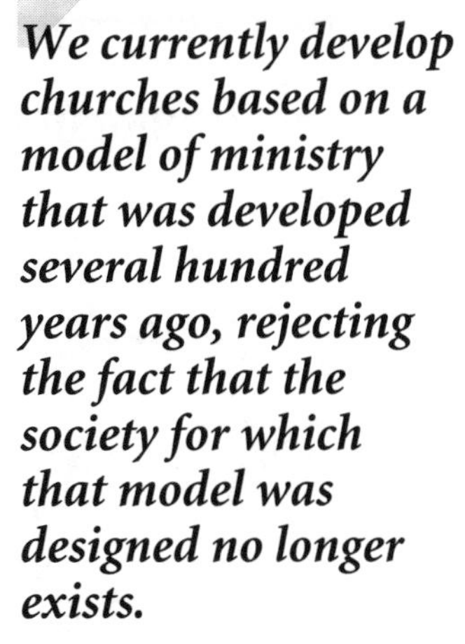

We currently develop churches based on a model of ministry that was developed several hundred years ago, rejecting the fact that the society for which that model was designed no longer exists.

GEORGE BARNA,
User Friendly Churches

NEW WINE DEMANDS NEW WINESKINS

Pastor Ken Sanders represents a growing company of ministers in this country and around the world who are forging a relevant and fruitful approach to Christian ministry. They have moved beyond merely hosting meetings and conducting services where people come together, take good notes, and walk away saying, "Wasn't that a fine sermon?" The fresh message these church leaders proclaim is affecting the traditional structure of ministry. This "new wine" is in fact bursting old wineskins.

In order for us to live out a message of Great Commandment love in the coming decades, our ministries may need to look significantly different. Any restructuring or altering of methods will be dictated by ministry objectives driven by both the Great Commission *and* the Great Commandment.

In order for us to live out the Great Commandment, our ministries may need to look significantly different.

For example, instead of simply preaching about accepting others, some leaders may opt to guide people in experiencing acceptance in the service. A pastor may pause in the middle of a sermon on the topic of edifying one another to allow parishioners to experience Ephesians 4:29. He may encourage parents to turn to their children and say something like, "I am so glad that God chose me to be your parent. No matter where you go or what you do, I'm proud that you are my child."

What kind of ministry objectives are needed to create suitable wineskins for relevant ministry in the twenty-first century? In these three chapters we will identify twelve specific principles for Great Commandment ministry to our culture. Many Christian leaders across this country and around the world are currently using these principles as the basis for ministry objectives and methods. How these principles are implemented in your local setting will depend on a number of factors.

The examples we give in the pages ahead are based on actual ministries following Great Commandment principles. Hopefully they will help you structure objectives and strategies that will facilitate more relevance in your ministry.

PRINCIPLE 1: GREAT COMMANDMENT LOVE THRIVES IN AN ATMOSPHERE OF VULNERABILITY

People are more likely to be affected by Great Commandment ministry when church leaders foster an atmosphere of openness and vulnerability. Vulnerable self-disclosure communicates, "We all need God, and we need one another." Vulnerable self-disclosure encourages people to humbly acknowledge their own needs and allow God to meet those needs directly and through others.

We must resist the common misconception that people in ministry are to be self-reliant and closed, carefully concealing imperfections and needs. Church leaders who hold to this false notion contend that the flock will not follow a shepherd who struggles, fails at times, and hurts as they do. In reality, people are inspired when they see God's strength made perfect in the weakness of their leaders.[1] Vulnerability helps our people know that we also struggle and need Christ's daily help.

Openness and vulnerability in church leaders are far more significant to church health and growth than any event or program.

Pastor Ken Sanders discovered that being open and vulnerable about his trials as well as his triumphs encourages his people to grow through their difficulties. When he talks about sadness from his childhood, church members sense that he understands where many of them are coming from. When he openly allows his present or past pain to be comforted, people are motivated to allow the God of all comfort to minister to their pain. When he reveals his struggle with anger and his journey toward freedom, others with anger problems are less alone and more hopeful of victory in their lives. And when

Ken shares his confession and repentance, others are encouraged to do the same.

The primary model for vulnerability in leadership comes from God himself. God became vulnerable, approachable, and knowable as the Word became flesh and dwelt among us.[2] Jesus, the Great Shepherd, modeled vulnerability by humbling himself, leaving heaven, and becoming not only a man but a servant.[3] Though sinless, he experienced the pain of rejection, loss, disappointment, and loneliness so he could empathize with our pain.[4]

Teresa and I have discovered that openness and vulnerability demonstrated by church leaders are far more significant to church health and growth than any event or program. Ministers like Ken Sanders display a winsome willingness to relate to their people, not just to teach them, correct them, or seek to change them. As you transparently share with others from your own struggles, whether in the worship service, a Bible study class, a small group, or in private conversation, people sense that you are as concerned about their aloneness as you are about their fallenness.

What does vulnerability look like in ministry? Here are several practical, transferable suggestions.

Experience the Word before You Expound on It

Many church leaders believe that their primary task is to bring people to Christ and help them to grow in him. We assume that our own spiritual growth will occur as a by-product of ministering to others. We study God's Word in order to preach it and teach it to others. But we rarely slow down long enough to contemplate what God wants to do in our own lives apart from what he does through us for others.

Thousands of ministers and lay leaders in this growing Great Commandment movement have changed the way they study God's Word. Instead of exegeting Scripture primarily to preach sermons, teach classes, or lead small-group Bible studies, they study in order to know and to love God more intimately. This approach seems consistent with Paul's testimony, "I consider everything a loss compared to the surpassing greatness of knowing Christ Jesus my Lord" (Philippians 3:8). These leaders seek to know and love God first for who he is and what he wants to do in their lives, and second for what he wants to do through their lives.

Let Your Sheep Know You

Many of us have been exposed to a damaging half-truth. It goes something like this: "As a good shepherd, you must know your flock. But it is not healthy for the sheep to know you." In reality, vulnerability in ministry is a two-way street. If you expect your people to be open about what is happening in their lives, you must be open about what is happening in yours.

This does not mean ministers, teachers, or small-group leaders are duty bound to itemize their sins and failures to their people each week. But within the bounds of propriety, you should be as honest about your joys, victories, and struggles as you wish your people to be with God, with you, and with one another.

When you fail to let people know you, especially your struggles, they may struggle with a sense of condemnation. "The leaders of the church have it all together. I guess I'm the only person who struggles with relational pain and living the Christian life."

As a result, their reluctance to share with God or with others is reinforced, their isolation increases, and ministry to them becomes irrelevant. Furthermore, the unchurched coming into such an environment will not sense it to be a safe place to be open about their life and burdens. The healing atmosphere of relational openness will flourish only when leaders allow people to know them "warts and all."

Verbalize Your Needs Honestly and Humbly

What is God presently at work to change in your life? Do you have a ready answer for that question? If you and your message are to be relevant to the needs of people, vulnerable self-disclosure of your needs is vital. And what better way to open yourself to others than to verbalize how God is at work in your life to bring you into conformity with his likeness.

Honest, humble sharing of the leader's struggles and needs is powerfully effective and refreshing. One layman commented, "When my pastor shared that he was struggling to be more patient when things get out of control, it not only helped me see my need for help in that area, but it raised my respect for him." Genuine accountability and encouragement can flourish in an environment where leaders are open about their needs.

PRINCIPLE 2: GREAT COMMANDMENT MINISTRY THRIVES WHEN THE FOCUS IS ON MEETING NEEDS

Imagine with me this scene from John 9. It is a warm Sabbath day morning in Jerusalem, and we are strolling with Jesus and his disciples. Having visited the temple, we follow the Master through the narrow, bustling streets. Then Jesus stops suddenly. The disciples whisper questions among themselves.

"What's going on?"

"Why are we stopping?"

"What is the Master doing?"

We approach Jesus to inquire, but we are quickly silenced by the intensity in his eyes. Following his gaze into a shadowy corner, we discover the object of his rapt attention: a blind beggar huddled alone beside this teeming river of humanity.

God dealt with sin for a purpose: to restore relationships—people to God and people to people.

The people who jostle past the beggar are as blind to his presence as he is to them. But Jesus notices him. The Savior's brow is furrowed with concern, but his face radiates compassion. We are gripped by the love pouring from him.

But before the Master moves to touch the needy, blind beggar, one of the disciples shatters the tender moment. "Master, whose sin caused this man's blindness? Did he do something wrong, or were his parents at fault?"

We are struck by the contrast. The Master's focus is, "How shall I minister to this poor man's need?" while his men are wondering, "How can we get this sinner squared away?"

Here is a significant insight into the irrelevance of the twentieth century church: God's heart is captivated by human need; God's people are too often preoccupied with human sin. Sin indeed separates people from God, and at Calvary God made provision for sin. But we must not stop there. God dealt with sin for a purpose: to restore relationships—people to God and people to people. God's heart longs for relationship. If we are to restore Great Commandment love to ministry, we must enter the compassionate heart of God, who is as concerned about human aloneness as human fallenness. We must align our focus with that of the compassionate Father who is intent on meeting people at the point of their total need.

Building relationships with people was an intentional, aggressive agenda for Christ. "He spent time with His disciples" (John 3:22). He lived by the principle that people respond when we reach out to them.

DANN SPADER AND GARY MAYES,
Growing a Healthy Church

Paul boldly declared, "My God will meet all your needs according to his glorious riches in Christ Jesus" (Philippians 4:19). Can you sense Paul's excitement about his God? He almost seems to be bragging, "My God is a need-meeting God!" He is convinced that God has both the concern and the resources to meet all his needs. In reality, that is how we experience God's love. We need acceptance and he gives it, we need forgiveness and he gives it, we need comfort and he gives it, etc.[5]

Imagine what ministry could look like if Christians began to boldly live out the truth that "we all need God and one another." Imagine the impact if we allowed God to minister through us to both the fallenness and the aloneness of our families, friends, and neighbors. Such caring would be the strong testimony of loving unity that is to characterize God's people.[6] And imagine what could happen if we equipped other church leaders and members to identify and meet specific relational needs in the lives of those around them. I believe that relationally relevant ministry would happen.

How do we develop a need-meeting mentality in the church? It must start at the top.

Minister to the Needs of Church Leaders

Caring ministry to the needs of the body of Christ begins with caring ministry to the needs of our fellow leaders in Christian ministry. Your efforts to meet spiritual and relational needs in your congregation, Bible study class, or small group will seem hollow if you fail to minister to the needs of those who serve with you in the ministry. Don's experience is a classic example.

Don came to me lamenting his lack of motivation in ministry. He had been associate director in a missions organization for more than a dozen years. "I know that Grace, our ministry's director, appreciates what I do for the organization," he told me. "Every year she gives me a nice gift along with a note of appreciation. But for some reason I don't really feel valued by her. I sense God's blessing and favor in what I do. But why do I sometimes lack the true joy of ministry in our mission?"

I shared 1 Corinthians 12:24-25 with Don and talked to him about God's plan for mutual care among believers. I reminded him of his role in serving Grace by meeting her needs. Next, I probed Don about needs that were not being met in his ministry relationships. "Tell me, Don," I said, "are there things Grace does or does not do that negatively affect your motivation?"

Don had a ready answer—a six-point list. He talked about the issue at the top of his list. "I spend days drawing up a detailed proposal for a ministry project. I itemize why we should do it, how we should do it, when we should do it, and what it will take to get it done. I take great care to be thorough and accurate. But when I bring the proposal to staff meeting, Grace doesn't seem to be interested. She glances at her watch and yawns impatiently as I present the detailed proposal to the staff. Finally, she interrupts and says something like, 'Don, I appreciate your attention to detail, but let's cut to the bottom line. How much will it cost and how soon can we do it?' Even though she appreciates me, I walk away from those meetings totally deflated and demotivated."

"Don, I'm afraid that, even after all these years, your ministry director may not really know you," I said.

Don looked puzzled.

"It is obvious to me that being appreciated is not a high priority to you," I went on. "Rather, you long to be valued for your insight, your meticulous assimilation of data, and your strategic long-range planning. You have a high need for respect, but apparently Grace doesn't know you well enough to realize it. All the appreciation she lavishes on you does not fill your need for respect. This may be why you lack joy and motivation in your ministry."

Many Christian leaders have lost the joy of ministry because vital relational needs are overlooked and unmet.

Don represents so many Christian leaders who have lost the joy of ministry because vital relational needs are overlooked and unmet. In such situations, Christ's body is not fulfilling the ministry of mutual care for one another that brings the unity of Christ's love. Do you know the top relational needs of each of your coworkers in ministry? Perhaps you, like Grace, fail to meet those needs because you have not identified them.

Here is a simple way to discover the top relational needs of any church leadership group you may work with: paid staff, lay leaders, deacons or elders, committee members. Ask each team member to complete this sentence: "I feel important to our ministry team when. . . ." The response will reveal needs you can help meet in each person's life.

For example, Don might say, "I feel important to our ministry team when they value my ideas and strategies." Don is revealing his need for respect. If the youth leader says, "I feel important to our ministry team when someone sees that I did a good job and tells me so," he reveals his need for appreciation. And if an administrative assistant says, "I feel important to our ministry team when someone notices that I am overloaded and gives me a helping hand," she reveals her need for support.

Once you identify key relational needs, you know how to minister care and compassion to those individuals, meeting their aloneness needs and freeing them for joy-filled, fruitful ministry.

Minister to the Needs of Volunteer Workers

Milt, the Christian education pastor in a large church, was puzzled by the high turnover rate among Bible teachers. Every year the church spent a considerable amount of time, effort, and money appreciating teachers with gifts, plaques, and an annual banquet. Yet attendance at the banquet was usually spotty, and a high number of teachers dropped out at the end of the year. Milt wondered what else could be done to show the volunteers how much he appreciated them and wanted them to remain on the team.

Understanding the importance of loving his coworkers, Milt put together a relational needs inventory and asked all his teachers to complete it. He was surprised to learn that fewer than 10 percent of his staff listed appreciation among their top three relational needs. No wonder the banquet and all the presents made such a small impact! Milt also discovered that 85 percent of his teachers listed respect among their top three needs.

Armed with this new information, Milt developed a questionnaire to solicit input from the teachers regarding curriculum. Up to this point, Milt made all the decisions about curriculum—the teachers were never involved in the process. The high need for respect among the teaching staff told him that they wanted to be heard in this area. Based on the input he received, Milt put together a list of acceptable curriculum options, and each teacher was allowed to choose the one that best suited his or her style and interests.

As the new term began, ownership level and excitement among the teachers were high. Month after month the Sunday school set new attendance records. And the next year, teacher turnover was at an all-time low—all without an appreciation banquet! This is one example of how demonstrating Great Commandment love to coworkers by ministering to their needs can solve the mystery of disappearing volunteers.

Minister to the Needs of Families

Keith and Janna sit in front of the new-parents class, ready for the first question. Theta, the teacher, often uses games and skits to help her group of new or soon-to-be parents learn practical ways to express parental love by meeting relational needs in their children. Today Theta has prepared a "quiz show" to review the material they have been studying, and Keith and Janna are the "contestants." Ten other couples and three single parents watch with interest.

"Here's your first question," Theta begins. "Little Bobby races into the room after preschool waving a finger painting in his hands. 'Mommy, Daddy, look what I did!' he yells. What is his need at the moment?"

As Keith and Janna huddle to discuss their answer, someone in the audience pipes up, "If he's my child, he probably needs art lessons," getting a good laugh.

Finally Keith and Janna answer, "Bobby is showing a need for approval."

"Right!" the teacher says. "And how can you demonstrate approval in this situation?" "Tell him what I like about his picture," Keith answers tentatively.

Janna chips in, "And tape it to the refrigerator door."

Theta affirms their answers by writing them on the white board. Then she asks the class for more ideas, which she adds to the list.

The new-parents class is one of several life-stage classes offered as

PARENT TRAINING

Using Intimate Life Ministries resources, lay leaders are conducting courses to equip parents to truly "know" and disciple their children. By learning to identify key relational needs, parents are better able to affirm each child's uniqueness. "Family nights" provide the opportunity for parents and children to deepen their relationships as they experience biblical truth together.

OWEN AND CLAIRE CONNOLLY, IRELAND

part of the Christian education ministry in a church practicing Great Commandment principles. There is also a class for parents of elementary-age children, parents of teens, and empty nesters. Classes are also available to help single adults identify and meet needs in friendships and work relationships. Each class is offered as a quarterly option, along with standard Bible survey and doctrinal studies. Though many different topics are covered in these classes each quarter, a primary goal is to help individuals learn to identify and meet relational needs in their spouses, children, friends, and coworkers.

A primary goal is to help individuals learn to identify and meet relational needs in their spouses, children, friends, and coworkers.

Family ministry is too important to be relegated to spot treatment through the year: an annual couples retreat, an elective adult education class in the spring, a four-week sermon series on marriage and parenting, etc. How would your church fare if nursery ministry were conducted that way—providing care for infants and crawlers only three or four times a year? Not well, I'm sure. The nursery ministry is ongoing week by week because the needs of small children are ongoing.

The relational needs of husbands, wives, parents, and children may not always seem as obvious as those of the nursery dwellers, but they are every bit as important. Therefore, equipping families and individuals to meet relational needs should be a priority in a Great Commandment ministry.

Hundreds of churches in the Intimate Life network across the country now provide ongoing ministry to teach husbands, wives, singles, and parents vital need-meeting skills. Many churches require their married church leaders to participate regularly in ongoing marriage and family enrichment in order to nurture Great Commandment love at home.

Minister to the Needs of Unbelievers

In relevant Great Commandment ministry, evangelism means ministering in love to unbelievers at the point of their need rather than just urging them to believe what we believe. This is the Zacchaeus Principle: looking beyond faults to see needs. Once the crooked tax collector was convinced that Jesus was interested in him personally, his life changed spiritually and behaviorally.

Similarly, as unbelievers are lovingly accepted, comforted, and cared for by believers, they will begin to wonder, "Where did you receive all the acceptance, comfort, and care you have shared with me?" At this point, well-equipped believers are ready to give an account of the hope that is within them.[7] As the saying goes, "People don't care how much you know until they know how much you care." Here's another way to say it: Surrounding the unbeliever with Great Commandment love opens the door for Great Commission sharing.

What does evangelism look like in a Great Commandment ministry? Meeting the relational needs of unbelievers may take the following forms:

- Worship services where the unchurched sense acceptance and where God's truth is experienced and practically applied to everyday life.
- Classes or support groups offered to the community—divorce recovery, parenting skills, substance-abuse recovery,

THIS STUFF IS SO REAL!

We led our children in a time of hearing from us repentance and apologies on how we'd hurt them. All five of our children cried tears of sorrow, pain, hurts, anxieties. Then we comforted, loved, and affirmed them through a wonderful time of healing. It was awesome.

On Wednesday nights our church is going through Intimate Life materials. Our people are being transformed. Their marriages, relationships, children are all being helped and renewed. This stuff is so real.

CORNERSTONE CHRISTIAN FELLOWSHIP, SARALAND, ALABAMA

marriage enrichment, etc. Each group is focused on experiencing the practical application of biblical truth.
- Small groups in homes and other nonchurch settings where friendships deepen and vulnerable sharing and ministry occur.

Surrounding the unbeliever with Great Commandment love opens the door for Great Commission sharing.

- Backyard barbecues or neighborhood popcorn parties for the unchurched, where the relevance of God's love in everyday challenges is shared through the lives of "living epistles."
- A youth center where fun, food, fellowship, and caring involvement with unchurched kids provokes a hunger for our need-meeting God.

Todd, a high school senior, testifies about the youth group that actually "loved him to Christ." He relates the encounter this way:

"A girl from school invited me to one of her youth group's parties. I told her I would go, but I didn't want anyone pushing religion on me. She assured me it wouldn't happen—and it didn't. I had so much fun at the party that I decided to keep attending church events until someone started preaching at me. But no one ever did, at least not with threatening or condemning words. I had a great time, and when I was down, they showed their concern for me and supported me.

"After a few months, I finally asked Bart, the group leader, why he and the others cared about me so much. Bart explained that he and the kids loved me because God loved them; they were just sharing his love with me. That didn't seem like preaching at all. So, not long afterward, I accepted Christ as my friend, Lord, and Savior. Now I am a member of the group, and I'm loving my non-Christian friends the same way the group loved me."

When you look beyond faults to meet needs, opportunities to share the truth about Christ will be natural and effective.

Minister to the Needs of Other Cultures

Worldwide evangelism takes on new excitement as ministry to relational needs promotes cross-cultural relevance. No matter what language they speak, people everywhere need love expressed through acceptance, approval, encouragement, support, affection, security, respect, attention, comfort, appreciation, etc. Ministry to needs may differ from culture to culture, but the needs are the same everywhere! Great Commandment missions training focuses on the task of equipping missionaries to identify and meet relational needs and to share Great Commission truth when the opportunities are ripe.

Minister to the Needs of the Shepherd

Christian leaders who serve the needs of church congregations and other ministries also have needs. Since Great Commandment ministry is a two-way street, it is the responsibility and privilege of those being served to provide loving care for those who serve them. Imagine a church taking minister care to heart in response to the following incident between a young pastor and his son.

For weeks, six-year-old Chad had been asking his father to take him to the new Toys "R" Us store. The boy had even saved up his allowance to buy something. Stan had promised to

MARRIAGE ENRICHMENT OUTREACH

After attending an ILM retreat, the pastoral staff introduced a new ministry for marriages and families. When the church scheduled a day-long Great Commandment marriage conference, over 1,000 people attended. Following the conference, 300 people—many of them unchurched—signed up for continuing marriage enrichment through small groups or classes!

SCOTTSDALE BIBLE CHURCH, SCOTTSDALE, ARIZONA

take him to the new store, but he was very busy with church duties and kept putting it off. Finally one Saturday, after much begging by his son and a little nagging from his wife, Marsha, Stan took Chad to Toys "R" Us.

Father and son toured the store, and Chad picked out a toy. On the way to the checkout stand Stan ran into Phil, one of the deacons in his church. The two men chatted for a few minutes while Chad made his purchase. As Stan and his son walked away, Phil heard Chad say, "Thanks, Dad, for taking me to the store. Maybe next time you will *want* to come."

As Phil drove home, he thought about Chad's comment. The little boy was hurt, and Phil felt his pain. The deacons had admonished Stan to make his wife and children top priority and had promised in love to hold him accountable. An overloaded church schedule was apparently interfering with Stan's ministry to his own family. Phil knew something had to be done.

Phil met with Stan the next Monday to express his love for the pastor and his concern over the demanding schedule. Stan was touched by Phil's loving interest. The two men prayed together; then Phil suggested the next step. The deacon board met with Stan after the midweek service to discuss his workload and explore ways the pastor could reorder his family and ministry priorities. A deep, loving relationship already existed between the pastor and deacons, so the meeting was positive and productive.

On Sunday morning, Stan's text was 1 Corinthians 12:24-26, Paul's instruction for members of the body to care for one another, especially those who are suffering in some way. "This week I experienced this passage in a new and hopefully life-changing way," he began. "God challenged me to review my relationship with the most important people in my life: my wife, Marsha, and our son and daughter." He told the Toys "R" Us story and how he had wounded his son Chad by failing to meet his need for attention. Then he assured the congregation that he had asked for and received Chad's forgiveness.

Stan invited Phil to address the congregation on behalf of the deacons. Phil stepped to the platform and invited other deacons to stand with him. Then he called the family—Marsha, Karen, and Chad—to join Stan and the deacons in front of the congregation.

Phil said, "The deacons realize that we have not been as supportive of Pastor Stan and his family as we should be. How can our pastor serve the needs of his family when church activities take him away from home most nights of the week and many Saturdays?"

Turning to the pastor and his family, Phil said, "You have been so diligent to serve us and care for us, but we have failed to do the same for you. So we apologize to you, Stan, Marsha, Karen, and Chad, and ask you to forgive us for allowing some of your vital needs to go unmet."

A round of tearful embraces demonstrated that the apology was accepted and forgiveness granted.

Phil turned back to the congregation. "From now on, we promise to honor our pastor's needs for time with his family. We have established a ministry-care team composed of three couples on the deacon board. The team's role is to ensure that our leader's family is nurtured and cared for in love. The team will encourage Stan to take his regular days off and to schedule dates with Marsha, family trips, and vacations. We will make sure the pastor and his family are not interrupted by church activities at least three nights a week. And we call on the entire congregation to support our pastor and his family by guarding the privacy of their home life and by participating in an annual churchwide pastor appreciation day."

Like Stan's church, may all of our congregations grow in sensitivity to meet the vital relational needs of ministers and their families.

PRINCIPLE 3: GREAT COMMANDMENT MINISTRY THRIVES WHEN RELATIONSHIPS TAKE PRIORITY OVER RELIGION

When I became a Christian at age twenty-one, someone gave me a popular Bible study plan to follow. Each day I was to read a chapter of Scripture and answer a number of questions about the passage: Is there a command to obey? Is there a sin to avoid? Is there a promise to claim? Is there a behavior to change? etc. I dived into the project energetically, determined to change my behavior in accordance with what I learned.

After about three weeks of furious study, a penetrating thought stopped me dead in my tracks. *This is not the God who saved me. This God is concerned primarily with commands, sins, beliefs, and behaviors. I want to know the God who loved me in my sin, touched my heart with his compassion, and called me into an intimate relationship with himself.* I was captivated by Psalm 103:7: "[The Lord] made known his ways to Moses, his deeds to the people of Israel." I wanted to learn more about God than his deeds; I wanted to know his ways, the how and why behind the deeds.

Religion cannot produce a transformed life. Only a relationship with the Redeemer can do that.

So I set aside the arduous Bible study plan and determined to know this God of love. I still studied the Scriptures and memorized many large passages. But my motivation was different. I still wanted to know what to believe about God and how to behave toward others. But I also wanted to know how to love this loving God with all my heart, mind, and soul. That longing to know him and his ways early in my journey as a Christian changed my life and eventually shaped my ministry.

Great Commandment ministry undergirds its commitment to right beliefs and right behaviors with a priority commitment to loving relationships. Believing and behaving correctly are essential to the Christian life but not sufficient in and of themselves. Belief and behavior alone constitute Christian religion, but religion cannot remove aloneness. Only deep, intimate relationships with God and others can do that. Religion cannot produce a transformed life. Only a relationship with the Redeemer can do that. Therefore, relevant ministry must equip people to believe, behave, and love correctly.

Encourage a Love Relationship with God

Leaders in Great Commandment ministry must never assume that a call to, and involvement in, Christian ministry automatically guarantees intimacy with God. Each individual must wholeheartedly pursue a growing, personal love relationship with God. Personal devotions must go beyond *studying about* him to *relating to* him. The heart cry of every minister should be to know God intimately. The "business" of the ministry must not drown out a passion for loving God, learning his ways, and experiencing his heart. When we model and teach the priority of a love relationship with God at all levels of church life, we have relevant ministries.

In Great Commandment ministry, worship services, regardless of worship style, are opportunities to relate to God corporately. Various elements of the service—from congregational singing to the proclamation of the Word to a time to "be still, and know that I am God" (Psalm 46:10)—are geared to call the church to encounter God relationally through experiencing his Word. Scripture may be experienced together at times as people rejoice with those who rejoice, mourn with those who mourn, and fellowship in Christ's joy and sorrow. Testimonies and rejoicing over God's mighty acts are balanced with moments of quiet reverence and wonder at contemplating his love.

Worship services, regardless of style, are opportunities to relate to God corporately.

Putting love relationships first in a teaching session may look something like this. Pastor Dale Bellamy has just read the Ten Commandments. Lifting high the large open Bible in his hand, he declares, "The Ten Commandments, which were given by God to Moses on Mount Sinai, constitute the best-known codification of truth in the history of civilization. But God did not deliver the Decalogue just to legislate how we should live. May we explore together the greater reason why God gave these laws to Israel and to us?"

Pastor Dale surveys his class, then continues. "Yes, God gave his laws to teach us right from wrong. But the primary reason God gave us the Ten Commandments was to reveal his heart. Did you catch that? Almighty God has revealed to us his very heart. He discloses to you and me in this book what he is really like.

"Moses prayed, 'If you are pleased with me, teach me your ways so I may know you' (Exodus 33:13). Dear people, God's ways—his laws—are a means to knowing God's heart. God commanded us not to lie or cheat or steal, not to commit adultery, and not to murder. But why? If God's laws reveal God's heart, what do these prohibitive commands reveal to us about the heart of God?"

Pastor Dale pauses to let his class ponder the question. Then he says, "In Deuteronomy 10:13, God states that his commands are *for our own good.* Did you hear that? Every prohibitive command reflects God's loving heart, which longs to provide for our needs and protect us from harm. God prohibits certain behaviors because he knows the pain and suffering they will bring us. And when our sin brings us pain, the loving Father hurts too. God sorrows at the pain of his children.

"Pause a moment and allow your heart to be stirred by this truth: God hurts when you hurt. Allow his love to warm your heart and fill you with joy. His laws exist to protect us and reveal his loving heart. Understanding God's compassionate heart, my fellow believers, will produce in us what the apostle Paul calls the constraining love of Christ. This love relationship is God's top priority."

Pastor Dale lays his Bible down. "Now I would like you to experience God's loving heart in the Ten Commandments of Exodus 20. Turn to a family member or friend near you and read a commandment aloud. Then answer these questions together: How might God's heart be touched by our pain when we violate this commandment? How might God's heart be blessed when we obey this commandment? How does your heart respond to such a God? Enumerate the blessings and benefits of obedience and participate in God's heart of rejoicing. Then close your time with prayers of gratefulness for a God who cares. Now let's experience together the heart of God!"

The constraining love of God's heart is nearly impossible to resist. People are drawn to God and truly worship and praise him when they understand that his first priority is not to correct our behavior but to bring us into right relationship with him. Right behavior will be a natural by-product of a loving relationship with God. Jesus said, "If you love me, you will obey what I command" (John 14:15).

Encourage Love Relationships with Others

In addition to encouraging an intimate love relationship with God, Great Commandment ministry exists to encourage the God-ordained love relationships among people, beginning with spouse and children and extending to the whole world. Therefore, equipping individuals to develop and maintain love relationships should be a fundamental priority in ministry. When the relational needs of spouses and children are being met in the family, the church's overall health and relevance in the community are greatly improved. When friendships are vibrant and vulnerable through the ministry of mutual care, living epistles clearly declare God's life and love.

A key goal for ongoing marriage, family, and singles ministry should be to equip individuals to meet relational needs and foster growing intimacy, thus removing aloneness. Ongoing ministry by trained lay leaders and mentors should be the rule, with onetime events regarded as supplementary. For example, the annual couples retreat should not be a substitute for week-by-week ministry to couples in classes or small groups.

Great Commandment churches in the Intimate Life network provide these kinds of ongoing ministries to strengthen relationships:

- Classes and/or couple-to-couple mentoring in conjunction with required premarital counseling.
- Classes organized by life stages: single adults, premarrieds, young marrieds, single parents, parents of small children, parents of teens, blended families, empty nesters, golden-agers, etc.

- Classes organized by how-to topics: vulnerable communication, marriage "staff meetings," "family night" activities, marriage enrichment, becoming best friends, leaving father and mother, etc.
- Classes where parents, children, and youth attend together and interact as family units, including nuclear families, blended families, single parents with their children, extended families (kids, parents, grandparents, etc.), with singles meeting as small "family" units or invited to join the church family of their choice.
- Small fellowship groups or enrichment groups, where relational intimacy is encouraged through the discipline, accountability, encouragement, and interaction of ever deepening relationships. Some of these groups are formed out of life-stage or how-to classes.
- Frequent sermons or teaching series on intimacy, needs, vulnerability, compassion, etc., where attendees are led to experience biblical truth in relationships.
- Mentoring relationships for men, women, couples, families, singles, and teens, where relational skills are nurtured, God's Word is experienced, and an intimate walk with the Lord is cultivated.
- Strategic once- or twice-a-year events—retreats and conferences—with a focus on specific topics such as healthy friendships, marriage intimacy, parenting, sex, etc. Attendees are then encouraged to continue growing in ongoing classes, groups, and mentoring relationships.
- Trained ministerial and lay leaders available for troubled marriages, parent-child conflicts, or other relational problems.

PRINCIPLE 4: GREAT COMMANDMENT MINISTRY THRIVES WHEN SERVANT LEADERSHIP IS MODELED

Great Commandment ministry places people and their needs above programs and activities. Such a priority can happen only when we restore the biblical motive for loving and ministering to relational needs. Ministry motivated by the desire to propagate church programs will never produce meaningful relationships. Ministry motivated by duty and obligation will not spur people to truly love one another. Ministry motivated by the goal to grow a great church will not automatically produce a loving church. In order to grow a body of believers committed to loving God and one another, you must be motivated by a servant's heart. No matter what your ministry office or leadership role may be, you can have no purer motive than to serve the needs of others. And there is no greater model of servant leadership than our Lord and Savior himself.

The Heart of Servanthood

The dimly lit room was adequately furnished for the Passover meal. Jesus and his disciples arrived and observed the Feast of Unleavened Bread according to Jewish tradition. But during the meal, something very *un*traditional occurred. Let us join the disciples at the table and watch.

Without a word, Jesus rises from the table, removes his outer garment, and wraps a towel around his waist. As he pours water into a basin, imagine the disciples whispering their concern: "What is he doing?"

"Isn't that the servant's basin and towel?"

"Foot washing is a servant's job."

"Surely he is not planning to . . ."

The room falls silent as the Master kneels at the feet of John and unfastens the disciple's sandals. Jesus gently cleanses the dusty, callused feet and dries them with the towel.

Do you see Peter's face as he watches? His eyes are wide with disbelief—even shock. For once in his life, the outspoken fisherman is speechless. But when Jesus moves the basin in front of him, Peter blurts out anxiously, "Master, why do you want to wash my feet?"

"You don't understand now," Jesus replies, reaching to untie the disciple's sandals, "but someday you will."

"No, Lord," Peter protests, pulling his feet away, "you will never wash my feet! It's not right. You're the Master."

Jesus is unruffled by Peter's resistance. "If I don't wash you, you don't belong to me."

Peter's eyes dart from face to face around the room. We sense his embarrassment at having refused the Master's service. As usual, Peter goes into verbal backup, blustering, "Well, if washing is so important, then wash me all over, Lord, not just my feet!"

Jesus continues around the circle until he gets to you. Do you sense the tenderness and compassion as he pours water over your feet and towels them dry? Don't you feel blessed as the object of his loving service?

When Jesus returns to his place, he says, "Do you understand what I was doing? You call me 'Teacher' and 'Lord,' and you are right, because it is true. And since I, the Lord and Teacher, have washed your feet, you ought to wash each other's feet. I have given you an example to follow. Do as I have done to you" (John 13:12-15, NLT).

There it is: the perfect model of servant leadership. Christ gave us the only valid motive for ministry: to serve others as he has served us. Servant leadership, as modeled by Jesus, springs from his love, which takes the initiative to serve the needs of others. Loving service to others is God's love in action. Do you see it? Relationships thrive in an atmosphere where leaders take the initiative to humbly minister to the needs of others.

Christ gave us the only valid motive for ministry: to serve others as he has served us.

Servant Leadership Begins at Home

The Christian leader's nearest "neighbors" are God's ordained starting place for exercising servant leadership. Whether it is with spouse and children or dear single friends, servanthood begins with those closest to us. Christ's relationship with his disciples and his "singles group"—Mary, Martha, and Lazarus—is an example to every Christian single adult of servant love and leadership.

Even though he did not marry, Jesus is the example of servant leadership to every husband. Paul wrote, "Husbands, love your wives, just as Christ loved the church and gave himself up for her" (Ephesians 5:25). Christ took the initiative and made the ultimate sacrifice to serve the needs of his bride, the church. Husbands are to follow his example and take the initiative for serving the needs of their wives and children.

Without the example and testimony of God's activity in his home life, the pastor's messages risk becoming academic, shallow, and irrelevant.

The "excellent" wife of Proverbs 31 faithfully serves her husband and family in countless ways.

The leader's home is where the anger-dissolving gentle answer of Proverbs 15:1 is continually practiced and perfected. The leader's nearest ones are the first to benefit from edifying words that build up others according to their needs.[8] The leader's home is the proving ground for the daily expression of "love, joy, peace, patience, kindness, goodness, faithfulness, gentleness and self-control" (Galatians 5:22-23). In the leader's home, wrongs are quickly confessed and forgiven,[9] and emotional pain is lovingly comforted and healed.[10]

As the Christian leader boldly and obediently takes the lead to restore relational intimacy with spouse, children, and friends, the church will observe and follow. Without this example of servanthood in the leader's inner circle, the finest preaching and teaching about love will be a noisy gong and a clanging cymbal.

Preach What You Practice

We have all encouraged ourselves and others to "practice what you preach." I think we have that saying backward.

A ministry colleague of mine was in a Christian bookstore recently and overheard a pastor mention Intimate Life Ministries to another pastor.

"I tell you, Alex," the pastor said, "the Intimate Life message has revolutionized my church. I don't know why I didn't do this years ago." He went on to tell how his relationship with his wife and children had been radically changed for the better.

Finally Alex broke in. "Sounds great, Roger, but how did you get your board to adopt this new ministry emphasis?"

Roger chuckled. "I'm not talking about a new program they had to approve. It's a new way of ministering to my family and to my church. I'm being equipped to be the husband and father God always wanted me to be. I'm learning to be vulnerable about my own struggles and victories. I'm giving more compassionate care and less advice. I'm learning how to meet the real needs of my family. And when I preach, my messages include how God is working in *my* life. You can't believe the impact I'm seeing in my congregation."

Roger has the right idea: Preach what you practice. At home and in other relationships, he is practicing scriptural principles for expressing God's love, then sharing through his sermons what he is practicing during the week. This pastor is taking the initiative to serve the needs of others—beginning at home. Without the example and testimony of God's activity in his home life, his messages risk becoming academic, shallow, and irrelevant. His listeners will gain more from a finely exposited sermon when it includes the confirming testimony of a vulnerable "living epistle."

DEVELOPING AN atmosphere of vulnerability, focusing on ministry to needs, putting relationships first, and modeling servant leadership are critical steps to restoring Great Commandment love to the church.

In the next chapter we will continue with four more principles for relevant Great Commandment ministry. Our prayer is that the application of these principles will help restore our churches to supreme love for God and one another. As this happens, the unchurched will flock to our local congregations because they will see that we have been with Jesus.

great Flood. Verse 6 tells us that God's heart was filled with pain because of all the evil done by the people. Aaron, why does it hurt God when people are bad?"

Aaron looks puzzled. "Maybe it hurts God when people don't listen to him."

Renee adds, "When people do bad things, a lot of times they get hurt. And when people hurt, God hurts too."

Ruth smiles. "That's right, Renee. And when we are disobedient to God, we are not being good friends to God. Aaron, how do you feel when you lose a friend?"

"I feel lonely," he answers.

"Yes, Aaron, we feel lonely when the people we like don't want to be friends with us or suddenly leave us. I have felt lonely lately. Last month, my father died. I loved my father very much. He was not only my dad, he was a great friend, too. I know what it feels like to be left without a friend."

Jessica interjects, "My little brother went to live with my dad, and I feel lonely." Two other students share their experience with loneliness.

Ruth listens attentively, then says, "Now, how do you think God might feel when people act like they are not his friends?"

Mike speaks up. "He must feel sad that he lost a friend."

"That's right. God feels sad when we do wrong. He feels that way because, when we no longer treat him as our friend, we become sad and lonely. God must love us very much to try to warn us about things that make us sad and lonely. He really wants to be our friend and take away our loneliness. That's a God I'd like to know better. Wouldn't you?"

The students smile and nod in agreement.

"I'm thankful we have a God who wants to be our friend and who is sad when we're lonely. Let's tell God about our thankfulness. Psalm 103:2 tells us not to forget his benefits. Let's pray so we don't forget."

Experiential teaching leads to experiencing truth in relationships with God and others. A period of time may be reserved in a worship service, a small group study, or in a Bible study class just to be still and know that he is God. Specific passages may be shared so that the hearers of the Word may meditate reflectively on the God who longs to remove their aloneness. Learners may be allowed time to fellowship with Christ's sufferings[4] and experience godly sorrow.[5]

At other times, experiential teaching may lead people to sense the depth of love in the Father's heart.[6] Times of meditation that touch the heart of God stir the human heart to great joy and overwhelming gratitude. They help produce a constraining love that empowers right living.

PRINCIPLE 7: GREAT COMMANDMENT MINISTRY THRIVES WHEN PEOPLE ARE EMOTIONALLY FREE TO LIVE IN THE PRESENT

Christians suffer daily from emotional bondage. In John 10:10, Jesus declared, "I have come that they may have life, and have it to the full." But the promise was preceded by a warning in the same verse: "The thief comes only to steal and kill and destroy."

One of the most subtle ploys of the enemy is to rob all humans, including believers, of abundant life in the present by keeping them bound to their past, their future, or both. A person may be enslaved to the past by unresolved anger, bitterness, guilt, or shame. A person may be in bondage to the future through anxiety, fear, insecurity, or worry. If Satan can keep us preoccupied with negative events from the past or potentially negative events yet in the future, we are unable to enjoy the abundance Jesus promised in the present!

Roy had a rough home life prior to becoming a Christian. His father was an alcoholic, so his mother worked full-time to support the family. Roy's jobless uncle, Tom, practically raised the boy. During the day, Tom brought girls into the house for his own sexual entertainment. As a ten-year-old, Roy was enticed to participate in Tom's perverted behavior with his young girlfriends.

Fifteen years later, Roy, who was recently married, became pastor of a small church. Not three months into the pastorate, Roy was discovered fondling the twelve-year-old daughter of a church member. Investigating Roy's background, Social Services discovered that the young pastor was a repeat child molester. Roy's wife, who never knew about her husband's background, was devastated.

As a child, Roy was a victim of abuse, tortured by guilt and shame. As an adult, Roy victimized others. The enemy robbed Roy of abundant life in the present by keeping him bound in the guilt and shame of his unresolved past.

Great Commandment ministry can guide people to experience God's Word and find freedom from past hurts and fear of the future. It is vital that people come to a saving knowledge of Christ and receive instruction in Bible doctrine and training in righteous living. But freedom from emotional bondage and the pursuit of abundant life in Christ is equally important. This importance is underscored by the hundreds of thousands of Christians who struggle through life battling emotional issues.

Suppose someone invented a special X-ray camera that saw through a person's exterior and recorded human emotions on film. And suppose you used that camera every week to "look in on" those to whom you minister. As you look at the film, what would it tell you about the emotional state of your congregation, your youth group, your Sunday school class, your church board, etc.? How much hurt, anger, guilt, and shame from the past would these pictures reveal? How much anxiety, fear, insecurity, and worry about the future would you find?

You may not be surprised by what you see, but are you equipped to deal with it? In our work with Christian leaders across the country, we find too few who are prepared to help believers walk free of the shackles of the past and future, finding freedom to experience God's promised abundance in the present.

A Biblical Model for Living in the Present

We experience abundant life when we live in the present. Jesus is the obvious model when it comes to living in abundance. He is the only person born who lived every day of his earthly life in the present. He never awoke to a new day plagued by guilt or anger about something that happened the day before. He never embarked on a new day fearful of what might happen to him or worried that he would not get everything done.

Contrast Christ's example of living in the present with your own first thoughts this morning. Did you awake thinking, *I can't believe what happened yesterday!* or *There's no way I'll finish my to-do list today!*? Our ministries are relevant when we help people break free of the past—and the future—and move toward Christ's model of living in the present.

Christ set us free to live in the present.

Paul wrote, "It is for freedom that Christ has set us free" (Galatians 5:1). The sacrifice of Christ provided our freedom to be sanctified entirely: spirit, soul, and body.[7] Christ set us free to live in the present just as he lived in the present while on earth. If we are to have relevant ministries, we must equip people to live in the present. Such a ministry may have many facets. Here are a few examples.

A present-living ministry to couples. Consider gathering married couples together in classes or small groups to minister freedom in Christ. These are opportunities to identify hurts and pain from the past that need to be mourned and comforted, confessed and forgiven. As couples learn to share God's care, concern, and compassion with one another by experiencing his Word, the pain is healed. People are freed from the shame, anger, worry, or fear that has bound them.

A present-living ministry to parents. Consider conducting training sessions with parents to resolve unhealed issues from their families of origin. Breaking shackles to the past and future will help keep parents from repeating unhealthy patterns in their parenting. The training may then move on to equip parents to help their children live in the present.

"Joshua, it's time to come in for dinner," Miriam calls to her five-year-old as he enjoys hide-and-seek with his friends. Instead of complying, Joshua throws a temper tantrum that upsets Miriam, which in turn fuels the boy's anger. Furious, Miriam sends Joshua to his room without dinner and spends the evening feeling guilty for her outburst.

Imagine a ministry that equips parents to offer comfort and reassurance to disappointed, fearful, and sometimes angry children like Joshua. After such training, the scene with Miriam and Joshua may look more like this. When Miriam calls her son, Joshua comes in from play, out of breath. "What do you want, Mom?"

"Look at my watch," she says, pointing to her wrist. "It's six o'clock. The other night we agreed that playtime is from four until six o'clock, and six o'clock begins family time around the dinner table. It's time to eat."

"Mom, not now!" Joshua laments in an angry tone, ready to cry with disappointment. "I really want to play more."

Miriam drops to one knee and gently pulls her son close. "I know you feel sad when you have to stop playing, and I'm sorry that you're sad." The mother hugs her son. "You'll be able to play more tomorrow. Family time is important to your father and me, and I think it's important to you, too. Let's get ready for dinner. And remember, I love you!"

Miriam's gentle, anger-quelling response[8] is in sharp contrast to that of parents who return anger for anger. Parents who are taught how to live in the present, free of the past and the future, can establish healthy boundaries of discipline and minister comfort to a disappointed child.

A present-living ministry to all believers. Consider taking every new member of your church, class, or study group through training to develop skills for responding to people who struggle with hurt, guilt, anger, condemnation, and fear. You might include the following spiritual and relational skills in such a class.

Hurt is healed through the blessing of comfort. Relevant ministry teaches people how to experience Matthew 5:4 with others: "Blessed are those who mourn, for they will be comforted." Train people to offer words of comfort when someone mourns a relational hurt. Expressions like, "It hurts me that you were hurt that way" or "I feel really sad for you because I care" become common phrases in the dialogue of relevant church members. This comforting environment becomes an attractive place for regular attenders and seekers alike.

Guilt is healed through sorrow-filled confession to God and others. Teach and remind people what 1 John 1:9 and James 5:16 look like. When they sin, challenge them to quickly embrace godly sorrow, then confess their offenses to God and those whom they have hurt, gratefully experiencing cleansing and forgiveness. Guilt from the past must not be allowed to take root and steal the abundance Christ promised.

Anger is healed by sharing forgiveness with others out of the gratitude of first having been forgiven by God. "Get rid of all bitterness, rage and anger, brawling and slander, along with every form of malice. Be kind and compassionate to one another, forgiving each other, just as in Christ God forgave you" (Ephesians 4:31-32). These verses remind us of the depth of human sin and the greatness of God's forgiveness. We see forgiveness as an issue of genuine stewardship. The forgiveness we have received from God is not really ours! We are challenged to share his forgiveness with others. As gratitude for God's forgiveness grows, people are motivated to release the anger of the past and forgive those who have hurt us.

Feelings of condemnation are healed as people gratefully internalize God's truth about their identity in Christ. Satan the accuser seeks to chain us in the past by pummeling us with condemnation: "God can't forgive those horrible things you did since your conversion"; "You don't have any abilities God can use"; "You will never get over those old habit patterns." Resist the enemy's condemning thoughts by challenging people to gratefully affirm their scriptural identity in Christ[9] and find freedom from thoughts and feelings of condemnation.[10]

Fear is healed through reassurance that perfect love drives out all fear. Fear is rampant in our culture—fear of never being loved, fear of being unable to love, fear of parental divorce, fear of losing a job, fear of losing a spouse's love, fear of not being good enough at one's work, etc. Relevant ministry practices perfect love that drives out fear.[11] A relevant ministry is a refuge, a safe place where people find security among those who love them unconditionally.

PRINCIPLE 8: GREAT COMMANDMENT MINISTRY THRIVES WHEN MINISTRIES PROVIDE AN INTERGENERATIONAL FOCUS

"Easy, boy, easy now, that's it." Harry Elder steadies the horse as the chain stretches taut from the harness to the stubborn tree stump in the earth.

"Hold him there, Dad," Harry's son Sam calls out. "I have to work on the taproot again. Eric, hand me the saw."

Sam's teenage son quickly hands his father the saw. Then he takes a small spade and clears more dirt away from the root system. It is apparent that the three generations of Elders—and their horse, Old Red—are experienced at removing tree stumps.

After several minutes of sawing and chopping and adjusting the chain, Sam gives his son a nod. Eric wipes the sweat from his brow, then waves to the eldest Elder, who holds Old Red. "OK, Grandpa, it's time to pull it out."

Harry coaxes Old Red into action. The chain creaks, and small roots pop as the muscular horse lowers his head and pulls the mighty tree stump from its socket.

"Great job, Grandpa!" cheers Marcus, Eric's ten-year-old brother, watching from a safe distance.

"It wasn't me, Marcus; it was Old Red here," Harry says, patting the horse affectionately. A clanging bell in the distance interrupts them. It is a welcome sound to the hardworking foursome.

"That's what I've been waiting to hear," Harry says to his son and grandsons with a laugh. "What do you think your mother and your sister have cooked up for us tonight, Eric?"

"I don't know, Grandpa, but I could eat a horse."

Marcus chimes in, "Don't let Eric eat Old Red, Dad. I want to ride him back to the house. Can I, Dad?"

Sam nods, and Grandpa Elder lifts Marcus onto the horse's broad back. The four Elders make their way through the clearing toward the old farmhouse that has been in the Elder family for fifty-three years.

The year is 1898.

Like the Elder place, the neighboring farms have been in their families for generations. The small town just over a mile from the Elder farm boasts a general mercantile, post office, feed mill, school, and, of course, a church. The community works together, worships together, and plays together. Barn raisings and barn dances are common. When Eric Elder marries in a couple of years, he will build a small house on his father's spread. Eventually he and his family will take over the farm.

At the dawn of the twentieth century, families worked together, played together, and struggled to make ends meet together. Immediate and extended families enjoyed each other and depended on each other. The education of the children was the responsibility of the family. Each community pooled its resources, built a schoolhouse, and hired a teacher to assist them in the proper education of their children.

Churches did not conduct marriage or parenting seminars. There were no radio programs focusing on the family, no magazines aimed at building Christian homes, and no professional family counselors. Young parents learned to raise their children from Mom and Dad, Grandma and Grandpa, aunts and uncles, friends and neighbors. Though far from perfect, this close community of relationships provided loving support and accountability. Intergenerational focus in each community was the norm.

Times Have Changed

At the dawn of the twenty-first century, we have experienced an unprecedented migration of families from rural communities to urban settings. In the wake of this move, the extended family has all but vanished. Josh McDowell reports, "Fifty years ago some 60 to 70 percent of all households included at least one live-in grandparent; today less than 2 percent of households benefit from that resource."[12]

With the proliferation of the two-wage-earner household and the expanded influence of public education, we have a generation of latchkey kids living with overextended, overcommitted, and overwhelmed parents. Today's parents spend precious little time with their children. According to a 1994 George Barna study commissioned by Josh McDowell, many Christian youth in good Christian homes spend fewer than four minutes a day in meaningful conversation with their mothers and less than three minutes talking with their fathers. Staggering but true, many Christian kids spend 2,800 percent more time with Beavis and Butt-head and Madonna than they do with their own parents![13]

Intergenerational activity seems to have become a thing of the past in our culture, and we are suffering the consequences. Today's youth may be the first generation in history to be raised without the benefit of an extended-family environment. And many live with parents who, for the most part, have assigned primary educational responsibility to someone outside the home. Single-parent homes are all too common. And the lack of discipline and loss of values among youth has an adult population antagonistic toward them. According to a 1997 study, two-thirds of adults surveyed consider today's teenagers rude, wild, and irresponsible.[14] No wonder larger numbers of children today feel more alienated and alone than in any period of recorded history.

The signs of our time—breakdown in the nuclear family, a highly mobile society, rampant materialism, rising rationalism, etc.—have affected the training of our children. A large number of parents are without the necessary skills to help their children deal with the moral, relational, and spiritual issues of life. This may be a harsh indictment of today's family, but how else can we interpret the sad plight of so many dysfunctional families in our culture? Seemingly, the love of an entire culture has grown cold. We have lost the basic tools for raising our children in the nurture and admonition of the Lord.

If Great Commandment love is needed anywhere in twenty-first century culture, it is needed in the realm of parenting our children. But we must go beyond simply instructing, exhorting, and encouraging parents in church and expecting them to go home to parent effectively. Today's young parents are without adequate parenting models. We need the "new wineskin" of an intergenerational focus that brings families together to provide on-the-job training.

Parents and Small Children

Imagine parents attending children's church periodically. Here parents are taught how to enter their children's world and play with them in a meaningful way. Parents might also receive instruction in the skill of vulnerable self-disclosure. Imagine a parent sharing with her five-year-old, "I remember when I was five years old and my best friend moved away. I was really sad. I cried and cried. I needed someone to cry with me and comfort me." Think of the security that is created in that child when it comes time to deal with his own feelings of aloneness.

An intergenerational focus will redefine and rejuvenate youth ministry.

During periodic intergenerational events, parents can be trained to identify the needs behind a child's deeds by developing common interests with each child and asking open-ended questions. "Tell me the two best things about school today" will get a better response than "How was school?" Parents can also be trained how to show attention, how to express acceptance without judgment, how to comfort a sad child, how to meet a child's need for security, etc. Intergenerational activities allow parents the opportunity to hone their skills for removing a child's aloneness and developing intimacy in the child-parent relationship.

Parents and Teenagers

An intergenerational focus will redefine and rejuvenate youth ministry. Imagine bringing parents and teens together periodically to help them deepen their relational skills. For example, prior to a combined meeting, parents and teens would be instructed separately on the power of confession in relationships. Parents would be asked to contemplate the following questions: How have I hurt my teenager in our relationship? Have I been critical or controlling? Have I expressed anger or impatience? Have I been negative or demanding? Have I identified my teen's top relational needs?

In their own class, teens are challenged to consider questions like these: Have I been angry or bitter toward my parents? Have I tried to deceive them in any way? Have I showed disrespect for my parents? Do I know my parents' top relational needs?

After a personal experience of 1 John 1:9 and receiving God's forgiveness in their own groups, parents and teens come together to experience the power of James 5:16 with each other—confessing faults, praying together, comforting each other, and experiencing God's plan for healing hurts. In later sessions, parents and teens may compare and discuss their top three relational needs, asking, "How can I better meet your needs?"

Imagine parents communicating vulnerably with their teenagers in such a meeting. During a discussion on the topic of performance pressures, Dad shares how he failed to make the high school soccer team. Mom reveals her disappointment at failing sophomore English and not being elected a cheerleader. Teens share their pressures, and the family discusses how to deal with them. Teens come to know their parents as people with pressures and disappointments just like them. They are reassured that Mom and Dad were not perfect either, but they made it.

Parents and teens alike must be equipped in this skill of self-disclosure so they can communicate who they are and how they feel. As parents and teens come together for such guided sharing, aloneness is removed and intimacy is deepened.

INTIMATE FAMILY MOMENTS

On the first Sunday of each month, our "traditional" couples class of forty parents are joined by their children—fifty of them, ages five to ten—in a time of experiencing the Word together. As families experience together more of God's acceptance, comfort, and encouragement, they learn to take more of it home!

CYPRESS BIBLE CHURCH, HOUSTON, TEXAS

Parents and teens can also work together on life-skill issues, everything from balancing a checkbook to cooking meals to checking the oil in the car to making reservations to cleaning fish! A teen needs to develop a sense of adequacy because adequacy helps remove anxiety. The more skill competence a teen develops, the greater his or her sense of adequacy.

The objective in all intergenerational ministry is to provide on-the-job training where parent and teen learn the skills for Great Commandment loving, meeting each other's needs at the point of God's Word. These skills for loving can then be more fully lived out at home.

Sometimes, intergenerational focus between parents and teens may take the form of youth-style learning. Parents can experience the joy of laughing at themselves, joining in on ridiculous activities, and just having fun with other parents and teens.

The Entire Family Comes Together

Periodically the church may offer a family Bible study where parents, children, and perhaps extended family members experience Scripture passages together. The object of family Bible study is to deepen relationships through vulnerable self-disclosure and by learning how to identify and meet specific relational needs. These encounters allow adults, children, and youth to deepen intimacy with God and capture his heart of care and compassion for one another.

Great Commandment ministry will make special provisions to include single adults, teens without church families, widows and widowers, and single parents in the intergenerational focus. Those without families are folded into nuclear families as "adopted" parents or extended family so no one in the church is alone.

ESTABLISHING A Great Commandment ministry is no small task. Imparting the Word as living epistles, implementing experiential teaching, equipping people to live in the present, and maintaining an intergenerational focus require both a top-down and a bottom-up strategy.

First, Christian leaders must both embrace this concept in theory and implement it at the practical level. Every sermon, every lesson, every small-group meeting, and every event must be recast in the context of experiencing God's Word together to deepen relationships.

Second, church members must catch this vision and become living models of God's Word in action.

This may seem like an exciting but rather overwhelming task. The key to success, however, is to begin in "Jerusalem," living out Great

Commandment love with your nearest neighbors. Then move on to "Judea" and "Samaria"—people outside your immediate family. Challenge individuals in leadership positions—pastors, associates, music directors, Bible study teachers, youth and children's workers, board members, etc.—to practice these intimacy principles in their own lives and homes. You may want to start by studying this book together with your leadership teams.

Great Commandment love is contagious and compelling.

As you become a living model of Great Commandment love with your nearest ones, your experience will naturally and inevitably flow into how you structure ministry to others. Whether married or single, as you deepen these nearest relationships, relevant ministry will overflow to other friends and ministry colleagues. And as your relationships with peers and colleagues are enriched, you will be amazed at how easy it will be to share these principles with the unchurched to whom you minister. Why? Because Great Commandment love is contagious and compelling in the lives and ministries of those who seek to live in right relationship to God and their nearest ones.

➢ *We have designed a video training course with a workbook for each leader. This training can also be used as a new-members course. Intimate Life Ministries provides additional resources to assist you in your efforts to establish and implement a biblically relevant Great Commandment ministry. See the appendix for details.*

CHAPTER FOURTEEN

"Upon This Rock I Will Build My Church"

IT HAD been several long, insightful days for the twelve disciples. They had watched in amazement as Jesus cast out demons, restored the sight of the blind, and healed the lame (see Matthew 15). They marveled at this display of Christ's power and mercy, and with grateful hearts they gave glory to the God of Israel. To top it off, Jesus miraculously fed a crowd of well over four thousand on only seven loaves and a few small fish.

After Jesus dismissed the multitudes, he began probing the disciples on who people said he was.

"Well," they replied, "some say John the Baptist, some say Elijah, and others say Jeremiah or one of the other prophets."

Then he asked them, "Who do you say I am?"

Simon Peter answered, "You are the Messiah, the Son of the living God."

Jesus replied, "You are blessed, Simon son of John, because my Father in heaven has revealed this to you. You did not learn this from any human being. Now I say to you that you are Peter, and upon this rock I will build my church, and all the powers of hell will not conquer it. And I will give you the keys of the Kingdom of Heaven. Whatever you lock on earth will be locked in heaven, and whatever you open on earth will be opened in heaven" (Matthew 16:14-19, NLT).

What was this "rock," this cornerstone upon which Jesus would build his church? It was the supernatural revelation of the living

Christ. The foundation of the church is the revelation and subsequent glorifying declaration that Christ is the Messiah, the deliverer from sin and the provider of all needs. The powers of hell cannot diminish, subvert, or conquer this relevant revelation by the faithful body of Christ's believers. The early church endured tribulation, persecution, and death. Through it all they demonstrated so much Christlike love that they were branded with his name: Christians, literally "Christ-ones."

Great Commandment love transformed the disciples' cowering fear into a relevant, vibrant, and attractive message of hope to the world around them.

Speaking of all the tribulation and persecution aimed at separating the church from Christ's love, Paul wrote, "Despite all these things, overwhelming victory is ours through Christ, who loved us. And I am convinced that nothing can ever separate us from his love. Death can't, and life can't. The angels can't, and the demons can't. Our fears for today, our worries about tomorrow, and even the powers of hell can't keep God's love away. Whether we are high above the sky or in the deepest ocean, nothing in all creation will ever be able to separate us from the love of God that is revealed in Christ Jesus our Lord" (Romans 8:37-39, NLT).

Great Commandment love transformed the once cowering followers of Christ into a relevant, vibrant, and attractive message of hope to the world around them. The final four principles of Great Commandment ministry focus on the importance of recapturing the power of God's love in our ministry to the church and the world around us.

PRINCIPLE 9: GREAT COMMANDMENT MINISTRY THRIVES WHEN THE CHURCH IS MOTIVATED BY JOYFUL GRATITUDE TO GOD

It was Christ's love that empowered believers in the early church. It was Christ's love that caused these new believers to endure hardship and even death. The apostle Paul declared, "Christ's love compels us" (2 Corinthians 5:14). Profound gratitude to a loving, need-meeting God was enough to fuel Paul and the early church for a lifetime of wholehearted devotion and service.

Peter linked Christ's love to another inner motivation, writing, "You believe in [Christ] and are filled with an inexpressible and glorious joy" (1 Peter 1:8). Old Testament saints were also reminded regarding their service to God and others, "The joy of the Lord is your strength" (Nehemiah 8:10). And Jesus challenged his followers with the end result of obedience: "That my joy may be in you and that your joy may be complete" (John 15:11).

> **A Great Commandment church is compelled to right living and service to others by gratitude for Christ's love.**

A Great Commandment church is compelled to right living and service to others by hearts overflowing with joy and gratitude for Christ's love. This heartfelt gratitude lived out in daily life constitutes "the fragrance of life"[1] that the unchurched find so inviting. The relevant church encourages the motivation of Christ's compelling love in its members in two ways. First, we must purposely cultivate hearts of gratitude to God. Then we must guard grateful hearts from ineffective and unscriptural motivations.

Cultivate Grateful Hearts

Those involved in a Great Commandment ministry will be reminded of God's love and goodness as much as they are challenged to live in obedience to him. Cultivating grateful hearts may be accomplished in a number of ways in the week-by-week ministry of the church.

Emphasize the believer's identity in Christ. The apostle John referred to himself as the disciple Jesus loved.[2] He was not boasting or exalting himself above others. Rather, John was in awe of this wondrous truth. He was so deeply affected by the Master's love for him that it became his very identity. Believers who accurately perceive themselves as the disciples Jesus loves are ready to serve God and others out of humility and deep gratitude. It is important, therefore, that sermons, Bible lessons, and worship experiences relate some facet of God's boundless love for his people.

Promote an environment of freedom. Christ said, "If the Son sets you free, you will be free indeed" (John 8:36). Paul reiterated this truth: "It is for freedom that Christ has set us free" (Galatians 5:1). An atmosphere of freedom in a church, class, small group, or leadership team prompts heartfelt gratitude, while fearful control quenches it. Therefore, the ministry should allow plenty of freedom for members to give input and select between options.

For example, an alternate Saturday evening worship service may be a liberating option for members who work on Sunday morning or others who are just not morning people. People should also feel *free* to participate in church activities instead of feeling *pressured* to attend or coerced into taking an active role. And they should sense that their spiritual gifts and talents are welcome and needed in the church. People who are free to serve will serve gratefully.

Encourage giving by helping people learn to receive. Jesus taught, "Freely you have received, freely give" (Matthew 10:8). Many people have difficulty giving of themselves and of their substance in grateful service to God and others because they have not learned how to receive. Just as Peter resisted Christ's ministry of foot washing, believers today frequently model self-reliance rather than joy-filled receptivity.

Joyful gratitude for God's generosity grows as believers learn the skill of receiving.[3] For example, during a time of leading people to mourn with those who mourn[4], you might say, "When you express your hurt to someone and they mourn with you, receive the comfort they provide and maybe offer the simple words 'thanks for caring.'"

Christian leaders provide important examples of vulnerable receiving as clergy appreciation days, anniversaries, and other celebrations occur.

The first affections of men towards Christ, and holiness, and heaven are usually lively and warm. These lively affections will abate and cool if great care be not taken.
MATTHEW HENRY

Take time to recount God's blessings. King David admonished himself, "Praise the Lord, O my soul, and forget not all his benefits" (Psalm 103:2). In the next verse he itemizes God's goodness to him: forgiveness, healing, deliverance, abiding love, fulfilled desires, renewed youthfulness. We are usually quick to speak about our difficulties and submit our prayer requests. But hearts are enlarged with gratitude toward God when believers are also encouraged to recount God's blessings.

In every aspect of the church's ministry—worship, preaching, teaching, counseling, leadership training, fellowship, etc.—and at all age levels (adults, youth, children, intergenerational gatherings), allow time for people to consider and speak about God's goodness to them.

Focus on the Great Commandment. Regardless of the biblical text of a sermon or Bible study lesson, consistently lead people back to the supremacy of love for God and others. When teaching about the Ten Commandments or any other biblical admonitions, relate God's directives to some of the significant reasons he gave them: to protect us and provide for us, because he loves us. When teaching about sin and holiness, include an encounter with the loving God who grieves when our sin causes us pain, because he loves us. When teaching about God's sometimes harsh dealings with Israel, share the context of his faithful love and gracious provision behind the firm discipline. Consistent reference to the God who loves us and challenges us to love him and others encourages grateful obedience.

Guard Hearts from Fleshly Activity

Anne suggested to Pastor Brantley that groups be formed at Community Church to pray during each of the three weekly worship services. Since Pastor Brantley was committed to encouraging prayer in the congregation, he appointed Anne to head up the task, promising his full support. Leaders were recruited, small rooms in the building were reserved, and announcements were placed in the church bulletin. People were encouraged to attend one of the worship services and join a prayer group during one of the other services.

For the first few weeks, a number of people responded to the call to pray. But attendance quickly dropped off. More bulletin announcements were made, but attendance still declined. Anne encouraged the pastor to promote the prayer meetings in the service, which he did. Attendance revived for a week or so, then continued its downward spiral. After several months church leaders admitted that the prayer groups were a good idea but apparently not God's idea! As soon as they stopped pushing the program, it died a natural death.

It is vital that church leaders discern the origin of every ministry or program. Jesus said, "Flesh gives birth to flesh, but the Spirit gives birth to spirit" (John 3:6). We must protect our people from events, programs, and activities that are birthed and maintained by fleshly effort. The Spirit is well able to empower and sustain any ministry he initiates. Any program that must be continually pushed, promoted, or propped up to survive is likely a fleshly endeavor. Such activities rob God's people of joy and gratitude.

Every program and activity in the church should be subjected to prayerful, periodic evaluation as leaders seek to sense God's initiative, guidance, and expected blessing. We must ask, "Why are we doing this?"

Many logical answers may be given:

"We have always done it."

"The people like it."

"The community expects us to do it."

"It's in the budget."

"The bylaws require us to do it."

However, God blesses only the ministries he prompts. Solomon wisely proclaimed, "Unless the Lord builds the house, its builders labor in vain" (Psalm 127:1). Nothing in ministry robs people of joy and gratitude more than trying to build something God is not building or maintain something God is not seeking to sustain. Great Commandment ministry thrives when we are in partnership with God in Spirit-born, Spirit-led tasks.

Nothing in ministry robs people of joy and gratitude more than trying to build something God is not building.

Once a church initiative is acknowledged as a God-ordained ministry, leaders in Great Commandment churches trust God to get people involved. Hebrews 11:6 reminds us, "Without faith it is impossible to please God." When we pressure or cajole people into participation, we may not be exercising faith. Furthermore, such efforts subtly train people to respond to human pleading instead of the Holy Spirit's prompting. How much better it is to equip God's people to discern his prompting and direction and then trust God's people to God.

Here is an example of these contrasting motives. The leaders at First Church are confident that the annual men's conference at their church is a God-ordained ministry. But notice in the following worship service announcements two contrasting approaches to challenging men to become involved: "I want every man in the congregation to stand right now. What a great group of guys! Next Saturday is our annual men's conference. All of you men who have already registered for the conference may sit down. Now look around, guys. Those of you still standing need to get on the ball. You ought to be there next Saturday. Get to the registration table in the lobby right after the service. Don't miss out!"

What kind of motivation is employed in this announcement? How much faith in God is exercised? What impact might this kind of motivation have on any seekers present?

In contrast, consider another announcement for the event: "Next Saturday is our annual men's conference, and it will be a special time of encouragement and equipping for all men who attend. Information and registration are in the lobby. Let's pause for a moment of prayer right now and seek God's presence and ministry among our men next Saturday. Men, ask God to give you clarity of direction concerning your possible involvement in the men's conference. Thank you, Father, for giving discernment now and for your special blessing next Saturday. Amen."

Great Commandment ministry thrives as church leaders cultivate grateful hearts while guarding those hearts from fleshly pressures.

PRINCIPLE 10: GREAT COMMANDMENT MINISTRY THRIVES WHEN WORSHIP CENTERS ON INTIMATE ENCOUNTERS WITH GOD

Relevant corporate worship is not primarily the product of a large, well-rehearsed choir or soul-stirring praise choruses. Relevant corporate worship occurs when members of the congregation are led to experience deepened intimacy with their Creator.

> **Worship leaders become "shepherds of the soul," helping prepare hearts to receive the Word.**

Relevant personal worship is not produced by devotional programs or disciplined routine. Relevant personal worship for the individual believer occurs through deepened intimacy with the Creator.

Relevant worship cannot be programmed. It cannot be "worked up" by manipulating the tempo and volume of the music. It is not dependent on the platform expertise of the staff. Regardless of corporate worship style or personal worship routine, relevant worship occurs when attention is focused on a personal, intimate encounter with God.

How can people be equipped for personal encounters with God in worship? Emphasis is needed in the following areas.

Experiences of renewal . . . are God-centered in character, based on worship, an appreciation of God's worth and grandeur divorced from self-interest.

RICHARD LOVELACE

People Encounter God When They Find Inner Freedom

David's personal call to worship is expressed in Psalm 103:1: "Praise the Lord, O my soul; all my inmost being, praise his holy name." It is difficult to express worship and praise to God when our "inmost being" is distracted by pain, guilt, anger, or condemnation from the past or fear and anxiety about the future. Therefore, a significant element of relevant worship is helping worshipers find freedom from these distractions, thus equipping them to "enter his gates with thanksgiving and his courts with praise" (Psalm 100:4).

We enter his presence to *receive* freedom from past pain and future fears. A time of corporate worship is an opportunity to lead people away from the concerns of the past and future into freedom in the present. It is in the present that we can enter the depth of intimacy God desires in our personal encounters with him.

What might this type of corporate worship look like? Here is an example. Pastor Dale leads the congregation in two brief choruses of praise. Then, as the instruments play softly in the background, he says, "Sometimes, even as faithful believers, we are robbed of intimacy with God by self-condemnation. Perhaps you are struggling with that hindrance right now. Maybe something happened this week that left you feeling spiritually defeated or worthless. You stand here today under a dark cloud. You feel like God isn't interested in your worship because you are just not good enough. You may even have a specific weakness or failure in mind. Perhaps you are not as patient or forgiving as you should be. Maybe you have squandered opportunities to share Christ with your neighbors or coworkers this week. Does an issue come to your mind?"

Pastor Dale waits as the congregation ponders his question silently. Then he says, "At times, we all feel a little like the apostle Paul. He laments in Romans 7:15 that he found himself doing the things he *hated* to do instead of the things he *wanted* to do. Even during a time of worship we may find ourselves feeling with Paul, 'What a worthless person I am!' Bondage like this blocks our worship, and the Father longs for us to enjoy our freedom. But how can it happen?"

Pastor Dale continues, "Consider with me a liberating truth and see if it doesn't set your heart free to gratefully praise God. You may be disappointed by your inconsistencies and failures, but are these lapses a surprise to God? Did he not know about your criticism, impatience, anger, or unforgiveness long before he chose to birth you into his spiritual family? Did he not see all your sins of omission and commission—past, present, and future? And yet he chose to make you his child anyway. He knew about your weakness and sin, and he loves you in spite of them!

"Let your heart be free from condemnation and free to worship God with deep gratitude. Let this truth bring a smile to your face as you rejoice with the apostle who exclaimed, 'Thanks be to God—through Jesus Christ our Lord! . . . Therefore, there is now no condemnation for those who are in Christ Jesus, because through Christ Jesus the law of the Spirit of life set me free from the law of sin and death' (Romans 7:25–8:2). Let's sing our heartfelt praise together."

Corporate worship should challenge people week by week to find healing for the soul and express their gratitude to God. Worship leaders thus become "shepherds of the soul," helping prepare hearts to receive the Word as it is taught, resulting in abundant fruitfulness.[5]

People Encounter God When They Celebrate Their New Identity

Jesus said that we are *in* the world but not *of* the world.[6] Living in a world of tribulation, we can easily be robbed of this truth. Worship should be a constant reminder of, and grateful response to, *who* we are, *whose* we are, and *where* we reside. As believers are guided to reaffirm their spiritual identity and heritage, their focus is shifted to a personal encounter with a loving heavenly Father.

The dust of daily living often dulls the luster of our identity, inheritance, and destiny in Christ.

Who are we? The Scriptures declare that we are saints, new creations in Christ, redeemed. Whose are we? We are God's children, his masterpieces in progress, his heirs. Where do we reside? We have been raised with Christ; we are seated with him in the heavenlies; we are citizens of the Father's kingdom.

Yet the dust of daily living in this world often dulls the luster of our identity, inheritance, and destiny in Christ. Times of worship should serve to rid our minds and hearts of the world's idea of who we are and where we are headed. Songs we sing, meditations we lead, and Scriptures we read or recite in worship can pointedly affirm that we are in this world but not of it.

As this truth is regularly revisited, people will be encouraged to express the wonder and gratefulness of their identity in Christ. The world they reenter after worship may be as dusty and draining as ever. But an encounter with God and the affirmation of their identity in him will send them back into it with boldness and gratitude.

People Encounter God When They Experience His Heart

The destination of worship is the Father's heart. Beautiful choruses and stirring anthems may move people emotionally. But if we do not enter the Father's heart relationally during worship, the encounter with God is less relevant to worshipers than it should be. Music and meditations are often useful for leading people to an intimate encounter with God, but the means is no substitute for the end. A critical objective of worship is to experience the Father's heart.

Deepened intimacy with God sensitizes the human heart to him. Such encounters cannot help but affect our relationships with each other. As we fellowship with his sufferings, hurting that he experienced hurt, our hearts will be tenderized with love, first for God and then for others. As we rejoice with God over the things that cause his heart to rejoice—such as unbelievers who repent and believers who practice unity, we will experience his constraining love, which empowers us to be his ambassadors.

As we mourn with him over those things that grieve his heart, we will experience the stirring of his compassion for others who hurt. As we sorrow with him over our sins, which have brought sorrow to his heart, we will be empowered to walk worthy of our high calling, compelled in righteousness not to add further sorrow to the Father's heart.

Principle 11: Great Commandment Ministry Thrives When the Church Is Known as a Safe Place for All

A Great Commandment church is known as a safe, welcoming place for regular members, for the hurting within its reach, and for those beyond to whom it will minister sacrificially. These are the three concentric circles of concern for a body of believers. First, there must be an environment of Great Commandment love for all who attend regularly. This allows people to say, "I belong here; I am accepted and loved for who I am." A second concern is to provide intentional, compassionate ministry to hurting people who are drawn into this safe environment. Then, we must purposely reach beyond our comfort zone to conduct sacrificial ministry. When these priorities are internalized and implemented by church leadership, it will have an impact on the entire church and beyond.

Create an Environment of Great Commandment Love

Two key elements help create an environment where members and seekers sense they are welcomed and accepted. The first is the Zacchaeus Principle discussed earlier in the book. The church is viewed as a safe place when people sense that we are more burdened to meet their needs than to judge their deeds. Does this mean that sinful behavior is not confronted? Absolutely not. But sin is confronted within the context of an accepting relationship, not piously apart from it. Jesus never shied away from calling sin sin. But he was known as "a friend of tax collectors and 'sinners'" (Matthew 11:19). A Great Commandment church is known as the friend of sinners.

The church is viewed as a safe place when people sense that we are more burdened to meet their needs than to judge their deeds.

A second element that makes the church a safe place for members and visitors is maturity among the leadership regarding personal preferences, personal convictions, and biblical absolutes. Leaders should delineate these three areas in their thinking in order to clearly declare biblical absolutes while allowing freedom in the areas of preferences and convictions. When the leaders' preferences and/or convictions are foisted on the congregation as biblical absolutes, relevance is lost, and love is quenched.

What's the difference?

Personal preferences center on the leader's wishes, desires, or opinions without clear direction from God's Word. For example, a pianist may prefer contemporary praise songs over traditional hymns and anthems. A teaching pastor may like the New King James Version better than the New International Version. The Christian Education director may prefer to hold teachers meetings on Tuesday night instead of Thursday night. Individual preferences should be held lightly and relinquished quickly to accommodate the needs of others and to prompt unity.[7]

Personal convictions involve our sense of God's specific direction for our lives. One couple may feel led to home-school their children instead of send them to public or private school. A deacon may feel it is wrong for him to eat in restaurants that serve alcohol. A woman may sense God's leading to volunteer in a crisis pregnancy center. These individuals should observe their convictions as God has led them but allow others the freedom to find God's leadership in *their* lives. When personal convictions are lifted up as biblical absolutes, contention in the body of Christ may result, and the environment of safety is shattered.

> Unbelievers who enter our doors as seekers often live pain-filled lives.

Biblical absolutes are God's undeniable, clear truth for salvation and right living. These are the "thou shalts" and "thou shalt nots" of Scripture. Biblical absolutes must be presented lovingly but boldly and without apology. Church leaders must be prayerful and diligent to discern biblical absolutes from personal preferences and convictions and to allow others freedom in the latter two areas. Focusing on fewer "essentials" allows for greater unity and more effective ministry, creating an environment of safety for all.

Cultivate an Atmosphere of Compassion toward the Hurting

Reaching a pain-filled world with the relevant message of the gospel requires the compassionate heart of the Savior. Jesus' ministry in the Gospels is an example to every believer. While others around him responded to situations out of fear, judgment, or legalism, Jesus was moved with compassion and acted out of love.

The Pharisees saw the disciples picking grain on the Sabbath and condemned them for breaking the law, but Jesus was moved with compassion because his men were hungry.[8] When a blind man came to Jesus for healing, the disciples wanted to know who had sinned to cause the blindness. But Jesus was moved with compassion because the man could not see, and he healed him.[9] While some were eager to call down fire and judgment on the unbelieving, Jesus rebuked them[10] and later grieved over the unbelief of Jerusalem.[11]

Christ's exhortation to the Pharisees seems applicable to the twenty-first century church: "If you had known what this means, 'I desire compassion, and not a sacrifice,' you would not have condemned the innocent" (Matthew 12:7, NASB). Like Jesus, a Great Commandment church is as concerned about the pain and aloneness people suffer as it is about their sin and fallenness.

Unbelievers who enter our doors as seekers, who occupy the office or workbench next to ours, or who live near enough to borrow eggs and sugar often live pain-filled lives. Multitudes of the men, women, teens, and children we encounter during the week are victims of one or more of the "plagues" of twentieth-century culture: broken homes, physical violence, sexual abuse, addictions in the home. Yes, these people must eventually deal with their own sin issues in order to receive God's forgiveness and experience new birth. But will they be drawn to the Savior more effectively by our condemnation of their sin or our compassion for their pain? Christ's example compels us to share the Good News with these people through the doorway of compassion for them.

We now see people through the windowpane of compassion, understanding that they are trying to meet valid needs in sinful ways, rather than through the windowpane of judgment, viewing them only as having fallen short of God's commandments. Addressing people's aloneness and then their fallenness has drastically transformed every aspect of our lives.

ST. PETER LUTHERAN CHURCH, MABANK, TEXAS

How does a church cultivate a heart of compassion for people? First, those in leadership must pursue ever deepening intimacy with

God by sharing in the fellowship of Christ's sufferings and experiencing the blessing of his comfort in their own devotional lives. When we encounter someone in need, we can only minister his love as we sense Christ's heart of compassion for the hurting. As leaders begin to reach out to the hurting with compassion, others in the church will follow their example.

Great Commandment love cannot be limited to our comfort zone.

Second, leaders must maintain vulnerability in sharing their own pain and in giving and receiving comfort in their own families and friendships. If we are not practicing compassion consistently in our inner circle of relationships, we are ill equipped to reach beyond that circle to express compassion to others.

Third, the church, both in the personal devotions of its members and in corporate gatherings, must experience often the awe and wonder of worship in order to nurture and tenderize hearts for relevant ministry.

Minister beyond Your Comfort Zone

Every Christian leader and every church seem to have a comfort zone where care and concern for others is relatively easy for them. The comfort zone may relate to a socioeconomic stratum, ethnicity, education, or professional level. College-educated professionals may be more comfortable ministering to college-educated professionals. Ethnic churches may most easily reach out to those of their own race. Ministry to those who are most like us is the path of least resistance, and there is nothing wrong with employing this familiarity to good advantage for the gospel.

However, Great Commandment love cannot be limited to our comfort zone. This seems to be God's message to Peter in his God-ordained encounter with the "unclean" Gentile Cornelius (see Acts 10). As certainly as the first-century church broke through barriers of all types to minister to others, we should seek to provide a safe place for those in need by engaging in *purposeful* ministry beyond our comfort zone. For example:

> ***It is an act of love to show that we are willing to go out of our own way to have people from other cultural backgrounds sit in our pews.***
>
> T. D. JAKES

- A suburban, college-educated congregation may take on an inner-city ministry to unwed mothers on welfare.
- An inner-city, ethnic congregation may seek to develop a supportive sister-church relationship with a dissimilar ethnic fellowship.
- A congregation comprised largely of high-tech professionals may take on an English-teaching and day-care ministry to rural migrant families.
- A church with a strong base of nuclear families may target the residents of a single-parent apartment complex for compassionate ministry.
- A blue-collar church may embrace a hospitality ministry to international students at a nearby state university.
- A seminary or Bible-college church may give itself to seeking out AIDS or substance-abuse victims for compassionate ministry.

The initiative to include ministries outside a church's comfort zone comes from Christian leaders who are personally ministering outside their comfort zones. Such leaders pursue as a matter of course deeper death-to-self expressions of Christ's unconditional love in their personal relationships. They sustain a faith-stretching attack on fears of rejection and inadequacy. They maintain a tight focus on serving others, which limits the destructive tendency to compare themselves with others. As these qualities influence others in the local body, a safe, welcoming environment is produced.

PRINCIPLE 12: GREAT COMMANDMENT MINISTRY THRIVES WHEN THE CHURCH RESTORES COMMUNITY ONE RELATIONSHIP AT A TIME

Second Chronicles 14:7 declares, "The land is still ours, because we have sought the Lord our God; we have sought Him, and He has given us rest on every side" (NASB). The relationships of marriage, family, and the church are God's "land." He ordained these relationships, along with our intimate walk with him, as part of his provision to remove the aloneness he proclaimed to be "not good." A Great Commandment church is to bring healing to relationships at all levels as men, women, teens, and children are nurtured in life-changing intimacy with Jesus Christ and each other.

The result of a focus on restored relationships is "rest on every side"—healthy and fulfilling relationships, fewer conflicts and divisions. Newlyweds find rest through a ministry of effective prewedding preparation and ongoing enrichment. Marriages in trouble find rest through loving intervention and mentoring. Single adults find rest from loneliness, performance pressures, and worldly temptations through nurturing friendships and extended family relationships within the body of Christ. Parents find rest as they are equipped to cherish their children by meeting their needs for security, appreciation, affection, attention, and comfort. Families of all types—nuclear, blended, single-parent—find rest through extended family relationships within the church. Local bodies of believers can become communities of true fellowship, ministering mutual care to one another "so that there should be no division in the body, but that its parts should have equal concern for each other" (1 Corinthians 12:25).

As intimate relationships are established with God and within friendships, marriages, families, and the church, both the community and the surrounding culture are positively affected. God-honoring friendships become positive examples to children and teens. Couples building strong marriages become mentors to newlyweds. Troubled marriages in the community can be rescued, even reducing the divorce rate. Families are enriched and restored to their intended place of safety and refuge. Child abuse, violence, and teen suicides diminish.

Such bold predictions are not the result of a cultural revolution but of a restoration of biblical Great Commandment love.

Great Commandment Ministries Champion God's Purposes for Marriage and Family

The relevant church aggressively promotes biblical standards for relationships in the home. When those who freely receive God's abounding love fail to freely express it at home, love grows cold and relationship crises result. The following are examples of how God's priority of marriage and family can be championed in a ministry setting.

International Marriage Week. Our culture recognizes the week of St. Valentine's Day as International Marriage Week. Thousands of churches now take advantage of this highly visible occasion to lift up God's design for marriage. Some churches hold special worship services and conduct public-awareness campaigns to emphasize God's ideal: one man and one woman for life. Some churches invite couples in the community to a special ceremony to renew their marriage vows, using the opportunity to relate marriage as God's picture of Christ's love for the church.

A culture that refuses to cherish children will soon be a culture in crisis.

Cherish the Children. A culture that refuses to cherish children will soon be a culture in crisis. A number of churches utilize the month between Mother's Day in May and Father's Day in June to emphasize parenting responsibility and skills. Sermons, seminars, conferences, home groups, and other events challenge and equip parents to cherish their children as gifts from the Lord.

A special worship service emphasis based on 1 Kings 8 leads families through a time of "home dedication" as both parents and children declare their commitment to God's plan for their family. The end product of this emphasis is that children hear more clearly from their parents the unqualified affirmation Jesus heard from his Father: You are my child, whom I love; with you I am well pleased.[12]

Teens "Never Alone." Never Alone, an international church and parachurch emphasis for teenagers, ministers to the aloneness that gives rise to much teen substance abuse, gang violence, and sexual acting out. Through this ministry, hundreds of thousands of teens will be equipped with the skills of relational intimacy. Never Alone focuses on helping teens build close relationships at three levels: with parents and other meaningful adults; with peers in positive friendships; and most important, with Jesus Christ. Ministries like this one have a positive impact on teen crime, substance abuse, school dropout rates, suicides, and future divorce.

Great Commandment Ministries Declare Dependence on God

Our only hope for making a difference in relationships is God's activity in us and through us. John said it succinctly: "We love because [God] first loved us" (1 John 4:19). The ministry of restoring relationships will be no more relevant than our dependence on divine provision. If love is to be shared with others, it must first be received from the God who is love (see v. 7). If acceptance is to be shared with others, it must first be received from the God who has first accepted.[13] If comfort is to be shared with others, it must first be received from the God of all comfort.[14]

We are incapable of generating and perfecting love for others. We are simply called to give what we have received from God, "faithfully administering God's grace in its various forms" (1 Peter 4:10). If we exalt self-sufficiency and diminish receiving from God, our ability to give to others is reduced. Proudly declaring that we do not need anything from God[15] results in our having nothing to give. A prerequisite for restoring relationships in families, friendships, church, and community is wholehearted dependence on God for anything we hope to give to others.

A number of churches across the U.S. and abroad focus on the importance of receiving from God in an event referred to as Declaration of Dependence. Churches in America often capitalize on Independence Day for a communitywide emphasis on God as our only source for healthy relationships and community peace. The event calls individuals and families to declare their dependence on God and commit to "act justly and to love mercy and to walk humbly with your God" (Micah 6:8). Some churches invite families to sign covenants of dependence on God.

Throughout the year these churches emphasize and support community events that call people to divine dependence: times of prayer and fasting; times of praise, worship, and celebration to acknowledge God as the great physician and provider of all good things.

Great Commandment Ministries Model Divine Unity

Unity among believers was important to Christ. He told his disciples, "By this all men will know that you are my disciples, if you love one another" (John 13:35). Later he prayed for believers, "that all of them may be one . . . so that the world may believe that you have sent me" (John 17:21). The fulfillment of Christ's prayer for unity not only touches homes and congregations, but it will also affect the community of faith by removing walls between churches. A Great Commandment church will practice unity across denominational, racial, and social lines by "majoring on the majors."

Unity among churches can be displayed in events such as community praise gatherings, where all churches join together for a specific time of worship and praise to God. Hundreds of ministry leaders in the U.S. and Europe are coming together around community marriage covenants. These leaders are agreeing to help build up what God has joined together, linking arms to provide community marriage enrichment programs.

Where ministries like Mission Mississippi are fostering unity among believers, racial and religious barriers are giving way to the Spirit's oneness.

By making unity a high priority in our churches and the Christian community, we fulfill in practical, need-meeting ways Paul's admonition to "make every effort to keep the unity of the Spirit through the bond of peace" (Ephesians 4:3).

AMBASSADORS IN THE MINISTRY OF RECONCILIATION

The dawn of the twenty-first century finds our world facing multiple crises. Our newspapers and news magazines starkly proclaim: "AIDS Crisis Mounts"; "Teenage Pregnancy Hits Crisis Level"; "Marriages and Families in Crisis." Like a forest fire whipped by fierce winds, the crises in our culture seem to get worse by the hour, and more lives are consumed by the flames. The hurt is real. The pain is deep. Anxiety, emptiness, disconnectedness, alienation, and aloneness reign in the human heart. Inner turmoil surfaces in broken relationships, violence, abuse, addictions, and suicide. The "not good" of human aloneness cries out for a solution.

Ultimately, our culture's problems cannot be remedied by political, social, or economic means. We throw more laws, more programs, and more money at these problems every year, yet they continue to mount. The solution to the alienation and aloneness of the human condition can be found only in God's offer of reconciliation through his Son, Jesus Christ. As individuals establish and maintain an intimate relationship with their Creator through the power of new life in Christ, meaningful relationships with others are possible, and aloneness is removed.

Our culture's problems cannot be remedied by political, social, or economic means.

It is this ministry of reconciliation that Christ has entrusted to us, his church. God is at work in us, calling a hurting world to himself.[16] God is the solution to our culture's aloneness and fallenness. And since he is in us and we are in him, we have the awesome ministry privilege of co-laboring with him to see people reconciled to God and one another, providing a shelter in stormy relationships, a refuge

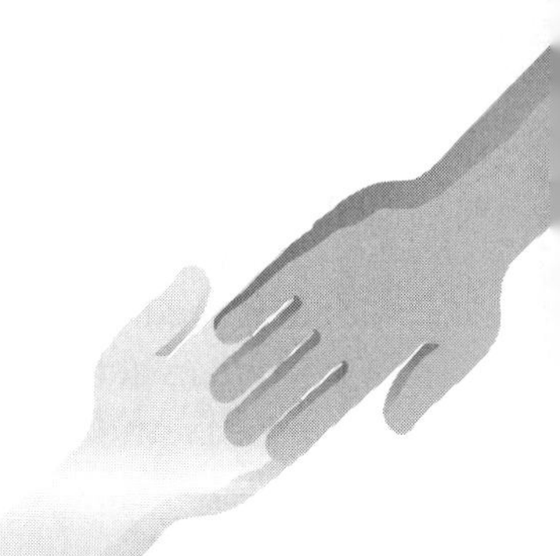

from life's pressures, a sanctuary of hope where sins are forgiven, needs are met, and hurts are healed.

Paul's inspired message to the Corinthian church is as pertinent today as it was then. "Working together with Him, we also urge you not to receive the grace of God in vain . . . in order that the ministry be not discredited, but in everything commending ourselves as servants of God" (2 Corinthians 6:1-4, NASB). This call from God is being restored to the twenty-first century church. He desires that our ministries not be discredited or *irrelevant.* The call is to relevance in ministry, applying the Great Commandment principle of love to his church. Only as we hear and heed his call will we give evidence that we are his disciples.[17]

One of the greatest signs of the truth of the gospel is racial reconciliation.

JOHN PERKINS, EDITOR, *Restoring At-Risk Communities*

I'm convinced that when we truly experience the Great Commandment principle of love in our lives, it will startle the world around us. I'm often reminded of Jesus' ministry. People were startled by the things he said: "Stretch out your hand"; "Arise and walk"; "I and the Father are one"; etc. They were startled by the things he did, such as turning water into wine, walking on water, eating with tax collectors, etc. But most important, the world was startled by his love. His love startled the woman at the well, the leper, Zacchaeus, and the woman caught in adultery, to name a few.

Yet the most startling expression of his love was the giving of himself as a sacrificial atonement for a skeptical and rebellious world. Aren't you startled by a love that is so giving to a world so undeserving?

He loved us when we were unlovable. He was moved with compassion when, from his eternal perspective, he saw us suffering in our alienation and aloneness. So his love led him to a cruel cross to make abundant provision for you and for me. Hear his startling cry of love for those who betrayed, tormented, and rejected him. "Father, forgive them, for they do not know what they are doing" (Luke 23:34).

We, too, are the beneficiaries of such forgiveness. Humbled by such matchless grace, we have been made partakers of his love. Yet our world—a world in crisis—needs to be startled by such love too. They need to see a living model, the Great Commandment principle of love in action. Let us go forth with gratitude and compassion this very day and begin to startle our world with God's love!

APPENDIX
About Intimate Life Ministries

WHO AND WHAT IS INTIMATE LIFE MINISTRIES?

Intimate Life Ministries (ILM) is a training and resource ministry, headquartered in Austin, Texas, whose purpose is *to assist in the development of Great Commandment ministries worldwide,* ongoing ministries that deepen our intimacy with God and with others in marriage, family, and the church.

Intimate Life Ministries comprises:

- A network of **churches** seeking to fortify homes and communities with his love;
- A network of **pastors and other ministry leaders** walking intimately with God and their families and seeking to live vulnerably before their people;
- A team of **accredited trainers** committed to helping churches establish ongoing Great Commandment ministries;
- A team of **professional associates** from ministry and other professional Christian backgrounds, assisting with research, training, and resource development;
- **Christian broadcasters,** publishers, media, and other affiliates, cooperating to see marriages and families reclaimed as divine relationships;
- **Headquarters staff** providing strategic planning, coordination, and support.

HOW CAN INTIMATE LIFE MINISTRIES SERVE YOU?

ILM's Intimate Life Network of Churches is an effective ongoing support and equipping relationship with churches and Christian leaders. There are at least four ways ILM can serve you:

1. Ministering to Ministry Leaders

ILM offers a unique two-day "Galatians 6:6" retreat to ministers and their spouses for personal renewal and to reestablish and affirm ministry and family priorities. The conference accommodations and meals are provided as a gift to ministry leaders by cosponsoring partners. Thirty to forty such retreats are held throughout the U.S. and Europe each year.

2. Partnering with Denominations and Other Ministries

Numerous denominations and ministries have partnered with ILM by "commissioning" us to equip their ministry leaders through the Galatians 6:6 retreats along with strategic training and ongoing resources. This unique partnership enables a denomination to use the expertise of ILM trainers and resources to perpetuate a movement of Great Commandment ministry at the local level. ILM also provides a crisis-support setting where denominations may send ministers, couples, or families who are struggling in their relationships.

3. Identifying, Training, and Equipping Lay Leaders

ILM is committed to helping the church equip its lay leaders through:

- *Sermon Series* on several Great Commandment topics to help pastors communicate a vision for Great Commandment health as well as identify and cultivate a core lay leadership group.
- *Community Training Classes* that provide weekly or weekend training to church staff and lay leaders. Classes are delivered by Intimate Life trainers along with ILM video-assisted training, workbooks, study courses, etc.
- *One-Day Training Conferences* on implementing Great Commandment ministry in the local church through marriage, parenting, or singles ministry. Conducted by Intimate Life trainers, these conferences are a great way to jump-start Great Commandment ministry in a local church.

4. Providing Advanced Training and Crisis Support

ILM conducts advanced training for both ministry staff and lay leaders through the Leadership Institute, focusing on relational ministry (marriage, parenting, families, singles, men, women, blended families, counseling, etc.). The Enrichment Center provides support to relationships in crisis through Intensive Retreats for couples, families, and singles.

For more information on how you, your church, or your denomination can take advantage of the many services and resources, such as the Great Commandment Ministry Training Resource, offered by Intimate Life Ministries, write or call:

Intimate Life Ministries
P.O. Box 201808
Austin, TX 78720-1808
1-800-881-8008

ENDNOTES

CHAPTER 1

1. Josh McDowell and Norm Wakefield, *Friend of the Lonely Heart* (Waco, Tex.: Word, 1991), 11.
2. George Barna, *The Barna Report* (Ventura, Calif.: Regal, 1992), 26.
3. Ibid., 67–69.
4. Rick Warren, *The Purpose-Driven Church* (Grand Rapids, Mich.: Zondervan, 1996), 191–192.
5. Josh McDowell and Bob Hostetler, *Right From Wrong* (Waco, Tex.: Word, 1994), 254–263.
6. Barna, *The Barna Report,* 68.
7. David L. Goetz, "Forced Out," *Leadership* (winter 1996): 42.
8. H. B. London Jr. and Neil B. Wiseman, *Pastors at Risk* (Wheaton, Ill.: Victor, 1993), 11.
9. *The Fuller Institute of Church Growth Report* (Pasadena, Calif.: 1991).
10. David L. Goetz, "Is the Pastor's Family Safe at Home?" *Leadership* (fall 1992): 38–44.
11. See 1 Corinthians 13:1-2.
12. See James 1:22.
13. Warren, *The Purpose-Driven Church,* 221.
14. See Acts 4:13.
15. See 2 Corinthians 5:20.

CHAPTER 2

1. See Matthew 9:36; 14:14; 15:32; 20:34; Mark 1:41; 6:34; 8:2.
2. See Genesis 1:4-25.
3. See Genesis 1:28-30.
4. See 1 Corinthians 12:21.
5. Ivor Powell, *Mark's Superb Gospel* (Grand Rapids, Mich.: Kregel, 1985), 318.
6. See Galatians 5:14; James 2:8.
7. George Barna, *The Barna Report* (Ventura, Calif.: Regal, 1992), 67–69.

CHAPTER 3

1. See Romans 5:8.
2. See Matthew 10:8.
3. See Philippians 4:19.
4. Adapted from *Merriam-Webster's Collegiate Dictionary,* 10th ed. (Springfield, Mass.: Merriam-Webster, 1995).
5. Ibid.

6. See Romans 5:8.
7. *Merriam-Webster's Collegiate Dictionary.*
8. See Ephesians 1:5; Romans 1:7; Romans 8:17; 1 Peter 2:9.
9. Adapted from *Merriam-Webster's Collegiate Dictionary.*
10. See Exodus 20:12; Leviticus 19:32; 1 Peter 2:17.
11. See Romans 13:7.
12. Adapted from *Merriam-Webster's Collegiate Dictionary.*
13. Ibid.

CHAPTER 4

1. Josh McDowell and Dick Day, *How to Be a Hero to Your Kids* (Waco, Tex.: Word, 1991), 127.
2. See 2 Corinthians 1:3-4.
3. See Matthew 19:13-15.
4. See Genesis 1:26; 9:6; James 3:9.
5. McDowell and Day, *How to Be a Hero,* 92.
6. See Ephesians 4:29.

CHAPTER 5

1. *Eerdmans' Handbook to Christianity in America* (Grand Rapids: Eerdmans, 1983), 313.
2. See Matthew 7:9-10.
3. *Marriage in America Report,* Institute for American Values (New York: 1995).

CHAPTER 6

1. See Philippians 4:19.

CHAPTER 7

1. *The Fuller Institute of Church Growth Report* (Pasadena, Calif.: 1991).
2. David L. Goetz, "Is the Pastor's Family Safe at Home?" *Leadership* (fall 1992): 38–44.
3. *Fuller Institute Report.*
4. George Barna, *Today's Pastors* (Ventura, Calif.: Regal, 1993), 59.
5. See Acts 1:4.
6. See Mark 1:35.
7. See 2 Corinthians 5:21.

CHAPTER 8

1. See James 4:6.
2. See Ephesians 3:20.
3. See Ephesians 2:4.

CHAPTER 9

1. See Psalm 51:17; 2 Corinthians 7:10.
2. See 2 Corinthians 7:8-10.
3. See Romans 14:12.

CHAPTER 10

1. Dennis Rainey, *The Tribute* (Nashville, Tenn.: Nelson, 1994).
2. See 1 John 1:9.

CHAPTER 11

1. See 2 Corinthians 3:2.
2. See 1 Thessalonians 2:7-8.

CHAPTER 12

1. See 2 Corinthians 12:9.
2. See John 1:1-2, 14.
3. See Philippians 2:6-8.
4. See Hebrews 4:15.
5. See Romans 15:7; 1 John 1:9; 2 Corinthians 1:3-4.
6. See John 17:21; 1 Corinthians 12:24-25.
7. See 1 Peter 3:15.
8. See Ephesians 4:29.
9. See 1 John 1:9; James 5:16; Ephesians 4:32.
10. See Romans 12:15; 2 Corinthians 1:2-4.

CHAPTER 13

1. See Hebrews 4:12.
2. See Acts 6:4 (NASB).
3. See John 14:23; 17:17-26.
4. See Philippians 3:7-10.
5. See 2 Corinthians 7:8-10.
6. See Romans 5:17; 8:32, 36-39.
7. See 1 Thessalonians 5:23.
8. See Proverbs 15:1.
9. See 2 Corinthians 5:17.
10. See Romans 7:25–8:1.
11. See 1 John 4:18.
12. Josh McDowell and Bob Hostetler, *Right From Wrong* (Waco, Tex.: Word, 1994), 37.
13. Ibid., 35–36.
14. "Kids These Days: What America Really Thinks about the Next Generation," *Akron Beacon Journal*, 26 June 1997.

CHAPTER 14

1. See 2 Corinthians 2:16.
2. See John 13:23.
3. See Romans 8:32.
4. See Romans 12:15.
5. See Matthew 13:23.
6. See John 17:16.
7. See Philippians 2:1-4.
8. See Matthew 12:1-8.
9. See John 9:1-7.

10. See Luke 9:51-56.
11. See Matthew 23:37.
12. See Matthew 3:17 (paraphrased).
13. See Romans 15:7.
14. See 2 Corinthians 1:3-4.
15. See Revelation 3:17.
16. See 2 Corinthians 5:18-21.
17. See John 13:35.

About the Author

DAVID FERGUSON and his wife, Teresa, are directors of Intimate Life Ministries, serving thousands of churches and ministry leaders worldwide with a message of how to deepen intimacy with God and deepen relationships in marriage, family, and the church. Early in his church ministry, David, like so many in Christian ministry, tried unsuccessfully to achieve balance between ministry and family demands. Out of an intense desire to honor God and minister to the needs of his family, he rediscovered a biblical principle that transformed his life, his family, and his ministry to others. For the past twenty years, the Fergusons have been sharing that message in print and through ministry retreats, media, and speaking engagements around the world.

David's graduate work in theology, counseling, and the social sciences focused on the Great Commandment principle and its impact on relationships, ministry, and culture. David has a masters of education from Southwest Texas State University and doctor of philosophy and doctor of letters degrees from Oxford Graduate School. He is a member of the Oxford Society of Scholars.

David and Teresa have been married thirty-five years and have coauthored several previous books and numerous articles. They reside in Austin, Texas, and have three adult children—Terri, Robin, and Eric.